BLUE CROSS

WHAT WENT WRONG?

BLUE CROSS
WHAT WENT WRONG?

SYLVIA A. LAW
PRINCIPAL AUTHOR

PREPARED BY THE HEALTH LAW PROJECT
UNIVERSITY OF PENNSYLVANIA

NEW HAVEN AND LONDON, YALE UNIVERSITY PRESS, 1974

Library of Congress catalog card number: 73-86907
International standard book number: 0-300-01728-6

The project reported herein was performed pursuant
to grants from the Office of Economic Opportunity
and the Department of Health, Education, and Welfare.
The opinions expressed herein are those of the author
and should not be construed as representing the
opinions or policy of any agency of the United States
Government.

Designed by Sally Sullivan
and set in Times Roman type.
Printed in the United States of America by
Vail-Ballou Press, Inc., Binghamton, N.Y.

Published in Great Britain, Europe, and Africa by
Yale University Press, Ltd., London.
Distributed in Latin America by Kaiman & Polon,
Inc., New York City; in Australasia and Southeast
Asia by John Wiley & Sons Australasia Pty. Ltd.,
Sydney; in India by UBS Publishers' Distributors Pvt.,
Ltd., Delhi; in Japan by John Weatherhill, Inc., Tokyo.

In the crucial stage of evolution immediately ahead voluntary health insurance may determine its own role, and, indirectly, the role of the government for many years to follow. . . . Of primary importance is the recognition of Blue Cross's "public utility" role and the needed increase in public and consumer representation on its policy making bodies. . . . At the moment the power of decision still rests to a major extent with the providers of service and the insurance carriers. If they default or fail the major influence in public policy determination may move into other hands.

> Herman M. and Anne R. Somers, in
> "Private Health Insurance: Problems,
> Pressures and Prospects," *California
> Law Review*

CONTENTS

FOREWORD

This book is a collective effort of the Health Law Project of the University of Pennsylvania. The Project began in the fall of 1970 with a grant from OEO to pay the salaries of four and a half lawyers, a community organizer, a sociologist, a librarian, secretaries, and several students. Our purpose has been to gain an understanding of how health care is delivered and financed in America and to figure out ways in which consumers can have a larger voice in determining the nature of the health services they receive. In the three years of its existence the Project has produced scholarly analyses of major aspects of health services delivery; some examples are studies of emergency room services, a report on health care and conditions in Pennsylvania's prisons, and a study of class differences in the provision of hospital care. We have prepared teaching materials for use in law schools to train lawyers to represent health consumers and have encouraged the development of such training. We have done original empirical research. We have developed models for organizing consumers and providing advocacy services by doing such work and analyzing and disseminating the knowledge that we gained. In the past we have gone to court and to state and federal agencies to advocate changes that seemed sensible and legally required.

In all of this we have tried to work collectively, with students, lawyers, and other professional and lay people (from members of our Board to members of our secretarial staff) making judgments as to what work should have priority, evaluating work that is in process, encouraging and supporting one another. We have also tried to combine scholarly detachment with the definite point of view that social institutions should be made accountable to the people who use and finance their services.

Dozens of people contributed to this book. Many were drafted, since compared to litigation or service to individual clients this work was tedious and did not offer immediate gratification. A few people deserve special mention. Ann Taylor did the bulk of the research and writing on the Federal Employees Benefit Program. Harvey Makadon did much of the research on the legislative history of Medicare and used his lively curiosity and intelligence to ferret out pieces of information throughout the process. Paul Tully first understood the mechanics and significance of the process of allocating hospital costs between government and privately financed patients and made many of the complex problems of hospital costs clear to us. Lotte Gottschlich assembled and maintains the invaluable Project library and organized cite checkers, proofreaders, and typists through several drafts. Edward V. Sparer is a continuing source of insight, and Harry Becker taught us the lessons of a lifetime of working for better health services for ordinary people. The principal writer and researcher of this book, its driving force, and the first Staff Director of the Health Law Project is Sylvia A. Law.

Please note that in writing this book, the pronoun "he" is sometimes used for convenience where "he or she" would be more accurate, but awkward.

The Health Law Project

1. INTRODUCTION

The crisis in medical care has arrived as an American public issue. It is fast becoming a tradition for both popular and scholarly articles to begin with a litany of figures contrasting spiraling costs with appallingly bad American health indices.[1] The nation now spends a larger portion of its total gross national product on health care than does any other country in the world—$67.2 billion, or 7 per cent of the gross national product in 1970.[2] In 1950 per capita health expenditures were $79; in 1960 they were $145; and in 1970 they were $324. This represents an average increase in health costs of 7.3 per cent a year, while during the same twenty-year period American wages increased at an average of only 4.3 per cent a year.[3] Hospital costs have risen at rates even more astronomical than other health care costs; according to the Bureau of Labor Statistics, hospital daily service charges increased 15.4 per cent in 1968, 13.2 per cent in 1969, and 12.4 per cent in 1970.[4] And the rate of increase in Blue Cross's operating expenses has been even sharper; from 1965 to 1969, Blue Cross's operating expenses per enrollee rose 66.2 per cent, or an average of 16.5 per cent a year.[5]

By contrast, in 1969 the infant death rate in the United States was 22.4 per 1,000 live births, exceeding that of fourteen other industrial countries. Nonwhite American babies died at a rate nearly twice that for white American babies. American males have a shorter life expectancy than the males of nineteen other industrial countries. Nonwhite Americans have a life expectancy seven years shorter than that for white Americans.[6] Unless the system of providing health care is improved, the health of Americans will become even less satisfactory, despite massive increases in costs.[7]

It is widely acknowledged that the American health care crisis is primarily one of organization, administration, and accountability. Blue Cross is at the heart of the administration of the present medical care delivery system.[8] Over $22 billion a year, about one-third of the national health care dollar, are spent in hospitals.[9] Blue Cross provides about half of hospital revenues, administering over $11 billion in 1970. Public funds comprised over half of Blue Cross payments to hospitals—$4.9 billion under Medicare, $1.2 billion under Medicaid, and $545 million under other federally financed programs.[10]

Blue Cross is a complex animal, impossible to characterize in a few words. For example, it may be seen as the financing arm of American hospitals, with a primary obligation to provide them, on an equitable basis, with a stable source of income to be utilized as they judge necessary. If this is regarded as its primary role, then Blue Cross's responsibilities to subscribers and to the public are to offer hospital insurance benefits at competitive rates, to maintain a financially sound rate structure, and to pay hospitals promptly for services provided to subscribers. Alternatively, Blue Cross may be seen as a quasi-public agency with primary responsibility to the public and to its subscribers. If this is its primary role, then its obligations are to offer benefits that will enable subscribers to obtain quality health care services economically, to monitor the quality of care provided subscribers in participating hospitals, to utilize the collective power of its payments to encourage hospitals to establish programs that will best meet subscribers' health needs, and to refuse to reimburse hospitals for charges that are excessive or do not meet subscribers' needs. Finally, with respect to the public funds it administers, Blue Cross may legitimately be viewed as an agent of the government, with an obligation to carry out the policies of Congress and of the administrative agencies responsible for publicly financed medical programs. Confusion as to the proper role of Blue Cross is common and pervades the organization itself, the state regulatory agencies, Congress, and the Department of Health, Education and Welfare.

In a nutshell, this book finds that Blue Cross is most accurately characterized today as the financing arm of American hospitals. It argues that money for hospital care, and health care generally, should be administered by an agency—whether Blue Cross or some other—which is primarily responsive and accountable to the public interest, and particularly the interests of the individuals who use and pay for health care services. It is useful at the outset to consider some basic themes and assumptions that recur in the detailed discussion that follows. These themes are not ideological preconceptions but rather generalizations that have emerged from an effort to understand and analyze the administrative structures of hospital care financing.

One assumption is that the issues involved in the financing of health services are fundamentally ones of public and social policy. An example is a hospital's decision whether to add a hyperbaric chamber or to install a more effective nurse call buzzer system, given a limited capacity for expansion.[11] Hospital and medical expertise are essential to provide the technical information upon which such a judgment can be made. How much will each innovation cost? How many patients will each affect? How significant is the impact of each on the treatment and eventual recovery of patients? How significant is each in enabling the hospital to attract and retain skilled personnel? In this example, it is likely that the hyperbaric chamber would be a factor, though of uncertain importance, in attracting surgeons, while the nurse call system would be more significant to nursing personnel. Thus, it is relevant to know the personnel needs and problems of the institution. When all of the information has been collected, the question still remains: which expansion will best meet the needs of the community served? While the issues are not normally posed in these either/or terms, many such decisions are made every year in American hospitals; collectively, they determine the nature and cost of hospital services.

A second theme, or assumption, is that, in the absence of countervailing pressures, any organization or bureaucracy will attempt to maximize institutional autonomy and stability, particularly financial stability. Institutions will be responsive to those forces, within and outside, that have power to affect their autonomy and stability. To recognize this is not to make a moral judgment. It is a natural, morally neutral tendency, and, indeed, a measure of autonomy and stability is essential if an organization is to function effectively, have a capacity for innovation, and develop a sense of responsibility. These observations may seem obvious, but they go to the very core of the problems of the administration and organization of health care services. Hospitals have attained a large measure of institutional autonomy and stability, and the development of Blue Cross as the principal vehicle for hospital financing has been a key element in preserving it. In the example cited above, a critical factor in the decision whether to install a hyperbaric chamber or a nurse call system is the availability of money. In this case, the cost of either innovation would be paid by Blue Cross, which would not urge the hospital to adopt one alternative or the other. The hospital is thus an autonomous institution with respect to the question posed. Detailed examination of the forces that affect decision making within hospitals is beyond the scope of this book; in general, however, it can be said that hospitals are hierarchical organizations in which physicians exercise dominant influence.[12] We will consider here the issue of institutional autonomy and examine the countervailing sources of power within and outside the hospital only as they relate to the role of Blue Cross. To what extent is Blue Cross an independent power affecting the institutional autonomy of hospitals? To what extent is Blue Cross in turn affected by subscribers, state and federal regulatory agencies, hospitals, competitors, and countervailing forces within the organization?

A third major theme is the fundamental powerlessness of the consumer of health and hospital care. The individual patient has very little to say about when or where he or she will be hospitalized, these judgments normally being made by physicians. Competition, at least competition directed at the consumer of services, is simply not a significant factor in determining the nature and cost of hospital services under present structures. Further, the individual consumer's purchase can have little impact on the availability, quality, and cost of services that are technically complex and are provided in highly structured organizations. Consumer and public influence could be organized and made potent through collective purchasing, and this could be an important role for a Blue Cross organization. The extent to which Blue Cross has served this role is examined in detail.

Consumer and public power could also be exercised through the public regulatory agencies that have direct jurisdiction over Blue Cross or the hospitals or through those state and federal agencies responsible for the administration of public health benefit programs. The fourth, and perhaps most disturbing, theme of this book is the massive failure of the public regulatory agencies to regulate either Blue Cross or the hospitals in the interests of consumers. Public regulation of industry is traditionally ineffective and tends to be controlled by the industry regulated.[13] This thought is hardly original and hardly unique to health. However, if we are to devise more effective means of organizing health care services and of assuring that those services are made accountable to the public interest, it seems useful to examine the nuts and bolts of existing sources of regulatory power and present regulatory operations.

The book consists of two parts. The first is an analytical description of Blue Cross, its history, its status under state law, its relationship to state regulatory agencies, its internal governance, the relationship between local plans, the national Blue Cross Association (BCA) and the American Hospital Association (AHA), and the legal role and status of Blue Cross under the federal health insurance programs. The second part considers in detail the role of Blue Cross with respect to two major problems: reimbursement for hospital services and review of the medical necessity of hospital services provided to individuals. These issues were chosen because they are important in any health services delivery system and because their resolution involves major public and social questions.

There are many other problems that are not considered beyond passing reference. For example, what role, if any, should Blue Cross play in monitoring and promoting high quality services? Should Blue Cross rate structures provide for uniform rates to all subscribers (community rating) or offer more favorable rates to those groups that are statistically healthier (experience rating)? What is the proper role of Blue Cross in developing lower cost alternatives to hospitalization? These are all issues deserving serious consideration. Examination of Blue Shield, the companion organization for the payment of doctors' services, is also not within the scope of this book. The two organizations are historically and functionally related, but there are fundamental differences in their operations. Blue Cross makes payments to fewer than ten thousand institutional providers of services, while Blue Shield pays nearly two hundred thousand individual private physicians.[14] Blue Cross payments to hospitals are generally made on some cost-related basis, while Blue Shield pays its doctors on the basis of customary and prevailing charges. Each organization operates under its own special state enabling legislation with disparate provisions on rate structures, board composition, and so forth.[15] The Social Security Act establishing the Medicaid and Medicare programs treats the two organizations differently.[16] The national Blue Cross Association has played a major role in coordinating the operations of local Blue Cross plans, while the National Association of Blue Shield Plans has less influence as a national trade association.[17] Examination of Blue Cross is a large undertaking in itself, and the policy questions raised by the operations of the two organizations are sufficiently different to justify separate consideration.

2. A UNIQUE AMERICAN INSTITUTION

Blue Cross is the child of the Depression and the American Hospital Association. The period from 1875 to 1915 was one of major development of medical institutions in this country, and by 1920 the now familiar pattern of community voluntary hospitals and local autonomy in health matters was established.[18] During the 1920s there was growing recognition of the need for some mechanism by which middle income people could finance extraordinary costs of hospitalization. Hospital insurance was virtually nonexistent.[19] In October 1927, the president of the American Hospital Association described the organization's "ultimate objective" as

> providing hospitalization for the great bulk of people of moderate means . . . [who are] confronted with the necessity of amassing a debt or the alternative of casting aside all pride and accepting the provisions that are intended for the poor . . . Let us keep in mind the *raison d'être* of our existence, vis.: the provision of hospitalization for the patient of moderate means, consisting of 80 per cent of the entire population. The wise solution of this great problem will inscribe the name of the American Hospital Association in the hearts of the people for all time.[20]

The solution most often proposed then was public education; people should be taught to save for large medical expenses.[21] The Depression, however, provided the impetus for a movement away from public education toward the development of the comprehensive Blue Cross network. Hospitals were hard hit by the Depression. In one year, from 1929 to 1930, the average hospital receipts per patient fell from $236.12 to $59.26. Average per cent of occupancy fell from 71.28 per cent to 64.12 per cent. Average deficits as a percentage of disbursements rose from 15.2 per cent to 20.6 per cent.[22] The hospitals had an immediate interest in developing a stable source of payment for services and also had the technical and financial resources to create such a program. Of 39

Blue Cross plans established in the early 1930s, 22 obtained all of their initial funds from hospitals, and five were partially financed by hospitals.[23]

There was by that time a variety of small, voluntary plans for the prepayment of medical expenses, particularly the predictable expenses incident to childbirth.[24] The largest of these plans, and the one generally credited as the progenitor of Blue Cross, was initiated in 1929 by Dr. Justin Ford Kimball in Dallas, Texas. As executive vice president of Baylor University, Dr. Kimball found the unpaid bills of many local schoolteachers among the accounts receivable of the university's medical facilities. In order to assure payment to the university, he enrolled 1,250 teachers in a program to prepay fifty cents a month for 21 days of semi-private hospitalization at the Baylor University Hospital.[25]

Under the Baylor plan and other early programs, subscribers could receive services only at the hospital that had organized the prepayment program. Most state insurance commissioners regarded these single hospital programs as group contracts for the sale of services by the hospitals to subscribing members and hence not subject to legal requirements applicable to insurance companies.[26] However, in some states insurance officials ruled that single hospital prepayment plans presented serious limitations to individuals and physicians by forcing them to select a hospital at the time of enrollment rather than at the time of illness. Consequently, during 1932 and 1933 "free choice" plans that covered care at a number of hospitals were organized in several cities. While the applicability of insurance laws to single hospital prepayment plans was an open question, the free choice plans were more clearly a form of insurance. The legal issue came sharply into focus when the United Hospital Fund of New York and the Cleveland Hospital Council were told that they would have to establish either a mutual or stock insurance company before making prepaid care available to the public.[27]

In response to this problem, the American Hospital Association and local hospital organizations sought state legislation to create a special class of nonprofit corporation and of hospital insurance. In the early 1930s, Dr. C. Rufus Rorem, associate director of the Julius Rosenwald Fund, studied the existing group hospital prepayment programs and was retained by the AHA to promote hospital prepayment and to seek the necessary enabling legislation. The following year the AHA promulgated seven "standards which should characterize group hospitalization plans.'' The standards were: (1) emphasis on public welfare, (2) limitation to hospital services, (3) freedom of choice of hospital and physician by subscriber, (4) nonprofit sponsorship, (5) compliance with legal requirements, (6) economic soundness, and (7) dignified and ethical administration.[28] In 1936, the AHA obtained a grant from the Rosenwald Fund to finance a special Committee on Hospital Service, and Dr. Rorem became its first executive director. In 1938 the committee established fourteen standards for nonprofit hospital care plans, including, for the first time, the requirement that the plan be approved by the AHA.[29]

The special enabling legislation sought by the AHA conferred the following advantages and privileges on the proposed hospital service corporations: exemption from the general insurance laws of the state; status as a charitable and benevolent organization; exemption from the obligation of maintaining the reserves required of commercial insurers; and tax exemption. The major justification offered in support of the special enabling legislation was the promise of service to the community, and particularly to low income families.[30] The AHA House of Delegates, in a 1939 resolution supporting the development of hospital service plans, cited the need for a program that would provide hospitalization ''among the low income groups'' and noted that such plans ''would reduce the need for taxation and philanthropy.'' [31] Dr. Rorem explained:

> Hospital service plans are unique, historically and geographically. . . . They deal with a service which has long been recognized as a community responsibility. *Hospital care must be provided for all persons regardless of their ability to pay.* Such a responsibility cannot and should not be assumed by a private insurance company, the first concern of which should be the financial interests of the policy-holders and stockholders . . . Government controlled hospitalization or health insurance is a second alternative to the nonprofit hospital service plan. . . . *But low-cost hospital service plans may reach many persons employed at low incomes who would otherwise require the aid of philanthropy or taxation.*[32] (Emphasis added.)

In 1934 the first hospital service plan enabling act was adopted by the New York state legislature.[33] With the support of the AHA, the bill had been promoted by the New York United Hospital Fund—a coalition of civic leaders, hospital administrators, hospital trustees, and physicians.[34] The New York act served as a model for other states, and by 1945 similar laws had been adopted in 35 states.[35] Currently 47 states have special enabling legislation for hospital service organizations,[36] and in 20 states such corporations are exempt from taxation.[37] Individual Blue Cross plans and the Blue Cross Association (BCA), the national trade association, are also exempt from the payment of federal taxes.[38]

Special corporate status and exemption from federal and state taxes seem to be based on a concept of social reform and utility rather than on any particular concrete characteristics of the Blue Cross plans. Neither the legislative history nor cases involving the validity of the tax exempt status provides much insight into the justification for the favored status of hospital service plans over commercial hospital insurers. State tax exemption has been challenged by tax collectors in five states.[39] In all but one, the courts held that Blue Cross was not entitled to exemption from payment of state taxes, even though it had been characterized as charitable or benevolent by the legislature.[40] The reasoning of the Georgia Supreme Court is illustrative. It examined the Blue Cross operation and found that it was "pure and simple insurance in direct competition with private concerns which are engaged in the same business," and hence not entitled to tax exemption.[41] The one decision squarely upholding the preferential state tax treatment of Blue Cross relies upon the close connection between Blue Cross and the nonprofit hospitals and reasons that if the legislature can confer privileged tax status upon the hospitals it can also exempt Blue Cross, "which is but an instrumentality of such hospitals." [42] Since Blue Cross guarantees full payment directly to participating hospitals for services provided to subscribers, while commercial companies make fixed cash payments to the individual insured, the distinction between Blue Cross and commercial insurers was "not so arbitrary that there is no conceivable basis in reason" for it.[43]

The Internal Revenue Service has given Blue Cross and the Blue Cross Association a tax exemption under Sec. 501(c)(4) of the Internal Revenue Code, which provides that "civic leagues or organizations not organized for profit but operated exclusively for the promotion of social welfare" shall be exempt.[44] While an organization exempt under Sec. 501(c)(4) does not pay taxes, contributions made to it are not deductible by the contributor as they are in the case of organizations exempt under

Sec. 501(c)(3). Because of this limited effect of a 501(c)(4) exemption, the IRS has tended to grant it liberally.[45] Since Blue Cross is essentially an insurance company in direct competition with commercial insurance companies, it is probably not technically entitled to the exemption, but the IRS has never issued an opinion or a ruling explaining the grounds for the exemption, and its validity has never been litigated.[46] Prepaid hospital insurance plans are not exempt from the payment of social security taxes as "corporations organized and operated exclusively for . . . charitable . . . purposes".[47]

No case can be found in which competing insurance companies have challenged the preferred tax and corporate status of Blue Cross, even though the exemption is one of the points of "differential treatment about which insurance companies are most vociferous." [48] Commercial insurance companies normally pay both premium taxes and state and federal income taxes.[49] Because commercial insurance companies may be able to allocate funds to policy reserves, and thereby avoid payment of substantial income tax, this difference between Blue Cross and the commercial companies may not be of great practical importance.[50] More research is needed to evaluate the actual relative tax burdens of Blue Cross and commercial insurers.

No case can be found in which subscribers have attempted to enforce the conditions upon which the privileged tax status of Blue Cross is predicated, although there is some precedent that would support their right to do so.[51] For example, subscribers who are paying a relatively high rate or who seek an opportunity to participate in the governance of Blue Cross might argue that equitable rates and subscriber participation in policy making are the conditions upon which the tax exemption and the preferred legal status of the organization are predicated. The difficulty is that the reason for the preferred status has never been made explicit. Further the tax law is an awkward and limited tool for shaping and controlling the nature and policies of social institutions.

From the 1930s on, the American Hospital Association sought to promote and control the development of monopolistic Blue Cross organizations. Preferred corporate status and tax treatment were important in the growth of Blue Cross, and these publicly conferred advantages were intensified by the private policy and control of the AHA. The enabling acts do not refer to Blue Cross by name but rather allow the establishment of "hospital service corporations." Although theoretically there could be several competing hospital service corporations in any one area, the enabling acts typically require that the corporation establish cooperative agreements with the majority of hospitals in the area served. Furthermore, AHA policy has required that, in order to use the Blue Cross emblem, a hospital service corporation must establish agreements with 75 per cent of the area hospitals,[52] and the AHA generally authorized use of the emblem by only one hospital service corporation in any given area.[53] Thus, historically, the combination of public enabling legislation and the private power of the AHA has assured that there is only one Blue Cross organization in any given area and that it is, to some degree, controlled by the hospitals.

By 1938, 1.4 million people in the United States had enrolled in 38 Blue Cross plans. Private insurance companies provided hospital insurance to only .1 million people. During the forties Blue Cross expanded at a rapid pace; the private health insurance industry also grew, but more slowly. Several factors contributed to the rapid growth of Blue Cross: it began writing contracts with employers and contracts having nationwide coverage; health insurance increasingly became a matter for collective bargaining, with labor supporting Blue Cross; and employment and wages mushroomed during World War II.[54] In 1945 Blue Cross claimed 61 per cent of the hospital insurance market, compared with the insurance companies' 33 per cent. But in 1951, for the first time, the number of people with private commercial hospital insurance (40.0 million) surpassed the number enrolled in Blue Cross plans (37.4 million),[55] and throughout the fifties and sixties Blue Cross was unsuccessful in competing with the commercial companies. At the end of 1969 Blue Cross had an enrollment of 70.6 million, or 35 per cent of the civilian population under 65, while the commercial insurance companies provided hospital coverage to 100 million people, or 57 per cent of the civilian population under 65.[56] The passage of Medicare and Medicaid legislation in 1965, however, gave Blue Cross a boost that reestablished its dominance in terms of hospital payments as a whole.

Two major characteristics have distinguished Blue Cross from most commercial insurance companies: payment of service benefits to hospitals rather than cash benefits to the individual insured; and community rating, that is, the provision of benefits to all members of the community at the same rate, rather than higher rates to high risk groups.

The Blue Cross commitment to the payment of service benefits to

hospitals means, simply, that while commercial insurers generally pay
the individual a fixed dollar amount per day or period of hospitalization,
and the individual bears primary responsibility for the payment of the
hospital bill, Blue Cross gives the subscriber the assurance it will settle
his bill with the hospital, with the subscriber bearing responsibility only
for the coinsurance, or deductible, specified in the policy. The original
American Hospital Association standards for the approval of hospital
service plans required that, "Benefits in member hospitals should be
expressed in 'service contracts,' which describe specifically the types
and amounts of hospital services to which the subscribers are entitled." [57] Over the years, however, as a result of competitive pressures,
an increasing number of Blue Cross plans have offered subscribers indemnity rather than service contracts. [58]

The second major distinction between Blue Cross and commercial insurers was the Blue Cross promise of service to the community. Initially
all Blue Cross plans offered hospital insurance to all members of the
community at uniform rates, [59] one rate for individuals and one rate for
families, while commercial companies offered more favorable rates to
those groups and individuals who were actuarially less likely to make
claims. [60] Since low income families and the aged tend to utilize hospital
services more than the general population, these groups are helped by
community rating. [61] During World War II, as organized labor began to
press for more adequate health benefits and other insurance companies
began to compete for this growing business, Blue Cross, after a decade
of internal struggle, abandoned its commitment to community rating. [62]
Today most Blue Cross plans offer group experience-rated contracts,
particularly for larger group policies, as well as community-rated policies for those individuals who are not able to obtain a group policy
through their work or otherwise. [63]

The adoption of experience rating was probably inevitable if Blue
Cross was to compete successfully with the commercial insurers for the
business of the low risk customer. [64] The alternatives were to persuade
low risk groups that Blue Cross was so useful as an organization serving
the entire community that low risk customers should subsidize the costs
of the higher risk groups or to offer a service so excellent that high risk
groups could be subsidized without fatal competitive disadvantage. [65]
Either of these alternatives would have been very difficult. Since a return to strict community rating is unlikely, the current major issue is

whether Blue Cross deserves its favored status under state and federal law.

SUPERVISION BY STATE GOVERNMENTS

In most states Blue Cross is regulated by the department or commissioner of insurance.[66] There is no general federal supervision of Blue Cross.[67] Several factors determine the nature of state supervision, including the statutory powers of the regulating agency, the number and abilities of regulatory personnel, and, most significantly, the attitudes of the state officials charged with this responsibility. As will be seen, some state officials with broad statutory powers often do little to supervise Blue Cross, while in other states insurance officials with vague and limited statutory authority attempt more comprehensive regulation. Courts, in accordance with the general rules, normally uphold the attitudes of regulatory personnel, whether lax or aggressive.[68]

Statutory duties of the insurance commissioner with respect to Blue Cross typically include: issuance and approval of certificates of incorporation, review of annual financial statements, and review of the rates paid by subscribers to Blue Cross and by Blue Cross to hospitals.[69] Proposed increases in Blue Cross subscriber rates must be filed with insurance departments in 20 states; in 7 additional states the insurance department has standing authority to review subscriber rates.[70] The statutory standards for judging subscriber rates are generally quite vague or unspecified. For example, in 7 states the law provides that the rates shall not be "excessive, inadequate, or unfairly discriminatory," [71] and 11 other states require that the rates shall be "fair and reasonable." [72] The vague statutory mandate to supervise subscriber rates gives state insurance commissioners a large measure of discretion to determine the extent to which they should examine and regulate subscriber rates.[73]

Statutes in over 20 states explicitly authorize the insurance commission to review contracts between Blue Cross and the hospitals, but often they provide no standard for evaluating rates paid to hospitals.[74] In some states there are such statutory standards. For example, the New Jersey act requires that Blue Cross rates to hospitals shall be reasonable and not in excess of the regular charges to the general public.[75] Massachusetts requires that rates "reflect reasonable costs or are based on charges made to the general public whichever is lower" and lists factors

to be considered in determining reasonable costs.[76] The New York statute is unusual in requiring that the commissioner of health, as well as
the superintendent of insurance, approve the rates of hospital reimbursement.[77]

Although statutes in most states are silent on the subject of regulation
of hospital reimbursement rates,[78] regulation of rates to subscribers
would seem to require examination of reimbursement to hospitals. For
example, the Pennsylvania statute requires review of subscriber rates
but is silent on the review of reimbursement rates to hospitals. In 1958,
the Pennsylvania insurance commissioner partially denied a requested
increase in subscriber rates, stating,

> The need of Blue Cross Plans for higher rates is directly caused by the
> increasing costs of hospital services . . . Since approximately 93
> cents out of every dollar received by the Blue Cross Plans from
> subscribers is paid over to hospitals to defray the costs of hospital
> care provided subscribers, any increase in hospital costs results in
> higher subscriber rates.[79]

However, the statutory framework is not the most important element
in determining the actual operation and effect of state regulation of Blue
Cross. The attitudes of regulatory personnel are critical, even where explicit statutory mandate to regulate hospital reimbursement rates exists.
For example, in New York, prior to 1969, prime responsibility for the
control of hospital costs rested on the superintendent of insurance, who
was required to certify the "reasonableness" of hospital reimbursement
rates.[80] In 1964 and again in 1969, private citizens and city officials
challenged subscriber rate increases; the resulting judicial review provides insight into regulatory attitudes. In 1964, Blue Cross requested
subscriber rate increases averaging 33 per cent. Subscribers objected on
grounds that the superintendent of insurance had relied upon inaccurate
data supplied to him by Blue Cross, "had failed and refused to inquire
into the reasonableness of the rates" to member hospitals, and had
failed to investigate abuses in Blue Cross operations.[81] The record
showed that the superintendent had conducted an audit of Blue Cross
three years before, as required by statute.[82] Because of the financial
needs of Blue Cross, the court affirmed the rate increase but warned that
the superintendent "so misconceives his duties and powers as to cast

doubt on the possibility of reasonable future rate request determination." [83] The court criticized the superintendent of insurance:

[There is no reason for his] assuming the role of a mere automaton, blindly approving mathematically correct adjustments (i.e., rate increases) in the formula. . . . The Superintendent does not and will not examine into the reasonableness and propriety of payments made to member hospitals by [Blue Cross]. Taking refuge behind the strict letter of the law, he asserts that it is his duty to determine the reasonableness of "rates" of payments, not reasonableness of payments themselves. He argues that examining into actual payments would be an overwhelming task. [84]

After consideration of New York's reasonable cost reimbursement formula for hospitals, the court continued:

Overseeing and controlling this mathematical labyrinth is [Blue Cross]. . . . So complete and unfettered is this control that when [Blue Cross] discovered that substantial overpayments had mistakenly been made to member hospitals, its review committee decided that no repayment was necessary but that these amounts would be set off against supplemental payments that might come due to the hospitals in succeeding years.

The Superintendent, meanwhile, would have us believe that he is to play absolutely no part in supervising or controlling this plan. He would have us believe that it is none of his concern whether payments are based on mistaken facts, fictitious charges, fictitious employees or even fictitious patients; nor that he should be concerned with making any independent evaluation of the reasonableness of . . . any of the myriad other details which would require him to go beyond the four corners of the balance sheet and ledger book. . . .

Both [Blue Cross] and the Superintendent seem intent on adopting the notion that no matter how costly operations become, for whatever reasons, eventually and inevitably, [Blue Cross] subscribers will shoulder the load. Small wonder that subscriber rates have increased 124% in the past five years. [85]

This judicial criticism had little effect on the New York superintendent. Five years later, in 1969, the New York legislature adopted a

hospital cost control law requiring that Blue Cross obtain certification
from the commissioner of health that rates to hospitals are "reasonably
related to the costs of efficient production of such service." [86] That
same year Blue Cross applied for an increase of 43.3 per cent in rates to
its community-rated subscribers for the next fifteen months. Before the
health commissioner had an opportunity to review the reasonableness of
the hospital reimbursement schedules, the superintendent of insurance
approved the requested rate increase, arguing that "there is no required
time sequence for regulatory approval of subscriber rates, on the one
hand, and regulatory approval of hospital payment rates on the
other." [87] A divided court of appeals accepted the argument and upheld
the rate increase. [88]

While the court's decision may be explained as a liberal application
of the principle that courts should defer to administrative discretion
unless patently arbitrary, it is difficult to understand why the superintendent would choose to exercise his discretion so as to undermine the
effect of the cost control legislation. As the dissenting opinion noted:

> If the Superintendent is precluded from determining hospital rates
> prior to the Commissioner's certification . . . and [Blue Cross's]
> principal cost of operation is hospital reimbursement (94%), how can
> the Superintendent ever determine the excessiveness of a proposed
> rate increase prior to certification? The answer is simply that he can-
> not. [89]

The affirmative reasons offered in support of the rate increase were that
the plan was near statutory insolvency, the commissioner of health had
testified that costs would continue to rise, the new cost control legislation would probably not be effective anyway, and a subsequent rate
increase would cause "expense and inconvenience" to Blue Cross and
its subscribers. [90] It is inherent and proper, however, that a regulatory
agency should cause inconvenience to the industry that it regulates, and
the prediction of ineffectiveness is self-fulfilling when made by those
responsible for implementation of the law.

In other states, insurance departments with less explicit statutory authority have begun to control excessive hospital costs and to institute
other measures for the protection of the subscriber by taking a more rigorous, adversary attitude toward Blue Cross. The Pennsylvania department is an outstanding example. It has required Blue Cross to institute

reforms to curb excessive hospital costs, to protect subscribers against unexpected hospital bills, and to allow some measure of subscriber participation in policy making. The Pennsylvania experience is considered in detail below (p. 28 ff.). In 1972 the New Hampshire commissioner, whose only statutory authority is to approve or disapprove proposed subscriber rate increases, rejected an increase because it did not take into account savings that could result from the institution of cost control measures.[91] He also prepared and introduced legislation that would allow increased subscriber participation in Blue Cross governance.[92] In Rhode Island the Department of Business Regulation, pursuant to statutory authority to modify proposed Blue Cross subscriber rate increases, instructed Blue Cross and the hospitals to devise a new reimbursement formula that would include cost-saving incentives.[93]

The attitude of the New York superintendent seems to be closer to the national norm. Even where statutory authority to examine hospital reimbursement rates exists, insurance commissioners in most states do not scrutinize them.[94] The official position of the National Association of Insurance Commissioners (N.A.I.C.) is that rising hospital costs should be controlled by direct regulation of hospitals rather than through the health insurance industry. Testifying in opposition to federal regulation of health insurance, an organization spokesman stated:

> Health insurance premiums are primarily a reflection of the underlying health care costs which have been skyrocketing in recent years.
> . . . Although some efforts have been made to exercise control through the insurance rate mechanism, since it was the only mechanism available, the leverage is too indirect for an overall effective solution. The minimization of health costs is primarily outside the scope of insurance regulation. The goal of providing health care benefits at reasonable cost is primarily a function of increasing efficiency in the health care delivery system and of control over prices charged by the providers of health services.[95]

A second related issue, and one on which there has been some change of attitude in recent years, is the question of public hearings on subscriber rate increases. Only four state laws explicitly mention public hearings,[96] and until the late fifties, they were rarely held.[97] A commissioner determined within the confines of his own department what rates were in the best interests of the state's citizens. Any communications he had with subscribers or other interested parties were on an unofficial and private basis.[98] Blue Cross officials objected to any public scrutiny of rates, because

> no information is developed in addition to what a commissioner already has available; a public place is provided for those with axes to grind; adverse publicity may be given to associations by newspaper reporting; large financial expenditures by associations are required; and an unwarranted delay in approval of rate increases may result.[99]

In recent years there has been some trend toward public hearings, though in the majority of states there remains no opportunity for public participation in the rate-making process.[100]

Practical factors of budget and personnel inevitably have some impact on the effectiveness of an insurance department. Effective regulation of hospital costs requires highly skilled personnel. Presumably, "most insurance commissioners and their staffs are trained and experienced in insurance principles, law and administrative theory," while supervision of Blue Cross requires "knowledge and sophistication in the field of hospital and medical economics."[101] The National Association of Insurance Commissioners asserts that current insurance department personnel are not capable of regulating hospital costs.[102] New York's Insurance Department has the highest operations budget and largest and best-paid professional staff in the United States,[103] while the Pennsylvania department has a far more limited staff and budget.[104] Yet the New York agency has done a lackadaisical job of regulating Blue Cross, while the Pennsylvania department has been uniquely effective in regulating costs and supervising Blue Cross operations. Thus, while budget and staffing are important, it is the attitude of the commissioner that most significantly determines the effectiveness of state regulation.

LOCAL PLANS, THE BLUE CROSS ASSOCIATION, AND THE AMERICAN HOSPITAL ASSOCIATION

Membership in the national Blue Cross organization is critical to a local Blue Cross plan. The advantages of membership include: use of the official Blue Cross emblem and seal; the right to exclusive provision of Blue Cross benefits within a territorial area; national advertising, public relations, and lobbying; the use of information gathering, processing, and dissemination apparatus; and mechanisms for coordination of national accounts and for the transfer and acceptance of subscribers who move from one plan's territory to another's. With the advent of Medicare, membership in the national organization became even more valuable. The national Blue Cross Association (BCA) contracted with the Social Security Adminstration for the administration of the Medicare program, and the BCA now serves as protector and interpreter for local plans vis-à-vis the federal government.

The name "Blue Cross" and the Blue Cross insignia were owned by the American Hospital Association until 1972.[105] The relationship between the AHA and Blue Cross plans has been close throughout Blue Cross history, as we have seen. In 1936, as part of its effort to promote the establishment of prepaid hospitalization plans, the AHA created a Committee on Hospital Services, which in 1946 became the Blue Cross Commission of the AHA.[106] Until 1960, the commission performed the national coordinating function among Blue Cross plans. In 1960, most of the commission's functions were transferred to the Blue Cross Association, a nonprofit Illinois corporation. The BCA and AHA maintained close coordination through interlocking directorates, with the AHA designating three members on the BCA board and BCA designating two members on the AHA board. Other functions, including the administration of the approval program for use of the Blue Cross insignia, were retained by the AHA. In 1971, the AHA and Blue Cross agreed in principle that the ownership of the Blue Cross name and insignia should be transferred to the BCA,[107] and this transfer became effective on June 30, 1972.[108] The two groups also agreed to eliminate their interlocking directorates and substitute a joint committee to facilitate communication between them.[109] AHA officials stated that the change was made as "a response to changing public attitudes" and emphasized that it did not represent a "cooling off" in the close relationships between Blue Cross and the AHA.[110]

The BCA follows the policies and practices of the AHA with respect to the use of the name and insignia. The AHA allowed plans that met its approval standards to enter into a license agreement with it for the use of the name and insignia. It conducted an annual written survey of each plan to make sure that it continued to meet approval standards. The standards required that a Blue Cross plan be a nonprofit community service organization [111] with a governing board "composed of representatives of both the public and the provider of service." [112] Plans had to offer benefits that "substantially" covered the costs of hospitalization, and at least 85 percent of subscriber income had to be paid out in benefits. [113] Plans had to be financially sound and maintain reasonable accounting and statistical records. [114] They were required to promise to cooperate with other Blue Cross plans and hospital associations in the area. [115] They had to provide the public with information on plan "functions, services, financing and responsibilities." [116] No plan could join the Blue Cross family unless it had "written agreements with at least 75 per cent of nonfederal short term hospitals registered by the American Hospital Association containing at least 75 per cent of these hospital's beds in the plan's service area." [117] This requirement assured that any organization using the Blue Cross name would be a major influence in the provision of hospital care in its territory and have the support of most hospitals.

The formal AHA approval process for use of the insignia was not demanding. It was administered by two individuals in the national office. Site visits were made every three years. Plans were judged on the basis of their answers to questions posed, without investigation of their actual operation. [118] No plan was ever disapproved for continued use of the insignia. [119] Recognizing that the Blue Cross name and insignia were of enormous commercial value, the AHA made a careful effort to protect its exclusive rights in these trademarks. [120] However, there is little evidence that the AHA utilized its formal approval program either as a mechanism for close monitoring of local plan operations or as a coercive device to obtain concessions from hospitals.

In 1969 the BCA had a budget of $4.4 million, contributed by the individual plans, and employed about 450 people. [121] It performs a variety of public relations functions; in 1971, $556 thousand were devoted to public relations per se. [122] In addition, the Washington Representation Division represents Blue Cross interests in Congress and the federal agencies. The External Relations Division carries on public relations work among consumer and provider groups and maintains intelligence on them. [123]

In addition to its public relations functions, the national organization performs a variety of services for local plans. It solicits and maintains national accounts, for example from labor unions and large companies, with much of the premium income going to the local plans. It administers the Inter-Plan Transfer Program, advises plans on premium rates and reimbursement rates, and maintains a data processing and telecommunications service. It conducts studies on health care economics and financing and publishes the magazine *Inquiry*. It provides local plans with legal advice on the administration of government contracts.

Many of the functions of the BCA are those of an ordinary trade association. As prime contractor under Medicare and other federal programs, however, BCA is more powerful than a trade association. Its bylaws, to which the individual plans adhere, provide that

> the association may make special studies . . . and may audit . . . all records of a regular member and make recommendations with respect thereto, first to the chief executive officer, then to the governing board of the member, and finally to official regulatory authorities where it appears desirable.[124]

In public statements, and especially in testimony before congressional committees, BCA officials emphasize the role of the national organization in reviewing and monitoring the quality of local plan performance.[125] Arrangements under Medicare and other federal health programs whereby the federal government contracts with BCA and BCA subcontracts with local plans assume that the national organization will oversee local plan performance.

In 1971, the Subcommittee on Antitrust and Monopoly of the Senate Committee on the Judiciary heard extensive testimony on the operation of BCA review of local plan performance, with particular reference to the Richmond, Virginia, plan. The hearings revealed that BCA's claim of national review of local plans is predominantly public relations puffing. Testimony showed that throughout the late sixties the administrative costs of the Virginia plan were among the highest of any Blue Cross plan in the nation.[126] Subsequent investigations prompted by public and congressional concern revealed gross mismanagement. For example, the plan had 119 rented automobiles and could not account for their use.[127] It paid for staff memberships in various country clubs and owned stock in a country club.[128] Two years after Medicare began, the plan moved into an $8 million office building. One million dollars was spent to decorate and furnish the building, and most of the purchases were made, without competitive bidding, from a firm whose sales manager was chairman of the Building Committee of the Blue Cross board.[129] The plan paid $198,000 to a profit-making data processing organization but received no identifiable service. The assistant general manager of the plan was also a member of the board of the data processing organization, but he never revealed this relationship, because he believed that there was no conflict of interest.[130]

In October 1968, while these policies were in effect, the Richmond plan was given a "Total Plan Review" by the BCA. This review was described as

> a review and analysis of the overall corporate structure of the plan, its organization, objectives, future plans and management controls, especially as they related to the effectiveness of the administrative system. Particular emphasis was given to the support function of data processing and financial activities.[131]

The final report, while noting low productivity and high cost per claim, was laudatory.

> The team was particularly impressed with the overall corporate structure and organization of the plan . . . The executive management group of the Richmond plan displays a progressive and confident attitude. . . . There is an atmosphere which is conducive to innovation and change aimed at improvement. . . .
>
> It was favorably noted that a good start has been made toward greater refinement of the budget, cost accounting, etc. in the financial area. The Richmond plan has made great strides towards attracting and retaining qualified personnel. This is true with respect to physical surroundings, progressive atmosphere, etc.[132]

Despite this clean bill of health, by early 1970 public attention prompted the BCA to reexamine the plan. Internal BCA memos subpoenaed by the Senate committee revealed that the 1970 investigation was primarily concerned with public appearances. One national official recommended that a BCA team be sent in "in the interest of preserving the National reputation as opposed to assisting the Plan." Another BCA official visiting Richmond concluded that BCA should

> refrain from moving in since we know the bad news that might erupt. . . . Richmond could blow up. It is a real "can of worms." But we know enough bad things without necessarily sending in a team to get

more information. However, I also recognize that the National Associations must preserve their dignity and be prepared to answer questions. . . . Nevertheless, this is another case of "locking the barn door after the horse has departed." [133]

It seems that local malfeasance is a subject for national concern only when it approaches the level of scandal or illegality. Even then BCA efforts are directed first toward preventing adverse publicity, then toward correcting the problems.

BCA internal memos do not suggest fear of state or federal sanctions. Senator Philip Hart asked why the Richmond situation was not reported to state regulatory officials, as provided in the BCA bylaws.[134] Walter McNerney, president of the BCA, stated, "The situation was sufficiently under cognizance by the board. . . . [No one] in the plan deliberately set out on a callous disregard of the public interest." [135] Richmond plan officials shared the view that the problems were not very great.[136] Even if timely reports had been made available, however, as a practical matter there was and is no regulatory authority to correct the Richmond mismanagement. State government had no authority, because in 1960 Richmond Blue Cross obtained special legislation removing itself from the regulatory supervision of the State Corporation Commission, which was previously responsible for regulating subscriber rates.[137] As will be seen, the federal Social Security Administration has no means of monitoring plan performance, even though over half of the Richmond plan's business is financed under Medicare and Medicaid.

Local plan officials did not recognize any supervisory power in the BCA. Asked about the relationship between the BCA and the local plan, the chief executive of the Richmond plan stated:

"We run our show. They don't. They haven't tried to run it since I have been in there, and it is much more like a trade association, as I view it. . . . They have no control. We are a separate legal entity, run the show our way." [138]

While corporate waste through high administrative costs is significant, it is not the central issue in evaluating Blue Cross performance. In Richmond, administrative costs represented only 5.4 per cent of the earned subscriber income, the balance being payments to hospitals.[139]

The key issue of public concern should be what Blue Cross does to ensure that hospital costs are reasonable. Not surprisingly, the evidence
was that the Richmond plan did not pursue any form of hospital cost
control. The executive director of the plan was asked, "What if your
audit [of hospital books] indicated clearly wasteful practices? What do
you do?" He responded, "Well, Mr. Chairman, I am not aware of our
audits ever uncovering wasteful charges, and I really wouldn't know
what we would do if we ran into them." [140]

Because of the difficulty in obtaining information about the internal
operations of Blue Cross, it is not possible to know whether the Richmond operation is typical. Probably it is not.[141] However, such mismanagement is not unique. For example, the General Accounting Office and a subcommittee of the House Committee on Government
Operations found that during 1966–67, Washington, D.C., Blue Cross
kept an average of more than $10 million in federal funds in noninterest-
bearing accounts in Washington banks. Larger amounts, estimated in
excess of $15 million, were kept in noninterest-bearing accounts from
1961 to 1965.[142] Several members of the Blue Cross board, including
the treasurer, were officers and board members of the banks in which
the monies were deposited.[143] From 1963 until 1971 Illinois Blue Cross
had between $7 and $15 million deposited in noninterest-bearing accounts in a bank at which the chairman of the board served as senior
vice president and an additional $2 million in noninterest-bearing ac-
counts in a second bank, one of the officers of which was also on the
Blue Cross board.[144]

Periodic investigations by congressional committees are obviously an
ineffective means to discover whether plans operate efficiently or to encourage such operation. As the facts concerning the mismanagement of
the Richmond plan unfolded, the Subcommittee on Antitrust and Monopoly grappled to find some mechanism of public accountability—some means by which the interests of the public and of
subscribers could be protected. Senator Hart asked, "There isn't any
outside discipline, either the Virginia Corporation Commission or legislative body or the National Blue Cross, that could do other than sort of
wonder. Nobody could correct, is that right, absent the internal discipline?" The chief executive officer responded, "Mr. Chairman, I
would say you are absolutely right, but that responsibility rests purely
on the shoulders of the boards of directors. . . . The moment they found

the level of spending which they couldn't quite stand, they acted immediately.'' [145]

It is extraordinarily difficult to obtain concrete information about Blue Cross operations. The BCA and published materials do not provide even basic information on the practices of various plans with respect to reimbursement of hospitals, claims review, determination of subscriber rates, governance, or state and federal regulation. Because of the lack of public information and the importance of concrete data on which to base an analysis and evaluation of Blue Cross, the author, on January 20, 1972, distributed a twelve-page questionnaire, covering the subjects listed above, to each Blue Cross plan. On February 1, 1972, D. Eugene Sibery, executive vice president of the BCA, wrote that the national association would be responding to the questionnaire on behalf of the local plans. Its response to most questions was that information was unavailable. [146] The questionnaire had originally been directed to the local plans precisely because the author was unable to obtain the information sought from the BCA and understood that the BCA did not have the data. Local plans may have been reluctant to provide information even if the BCA had not intervened. [147] BCA intervention assured the unavailability of the information.

Blue Cross Boards of Directors

The local Blue Cross board has the primary—and often the sole—responsibility for determining policy and assuring accountability within the plan. For example, the local board determines whether the plan shall offer community rates to all subscribers or experience rates based on the particular utilization patterns of groups of subscribers. It decides whether the plan shall offer benefits only for inpatient hospital services or provide more comprehensive benefits, including coverage for less expensive forms of care. It determines whether the plan shall pay hospitals whatever they ask or use the economic power of payments to force cost control and otherwise shape local hospital planning. It is responsible for establishing procedures for subscriber complaints and for determining the governing structure of the organization.

In the 1960s, the assertion that Blue Cross boards were publicly responsive was a major selling point in persuading Congress to give Blue Cross a key role in the Medicare program. [148] Although citizen control of local Blue Cross policy has always been emphasized in Blue Cross rhetoric, it is only within the past few years that there has been serious scrutiny of the actual composition of Blue Cross boards. Two major issues have been raised. First, what role, if any, should providers of service have on the board? Second, do the standards and procedures for the selection of public members of the board adequately ensure that they will represent public and subscriber interests?

Hospital representatives currently dominate Blue Cross boards. The AHA Standards for Approval, now taken over by the BCA, require that at least one-third of the board members represent the contracting hospitals, and some enabling acts require hospital representatives on the board.[149] In 1970, according to BCA figures, 56 per cent of the members of local boards were health care providers, 42 per cent representing hospitals and 14 per cent representing the medical profession.[150]

A case can be made that hospital representatives have no proper role on Blue Cross boards. Because the federal and state governments have delegated to Blue Cross the public functions of: (1) paying for publicly financed hospital care; (2) determining the reasonableness of hospital costs; and (3) using payment processes to encourage rational planning and utilization patterns, the place of provider representatives on Blue Cross boards can certainly be questioned. For example, the chairman of the Massachusetts Rate Setting Commission and special counsel for health affairs commented:

> If we regard Blue Cross as having a responsibility to "regulate" hospital costs—and I most certainly do—then we can look upon this arrangement as those who are regulated actually being the regulators of themselves. The counterbalancing and resolution of discrete interests which should be the heart of any regulatory process is lacking.[151]

Because of the close relationship between Blue Cross and the providers of services, Senator Philip Hart, after extensive hearings on the high costs of hospitalization, would exclude Blue Cross from any role in the administration of publicly financed health programs.[152] The West Virginia insurance commissioner disapproved a Blue Cross request for subscriber rate increases on the ground, among others, that the presence of provider representatives on the board prevented arms' length negotiation of a reasonable hospital reimbursement contract.[153]

The criticism of provider members on Blue Cross boards is not primarily that they are self-dealing or necessarily incapable of avoiding conflicts of interest.[154] Rather, the problem is that provider representatives are primarily responsible to hospitals rather than to subscribers or the public. It is unrealistic to expect that, as Blue Cross board members, hospital representatives will challenge hospital policies on cost control, area planning, or reorientation of services, when these are policies they have developed. Hospital representatives will seek to maintain the autonomy of the hospital.[155]

Several reasons can be advanced in support of continued hospital dominance of Blue Cross. The most serious is that hospital and medical services are technically so sophisticated that only experts in the field can properly determine what is useful and necessary. If the fear is that a public board would deny hospitals necessary financing simply out of ignorance, however, the problem could be met by a Blue Cross advisory board composed of hospital and medical experts.[156] A second, less legitimate argument for hospital domination of Blue Cross boards is that hospitals might refuse to contract with a lay-dominated Blue Cross organization. During the enactment of Medicare and Medicaid, accommodations were made to the medical profession and hospital industry in part because of a fear of doctor and hospital boycott.[157] However, given the current Blue Cross dominance of the hospital market and the increasing proportion of publicly financed hospital services, the threat of boycott becomes ever less potent.

In response to mounting criticism of hospital domination of its boards, Blue Cross, at least at the national level, has adopted a strongly proconsumer position. Walter McNerney, head of the BCA, states:

> Government and private programs need consumer input. Both tend to become obsessed with internal needs rather than effective service if all decisions are made by "professionals." To assure that care is rendered at a time and place and in a way satisfactory to the consumer, the consumer must participate in decisions. . . . None of this will come about without concerted programs involving orgainzational change and health education. . . . [It is] the beneficiary of service, less sidetracked by aspirations of personal achievement, who holds the key to service innovations and to change. The electorate is not enough, nor is the event of an out-of-pocket payment. . . .[158]

[With respect to relationships between Blue Cross and the hospitals we need] a certain amount of honest adversary relationship and a greater accountability through greater consumer as well as electorate input.[159]

As presently constituted, even the public board members often do not protect or reflect subscriber interests. Although in 1970 44 per cent of the members of local plan boards were "public" representatives, examination reveals that under present structures public representatives are an elite group with little resemblance to subscribers. In most Blue Cross plans public representatives are selected by the incumbent board.[160] In twenty-one plans they are selected by the hospital representatives.[161] In Washington, D.C., the public representatives are appointed by the commissioner of the district. Subscribers elect public representatives in only eight plans, including the Philadelphia plan.[162]

Compared to other plans the Philadelphia board has democratic selection procedures. However, it is not in fact open to subscriber control or participation. In 1971 the plan bylaws were amended to allow subscribers to vote for board members, with nominations made by the incumbent board or by petition with 300 subscriber signatures. In 1971 and 1972 subscribers nominated candidates to run against the nominees of the board. Through advertisements in local newspapers and through contacts with large organizations holding group contracts, the plan management solicited proxy votes for the board's candidates. In both years the plan refused subscriber requests to publish a ballot that would allow subscribers to cast votes for the insurgent candidates and to publish information about the position of various candidates on questions of plan policy. In 1971, the subscriber candidates received over 1,000 votes, but the management slate won with about 3,000 votes. In 1972, the subscriber candidates received over 4,000 votes, but management had increased its effort and obtained 16,000 proxy votes.[163] During the intervening year there had been substantial adverse publicity about Blue Cross, as Insurance Commissioner Herbert Denenberg criticized the plan for failure to hold down hospital costs. It is difficult to believe that the fivefold jump in votes for the incumbent board reflected a vote of confidence or popularity. The number of votes obtained by the management appears to reflect the amount of management resources devoted to the collection of proxies rather than subscriber endorsement of management policy and competence. The subscriber candidates had no financial support but depended on volunteer efforts of those concerned about Blue Cross policy. There are no limitations on the resources which the plan can devote to insuring the election of a board that will support current policies and management.[164]

The Philadelphia plan directors are not representative of the plan's subscribers. Twelve of the 32 directors are directors of banking and financial institutions. Two sit on the boards of major real estate companies, one is the president of a company with major interests in hospital supply, and others are business executives.[165] Two directors represent organized labor. The typical board member is white, male, over 40, and wealthy; departures from this norm are few. The Philadelphia board does not even reflect the broad range of the city's hospitals; in 1970 five of the city's most influential hospitals had more than one representative on the board.[166]

The pattern in Philadelphia is typical of the rest of the country. Blue Cross Association data show that the 824 members of local plan boards designated as public and consumer representatives include: 311 business executives, 116 physicians and surgeons, 90 retired people, 73 bankers, 54 lawyers, 39 labor leaders, 34 university and school officials, 23 investment advisers, 17 religious leaders, 8 real estate men, and 59 people in a variety of other positions.[167] Of these public representatives, only 18 are women.

Labor representatives on Blue Cross boards are often cited as the representatives of ordinary subscribers. There is no evidence that they have played such a role.[168] Further examination of labor members of Blue Cross boards is needed. One hypothesis is that labor representatives have been content to obtain relatively favorable rate treatment for their own members.[169] Blue Cross critics charge that community-rated subscribers, who pay substantially higher rates, subsidize the organized experience-rated subscribers.[170] No one would be the wiser if a plan were to offer favorable group rates based not on experience but on political influence, representation on the plan board, or other extraneous factors. Only Blue Cross has the information needed to determine whether such discriminatory rate setting exists. Insurance commissioners do not obtain sufficient information to know whether experience rates are justified on the basis of actual experience and administrative savings resulting from the group contract; certainly community-rated subscribers do not have access to such information.[171] Aggressive scrutiny of Blue Cross policies and pursuit of institutional reform would require enormous effort and tenacity and could quickly put labor representatives into direct conflict with plan administration and board members from the hospitals. Given that labor representatives constitute such a small minority on a Blue Cross board and given that they are accountable to a constituency that is probably not demanding reforms in the Blue Cross structure, it would not be surprising to find labor members playing a quiet role in Blue Cross governance.[172]

Within the present Blue Cross board structures, there are some reforms that can and should be instituted. Although neither the BCA nor the insurance departments presently scrutinize board members for direct conflicts of interests, such a probe could be conducted. It would be a fairly simple matter for the BCA, state insurance departments, or the federal government as administrator of Medicare to gather and publicize information on the affiliations of Blue Cross directors and on the major organizations with which the plan contracts and banks. Simply gathering such information and making it public would do much to curb the more flagrant abuses of Blue Cross power.

The more fundamental question of who governs Blue Cross, and to whom it should be accountable, requires a more comprehensive solution. It is an illusion to believe that effective public control of an institution as complex and influential as Blue Cross could be achieved easily or with minor reforms. Some of the criteria for effective reform of Blue Cross boards will be discussed after we consider its role as agent of the federal government and examine some of its major substantive policy-making powers.

3. BLUE CROSS AND FEDERAL
HEALTH PROGRAMS

THE FISCAL INTERMEDIARY CONCEPT IN MEDICARE

National health insurance is not a new idea in the United States. In 1915, the American Medical Association was "putting the final touches on the medical sections" of a model state act, and an informed observer predicted "fair prospects for legislative commissions to investigate in 1916 and for compulsory health insurance legislation in this country in 1917." [173] However, in 1920 the medical profession retreated sharply, and the AMA declared its opposition to "any system of compulsory contributory insurance . . . provided, controlled, or regulated by any state or the Federal government." [174] For five decades compulsory health insurance was analyzed, studied, and discussed. [175] Through the 1940s and '50s numerous unsuccessful national health bills were introduced in Congress. [176] Three major factors contributed to the failure to establish a comprehensive program of health insurance. [177] The first was the rapid growth of voluntary health insurance, which has been described. Second, there was a variety of piecemeal medical care programs, particularly for union members, veterans, and public employees who might otherwise have exercised influence in support of a comprehensive national plan. The last, and perhaps most significant, was the strong, well-organized opposition of the medical profession and the hospital and insurance industries.

During the early sixties, it became apparent that, at least with respect to the aged, the private programs were inadequate. In 1960 a special Senate subcommittee held hearings throughout the country and recommended a social-security-financed medical care program for the aged. [178] The 1961 White House Conference on the Aging also called for such legislation. [179] In 1964 the Senate Special Committee on the Aging found that only one-quarter of the aged had minimally adequate hospital insurance coverage and concluded:

Without a social-security-financed, hospital insurance program for
the elderly . . . [they] will, in effect, be priced out of Blue Cross
. . . [and] may have no recourse other than the public assistance
rolls when illness strikes.[180]

By 1960 broad-based support for national health insurance for the
aged was building in the public, if not in Congress.[181] Thousands of
people attended rallies in support of social-security-financed health insurance for the aged.[182] Under the pressure of election year politics,
Congress passed the Kerr-Mills Act providing federal grants to the
states to pay part of the costs of medical services to the needy aged.[183] It
was a stop-gap compromise measure that pleased no one.[184]

In 1961 the Democrats came to office committed to a social security
type of hospital insurance program for the aged. The administration introduced such a bill, which for the first time provided a role for Blue
Cross. The role was essentially one of bargaining agent for the hospitals.[185] The hospital industry and medical profession conducted a well-
organized campaign in opposition,[186] and no bill was reported out of
committee.

The major issues dividing Congress in the early sixties were: (1)
whether health insurance for the aged should be administered by the
states or by the federal government, and (2) whether medical care
should be financed by a social security type of fund raised by a tax on
wages and provided without means tests or should be financed from
general revenues and provided only to the indigent.[187] The medical profession and hospital industry were adamant in their opposition to federal
administration, social security financing, and universal eligibility.

In January 1962, however, the House of Delegates of the American
Hospital Association made a fundamental change in policy, adopting a
resolution supporting a social security type of health program on condition that the actual administration of the program was entrusted to Blue
Cross.[188] With this action, Blue Cross and the AHA broke sharply with
the American Medical Association, which remained steadfast in its opposition to social security financing and federal administration.[189]

The administration saw here an opportunity to develop a bill that
would meet the approval of Blue Cross and the AHA, have a better
chance of enactment, and, perhaps most significantly, avoid the danger
of a boycott by the core providers of services—the hospitals. An HEW

task force was quickly appointed to consider the use of Blue Cross and other insurers in the administration of health insurance for the aged.[190] After the report of the task force and private White House meetings,[191] a bill that for the first time contained the fiscal intermediary concept was introduced.[192]

Under Part A of the 1965 act, the fiscal intermediary is defined as "a national, State, or other public or private agency or organization" nominated by "any group or association of providers of services." [193] The secretary of HEW is authorized to enter into an agreement with an organization thus designated, whereby the latter determines the amount of payments to providers, subject to such secretarial review as may be called for in the agreement, and makes such payments. In addition, the secretary may arrange for the organization to do any or all of the following: (1) offer consultation to enable providers to join the Medicare program; (2) serve as a channel of communication between the providers and the government; (3) audit the providers' books; (4) perform other necessary functions.[194]

The secretary must not enter into an agreement with such a fiscal agent unless he finds that: to do so is consistent with the efficient administration of the act; the organization is able to assist hospitals in developing utilization review programs; and the organization agrees to furnish the secretary with any information acquired in the administration of the program which the secretary finds necessary.[195]

The act authorizes the secretary to make advances of funds to fiscal intermediaries and to determine the necessary and proper payments for administrative costs.[196] An individual hospital can choose the fiscal intermediary from which it will receive payment, or it may receive payment directly from the federal government. Hospitals may withdraw their designation of a fiscal intermediary and select another that meets the statutory requirements.[197] The statutory provisions on termination of agreements between the secretary and the fiscal intermediary are lopsided in that the intermediary may terminate the agreement at such time and on such notice as is provided by the secretary in regulations, while the secretary may terminate the agreement only after notice and hearing and upon a finding that the intermediary has "substantially failed" to carry out the agreement or that continuation is disadvantageous to the efficient administration of the program.[198] Finally, there are statutory provisions requiring surety bonds for disbursing officers and exempting the intermediaries and their officers from liability for incorrect payments in the absence of gross negligence or intent to defraud.[199]

The most striking fact about the legislative history of the fiscal intermediary provision is that Congress never considered the basic issue of whether it was a good idea to use Blue Cross to perform these critical administrative functions under the Medicare program. Even though bills containing the fiscal intermediary provisions were extensively debated in committee for three years, there is no evidence that this threshold issue was ever addressed. The provision on fiscal intermediaries enacted in 1965 was virtually identical to that introduced in 1962.[200]

The memorandum of the HEW task force in 1962 provides the most coherent statement of the alternative ways in which Blue Cross could be used in the administration of Medicare, but it does not address "the fundamental policy question of whether the apparent initial advantages of using private organizations would, on balance, outweigh certain long run disadvantages." [201] It urged that this threshold question be considered by Congress and expressed some reservations about the use of Blue Cross:

> A considerable price would be paid in order to get the initial public relations advantages with professional groups that might come from using Blue Cross, e.g., loss of direct contact with providers so that the Federal Government would not have detailed knowledge of problems and because of this, the loss of ability to react quickly to problems of administration, budget, program, etc.

Also, use of Blue Cross would involve duplication of effort, since the government "would have to audit not only Blue Cross operations, but a sample of hospitals to assure that Blue Cross was doing an effective job." Further, whether Blue Cross would be able to aid hospitals in establishing physician peer review of the quality and necessity of care provided "is a question on which there are differences of opinion." [202]

The task force outlined three alternative arrangements for the use of Blue Cross and other insurers in Medicare administration. They were: (1) to broaden the "negotiation" concept contained in the 1961 bill to allow the third party to act as an intermediary in the preparation of bills and receipt of payment; (2) to delegate *all* substantive administrative functions to private contracting organizations, including determination of which providers could join the program, negotiation of provider agreements, and review and payment of bills based on existing private reimbursement formulas; and (3) to contract out responsibilities to organizations nominated by the providers and meeting certain criteria to assure their efficient performance.[203]

The task force report recommended the third alternative [204] but cited certain dangers that should be controlled through careful drafting of legislation, regulation, or contract provisions. The secretary "must have recourse to direct Federal operation [if a] . . . private organization proves ineffective or impractical for any reason." The procedures for selecting intermediaries "should encourage the selection of organizations which have a public service orientation, . . . extensive experience in the provision of health insurance on a service benefits basis and the appropriate skills and personnel to administer the program." Also, the government must be assured "accurate and comparable data on utilization and costs." Federal review of the performance of all delegated functions and "ultimate Federal auditing responsibility" should be assured. Finally, "contracting organizations should be required to carry out policy and administrative practices which are established on a national basis."

The task force submitted two draft legislative guidelines. Under both, providers would designate particular organizations as fiscal intermediaries, and the secretary would be required to accept such designations unless the organizations were not qualified. One legislative draft contained specific statutory criteria for fiscal agents, and the second left the approval standards to the discretion of the secretary.[205] After consultation with Blue Cross and the AHA, the fiscal intermediary provision was drafted without the suggested statutory standards for evaluation of nominated intermediaries.[206]

It was not until three years later, on the Senate floor, after the Medicare bill had passed the committees of both houses, that the subject of the fundamental worth of the fiscal intermediary concept was taken up again.

Senator Wayne Morse, while indicating that he would vote for the bill, argued that administrative responsibility should rest with HEW and with state and local government agencies. He said:

Obviously to the extent that the administrative functions of medicare are rendered by Federal, State, and local governmental agencies, the overriding public interest is well served. Conflicts of interest may arise, however, where administrative responsibilities may be delegated or assigned by the Secretary of Health, Education and Welfare to non-public agencies. These are non-governmental agencies whose basic commitment is not to the beneficiaries of the program but to whom medicare is an incidental, profitable, and subordinate supplement to other business. . . . Blue Cross is essentially a creature and instrumentality of the hospitals . . . Thus, while Blue Cross can legitimately serve as the agent of the hospitals in dealing with the Government, it cannot possibly serve as the agent of the government. Blue Cross simply cannot meet the requirement that it "deal at arm's length." Further, Blue Cross plans may be affected by the amount of payments under the Government program—the larger the medicare payment the less the cost that might have to be met by Blue Cross. For example, hospitals incur substantial expense whether a hospital bed is occupied or not. A portion of the cost of maintaining unused hospital beds is passed on to Blue Cross. Thus, if Blue Cross were assigned responsibility for utilization review, it might be advantageous to approve overlong hospital stays by beneficiaries of medicare as a means of reducing its own cost for unused beds.[207]

Each year from 1963 until 1965 witnesses from the AHA and Blue Cross testified before the congressional committees considering Medicare. No one pressed the fundamental issue of whether private insurance companies should be used as fiscal intermediaries. Witnesses for these organizations presented two somewhat contradictory lines of testimony to the committees. First, they extolled the strengths of Blue Cross as potential administrator of the Medicare program, and second, they opposed bills containing the fiscal intermediary concept and sought instead a "national Blue Cross plan" for the aged, with the federal government as underwriter.

In 1963 the AHA representatives explained the differences between the fiscal intermediary concept and underwriting as proposed by the hospitals.

In underwriting someone pays a premium and the institution concerned then guarantees for that premium certain services. Whereas in the fiscal agent relationship, some agency responsible for the furnishing of care would contract with an agency like Blue Cross, which would handle the paperwork concerned with the provision of care but the Blue Cross plan would not be responsible for the total financings based on a premium.[208]

The president of the BCA advanced two arguments for a federally underwritten Blue Cross plan. First, underwriting would allow the government to determine annual costs in advance. Second, as a fiscal intermediary the ability of Blue Cross "to influence the program professionally and to contribute to attainment of its objectives is necessarily limited." [209] He explained that under an underwriting agreement

We are proportionately more excited to be sure that the money is well spent. This is simply a human fact, that having the responsibility, the risk, you are more intensely aware of how the benefits are cared for. Even though this can be recovered in part through a rate in the second period, this factor is there. Your good will in fact is on the line.[210]

Although conceptually the difference between a system of underwriting and the use of fiscal intermediaries is easy enough to understand, members of the House committee expressed puzzlement as to the concrete, practical basis of the objection to fiscal intermediary administration. Committee members inquired whether the BCA and the AHA objected to the reimbursement formula, [211] federal money per se, [212] the accreditation provisions,[213] or the requirements of hospital affiliation for nursing homes.[214] The AHA and BCA representatives stated that they had no objection to the particular provisions mentioned but returned again and again to the question of "administration." [215] Representative Ullman finally concluded:

Your opposition is really not substantive; your opposition appears not to be based on principle but rather on procedure. For the life of me, I cannot see that you have answered at all as to the question of opposition in principle. You seem to be saying that it will in some vague way interfere with your operations.[216]

Since the proposed bill already made Blue Cross a fiscal agent, the opposition rested on a desire for a greater autonomy without federal guidelines or supervision. In addition, an underwriting arrangement would have involved substantial advance payments to Blue Cross, which it could then invest and manage as it desired. The hospitals and

Blue Cross understood that, despite the statutory and regulatory formulas, critical decisions would have to be made in day-to-day administration, particularly with respect to reimbursement. Hence they pressed for complete autonomy in the exercise of those day-to-day administrative functions.[217]

The AHA and Blue Cross campaign for a national Blue Cross plan for the aged, underwritten by the government, was not limited to congressional testimony. Blue Cross launched a public relations campaign to pursuade Congress and the voters that private insurance could meet the needs of the aged with federal underwriting. In January 1962, Walter McNerney announced the formulation of a nationwide benefit program for the aged based on uniform rates, "without age limits, with no restrictions because of pre-existing conditions and no waiting periods," and stated that the general outlines of this service had been settled upon and only "technical language" needed to be worked out. In September and October, just before the congressional elections, the BCA placed half-page ads in major news weeklies announcing this new program and urging people to get details from their local plans. In fact, most plans had no information on the new program; only about ten local plans had any new program available for the aged. Senator Williams (D.–N.J.) criticized Blue Cross for utilizing subscriber funds to conduct a politically motivated advertising campaign that was essentially misleading.[218]

While pressing for a larger degree of Blue Cross autonomy in the administration of Medicare, Blue Cross and the AHA also sought to assure that, if the fiscal intermediary concept were retained, Blue Cross would have a major role. The main points made in support of a principal role for Blue Cross as fiscal intermediary were that Blue Cross would serve as a buffer between hospitals and the government and would make Medicare more palatable to the medical profession.[219] The Blue Cross and the AHA also stressed the logistical advantages of starting the program with an organization that already existed in many localities around the country. (It was not argued that use of Blue Cross would be more economical than direct federal administration but rather that use of fiscal intermediaries would be an administrative convenience, particularly at the beginning.) [220] Finally, Blue Cross and the AHA puffed the organization's experience and capacity to audit hospital books, determine reasonable costs, educate hospitals about physician peer review, and to perform other administrative tasks needed.[221]

The AHA strongly opposed any federal interference in hospital operations, though it did not explain why it believed that federal supervision of publicly financed hospital services provided under Medicare would be necessarily detrimental. A witness for the AHA explained:

> We believe that a free hospital system should be afforded the right to decide upon the administration of any program through which they elect to provide their services.[222]

> I think [a plan administered by Blue Cross] would have virtually universal acceptance by hospitals. The Blue Cross plans are hospital oriented and again I would say that I think that *hospitals should have the right to select the method by which the program should be administered.*[223] (Emphasis supplied.)

The force of the AHA's claim that it had a "right" to determine the administrative structure of Medicare was underscored by the possibility that the hospitals might boycott Medicare if Congress did not enact a program meeting with their approval. The possibility of a hospital strike was raised repeatedly. The AHA took no official position on the question but stated that it could not guarantee or predict hospital participation if Medicare were enacted.[224]

In 1965 three major proposals for medical care for the aged were introduced: the AMA-supported "Eldercare," which would have modified Kerr-Mills to encourage states to provide medical assistance for the aged, blind, and disabled in the form of private health insurance coverage; [225] the Byrnes bill, which would have established a voluntary federal health insurance program for the aged, financed from general revenues and from premiums paid by participants; [226] and the administration bill providing hospital insurance for the aged.[227]

After the hearings before the House Ways and Means Committee, Chairman Mills introduced a new bill, H.R. 6675, which provided for three related health insurance programs. The first was the basic program of protection against hospital and related health costs, similar to the program proposed by the administration's bill (now Medicare, Part A). The second was a voluntary program of protection against the cost of physicians and certain other medical and health services not covered under the basic program (now Medicare, Part B). This supplementary program was adopted from the Byrnes bill; it was to be financed by premiums from enrollees and a matching amount paid by the federal government and administered by local Blue Shield plans.[228] The third program (now Medicaid) was an expansion of Kerr-Mills, providing matching funds to enable states to finance health care to poor people receiving categorical assistance and additional persons of low income.[229]

The legislative history shows that Congress failed to give the question of administration of the Medicare program the serious attention that was necessary if the program was to succeed. This failing is perhaps understandable, given the magnitude of the political struggle required for the passage of any Medicare program in 1965. Throughout the congressional debate no distinction was made between the roles of the BCA and the AHA as technical experts, as self-interested parties, and as political organizations. Congress was dependent upon these organizations to supply the information needed to develop the Medicare program, including information on quality care standards and problems of hospital costs, accounting, management, and governance. Even today Congress does not have the independent technical resources to enable it to evaluate various proposals for national health insurance. It must depend primarily upon the industry and upon HEW for information and analysis. There was, and is, a paucity of scholarly sociological or economic studies of hospital prepayment mechanisms.[230] The hospitals and Blue Cross were the primary sources of technical information, and it was natural that they should have been relied upon in the development of Medicare.

However, it was also to be expected that as self-interested parties and as political organizations Blue Cross and the AHA would seek a program that would serve their interests and preserve and strengthen their institutional autonomy, financial stability, and sphere of influence. Their frank opposition to "governmental influence" presumably did not rest on a belief that there was no need for improvement in hospitals but rather on a desire to effect change in their own way and at their own pace.[231] The problem is that reform of hospital administration involves large questions of public and social policy. The director of the BCA recognized the social judgments involved in hospital reimbursement, noting that Blue Cross says to the hospitals, "These are the things that *we* think are in the public interest.'' [232] The public interest is never easily fathomable, especially in the absence of popular information, governmental control, academic study, free market, or any other mechanism for public expression of satisfaction or dissatisfaction. It is unlikely, in any case, that there will be perfect harmony between the interests of the public and the aged, on the one hand, and the hospitals and Blue Cross, on the other.

Congress was in a serious bind. Given its dependence upon the hospital industry for basic technical information and the difficulty of distinguishing issues of social policy from technical questions in an unfamiliar field, perhaps the best that Congress could have done in 1965 was to maintain healthy skepticism of the "facts" as presented by the industry and to attempt rigorous questioning. Unfortunately the lengthy debates reflect little effort to do this.

Selection of Medicare Intermediaries

In 1965, Blue Cross and the AHA urged that the fiscal intermediary provisions of the proposed Medicare bill be amended to: mandate the secretary of HEW to contract with private organizations as fiscal intermediaries; allow only one intermediary in each area, to be selected by competitive bidding or by the majority of the providers; and allow the secretary to contract with one national organization (the BCA), which would in turn subcontract with local plans. [233] The first two suggestions were not adopted, but the final bill did permit the secretary to contract with the BCA. [234]

During the year prior to the implementation of Medicare, Blue Cross and the AHA worked to assure that hospitals and extended care facilities would nominate Blue Cross as their fiscal intermediary. The AHA, on behalf of its member hospitals, nominated the BCA as fiscal intermediary; the BCA was nominated by 6,876 of the 7,906 hospitals participating in Medicare. [235] More than half of the participating extended care facilities also selected Blue Cross as their intermediary. [236]

The prime contract is between the federal government and the BCA. It was negotiated in 1964 and renegotiated in 1970. [237] The BCA subcontracts with local plans for the actual performance of the responsibilities allocated intermediaries under the contract and statute. Local plans subcontract with private companies for the performance of some functions, such as auditing and computer services. Major problems have resulted from the subcontracting arrangement. It creates a series of buffers between the government and the hospitals and insulates both the hospitals and the local plans from direct government scrutiny.[238] HEW has had difficulty communicating policy changes to the local plans. The BCA exerts an enormous influence on federal Medicare policy.

With respect to the flow of information from HEW to local plans, the current contract provides that the BCA is to

> Assist the Secretary in the preparation of manuals and operating instructions of general application . . . and with the approval of the Secretary, prepare and issue such additional manuals and instructions as may be appropriate . . .[239]

and

> serve as a center for and communicate to providers of services information or instructions of the Secretary, and serve as a channel of communications from such providers of services to the Secretary.[240]

The contract specifically provides that "the flow of inquiries and responses shall be from the provider of services to a plan, to the Intermediary, to the Secretary and return." [241]

This last provision has allowed the BCA to interpret the secretary's communications for the local plans, reshape the federal directives, and provide local plans with concurrent advice on means of avoiding federal directives. For example,

> For almost three years the St. Louis plan allowed hospitals to utilize the estimated percentage method of cost finding, regardless of their ability to utilize more sophisticated and accurate methods. In 1967, the Social Security Administration (SSA) issued a directive informing plans that the St. Louis interpretation was incorrect, and that the estimated percentage method was available only on a temporary basis to hospitals which had not yet developed a cost finding capacity. The St. Louis plan refused to follow the federal directive, stating that the SSA decision must be reviewed by BCA, and that they would continue to use the estimated percentage method "until specifically instructed by the Blue Cross Association to discontinue the procedure." [242]

There have been other instances in which Social Security Administration instructions to local plans have been countermanded by the BCA. Thomas Tierney, director of the SSA Bureau of Health Insurance, notes that the BCA "is quite jealous of its role" as communicator of federal directives.[243]

Apart from the policy-making powers it places in the hands of the BCA in its role as conveyor of information between the federal government and the local plans, the current contract with BCA provides that

> No regulation or General Instruction shall be prescribed by the Secretary for the administration of this agreement without adequate prior notice to the Intermediary and prior consultation by the Secretary with the Intermediary, with respect to the content of such Regulation or General Instruction and its effect upon the administration of this agreement.[244]

This provision assures the BCA substantial opportunity to shape the content of federal policy.

The prime contract with the BCA makes it difficult for the Social Security Administration to monitor the operations of local plans. Between 1965 and 1970, regional HEW officials who informed local plans of administrative problems were referred to the BCA in Chicago.[245] The 1970 contract attempted to alleviate this difficulty by providing that the secretary may inspect and evaluate local plans, after giving reasonable notice to the BCA,[246] and may communicate directly with them concerning matters covered in the plan subcontract, provided announcements of new policy are first communicated to the BCA.[247] While these provisions are helpful, they do not change the basic pattern requiring that communications be routed through the BCA.

Another major problem in contracting through the BCA rather than directly with local plans is that it creates pressure to accept all local plans, however ineffective. The Senate Finance Committee noted in 1969 that

> No local Blue Cross plan has been rejected by the Blue Cross Association for Medicare as being too small or inefficient. The administrative capacity and performance of the subcontractors range widely, yet the Social Security Administration has so far taken the good with the bad under this "all or none" prime contract arrangement.[248]

The prime contract with the BCA is silent on the power of the secretary to terminate a subcontract with a particular local plan. The subcontract between the BCA and local plans provides that the secretary may terminate an agreement with a local plan if continuation is "inconsistent with the efficient administration" of the program,[249] and the secretary has clear statutory authority to do so.[250] As a practical matter, however, the prime contract with BCA seems to have fostered an uncritical federal attitude of accepting all local plans, however ineffective or inadequate. The BCA has sought to protect local plans from federal scrutiny and has taken the position that "you have contracted with us to carry out these functions, now it is up to you to make an appraisal of our *overall* performance and see how we are doing it. It is not up to you to tell us how to do it." [251] The contracting structure and the attitude it fosters have undermined the selectivity and scrutiny necessary to effective use of fiscal agents.[252]

In response to this problem,[253] Congress amended the Social Security Act in 1972 to provide that the secretary may assign or reassign any provider to any intermediary "whenever he determines, in his sole discretion, that to do so would result in more effective and efficient administration." The provider's choice of intermediary should be taken into consideration, but it is not binding.[254] This amendment makes more explicit the secretary's authority to eliminate ineffective intermediaries from Medicare administration. However, it remains to be seen whether the statutory change will produce a change in attitude and administrative structure at HEW.

The Department of Health, Education and Welfare does not monitor fiscal intermediary operations on any regular or comprehensive basis.[255] The Social Security Administration has overall responsibility for the administration of Medicare, while the Medical Services Administration monitors state administration of Medicaid. There is no regular review of intermediary operations and no mechanism for review where there are indications that the intermediary may not be performing effectively. The HEW Audit Agency and the General Accounting Office review some aspects of the performance of some intermediaries.[256] Until 1972, the Contract Performance Review Branch of HEW conducted some formal reviews of fiscal intermediaries.[257] Though its reports were the most detailed source of information available on intermediary operations,[258] HEW refused to release them to the public or even to members of Congress. In January 1972, the Health Law Project of the University of Pennsylvania filed suit under the Freedom of Information Act to obtain these reports and other information on the operation of Medicare and Medicaid.[259] In September 1972, HEW proposed regulations making future reports available, and Congress subsequently amended the Social Security Act to require that they be made available to the public.[260] HEW has now stopped preparing these reports and has instituted instead a new series of reports to be prepared by the Regional Offices of the Bureau of Health Insurance, to be known as the Annual Contract Evaluation Reports (ACER). These are to be available on request.[261]

There has been dissatisfaction in Congress with the amount of supervision exercised over Medicare and Medicaid. In 1972, "after years of inquiry and extensive examination of the medicare and medicaid programs," the Senate Finance Committee found that these programs

> have suffered from the lack of a dynamic and ongoing mechanism with specific responsibility for continuing review of medicare and medicaid in terms of the effectiveness of program operations and compliance with congressional intent. . . . There is a pronounced need for vigorous day-to-day and month-to-month monitoring of these programs, conducted by a unit relatively free of constant pressures from various nonpublic interests.[262]

The Senate then proposed establishment of an Inspector General for Health Administration as part of the 1972 Social Security amendments. The Inspector General was to arrange, conduct, or direct reviews, investigations, inspections, and audits of Medicare, Medicaid, and other programs of health care established under the Social Security Act. However, this amendment was eliminated in conference.[263]

The deficiencies of HEW supervision of Blue Cross operations and its secrecy have made it difficult for academic or other outside analysts to scrutinize the actual working of the system.

The District Court for the District of Columbia ruled, with respect to the other information sought by the Health Law Project, that HEW is not immune from the requirements of the Freedom of Information Act and must provide information on the operation of Medicare and Medicaid unless there is some specific statutory justification for keeping the information secret.[264] This decision and the new Annual Contract Evaluation Reports could be important in making possible more broadly based examination of the operation of federal health programs than has thus far been feasible.

USE OF FISCAL INTERMEDIARIES IN THE
ADMINISTRATION OF MEDICAID

The Social Security Act makes no provision for the use of fiscal intermediaries in the administration of the Medicaid program. The act requires that states wishing to participate in Medicaid and to obtain federal reimbursement for medical services provided to eligible poor people designate a single state agency to supervise the administration of the plan.[265] The state plan itself must "provide such methods of administration . . . as are found by the Secretary to be necessary for the proper and efficient operation of the plan." [266]

With the encouragement of the BCA, many local plans came forward and requested a role in the administration of Medicaid.[267] In 1968, Blue Cross and Blue Shield were involved in the administration of Medicaid in 23 states, with Blue Cross paying about $1.2 million to hospitals and nursing homes for services to Medicaid eligibles. This is about one-third of the amount paid out by Blue Cross under its private contracts.[268] In some local plans the financial impact of Medicaid is even more significant. The New Mexico plan paid out three times as much under Medicaid as under its private business; in Los Angeles and Oakland, Medicaid payments were twice as large as private payments.[269]

Despite massive Blue Cross involvement in Medicaid administration, there are few federal standards for the use of Blue Cross in the program. The HEW Handbook of Public Assistance Administration sets out, in the most general terms, the provisions that must be included in a state contract with a fiscal intermediary.[270] However, there are no standards for payments to intermediaries for administrative costs. Until 1971 there were no federal regulations whatsoever on state arrangements with fiscal intermediaries, and the regulations finally adopted simply reiterate the vague provisions of the Handbook.[271]

Given the lack of federal standards, "the nature and extent of contractual involvement and the character of relationships between the

State program and the fiscal agent have been a matter simply of individual negotiation,'' [272] and there is wide variation in the rates paid to Blue Cross under Medicaid. In 1970, fifteen Medicaid programs utilizing fiscal agents on a no-profit/no-loss basis made payments for administrative costs ranging from $.70 to $2.70 per claim; nine states made payments at a fixed rate per claim of $.15 to $2.50. Other states reimbursed on the basis of actual cost, cost per line item, operating cost plus a percentage markup, reasonable cost, a specified percentage of the benefit expenditures, or other methods. [273] Some of the rate differences represent variations in services performed by the Blue Cross plan. However, the relative negotiating strength of the plan and the state agency are also significant rate determinants. For example, Indiana, Iowa, Pennsylvania, and Minnesota all reimburse Blue Cross on the basis of an amount per claim processed. Indiana pays from $.92 to $1.12 per claim; Iowa pays $1.19 per claim; Pennsylvania pays $1.50; Minnesota pays $1.88. [274] The services provided by the local Blue Cross are essentially similar, except that the Pennsylvania Blue Cross, which charges a relatively high rate, only processes the claims and turns them over to the state for payment, while the other plans both process and pay claims. [275] The contrast is even more striking in states paying a rate based on a percentage of the total amount of money processed. Kansas pays 1.29 per cent of all claims processed, less $1,590 per month. Alabama pays 1.75 per cent of sums paid for inpatient hospitalization. Vermont pays 4 per cent of total benefits paid to providers, and Massachusetts pays 6 per cent of claims paid. [276] The services provided by Blue Cross are similar in each of these states. [277] Apart from the unaccountable differences in the rates of payment for Blue Cross administrative services, payments based on a percentage of the amounts paid in claims create a disincentive to cost control or claims review.

The absence of federal standards for the use of intermediaries in Medicaid is a serious problem that is compounded by the lack of federal supervision of the state arrangements. Occasional reviews by the HEW Audit Agency and the comptroller general have been the primary form of federal monitoring. [278] These reviews have been harshly critical of Blue Cross. Common deficiencies are: failure to prevent duplicate payments after a beneficiary has died or eligibility has terminated; failure to determine actual ''customary charges'' in states where they are a basis for payment for services; failure to identify claims that might be covered in whole or part by the recipient's private insurance; failure to audit hospital books; failure to assist hospitals in instituting utilization review programs.[279]

Apart from these weaknesses in the system, there are problems that arise directly from the use of local Blue Cross plans in Medicaid administration, the most common being unaccountable and excessive payments to them. An HEW Audit Agency study describes, as "one illustrative example," the contract between the Texas State Department of Public Welfare (TSDPW) and Group Health Services, Inc., a subsidiary of Blue Cross/Blue Shield of Texas.

> The only information provided TSDPW as the basis for determining GHS administrative costs was a one page summary of estimated costs which totaled over $3 million. The summary listed 10 administrative costs items, one of which was "provider audits" at an estimated cost of $225,000. As of the date of our audit, no provider audits had been made and there were no firm plans to make any. . . .
>
> Another item was $1.2 million for "data processing." . . . There was no documentation available to show the relationship between estimated costs expected under the terms of the contract and the $1.2 million.[280]

Another item in the amount of $260,000 was listed for "executive, administrative, and legal" costs, but no itemization or allocation was ever requested or provided to show whether this amount was reasonably spent and reasonably attributable to the Medicaid operation.

Another HEW Audit Agency study found that there was no way of knowing whether the administrative costs paid to Delaware Blue Cross were reasonable or properly charged to Medicaid. The contract required Blue Cross to submit biannual reports showing costs and expenses together with supporting data, but Blue Cross failed to submit the information. The state agency accepted the Blue Cross figures without question, because it did not have the personnel to determine their accuracy. The state auditor of accounts audited the Blue Cross books but did not attempt to check the accuracy of its apportionments.[281]

Even though Blue Cross plans are nonprofit organizations, the administration of Medicaid can be a profit-making endeavor. For example, one profit-making Texas corporation (Electronic Data Systems Federal Corp., EDSFC) has contracts to perform all data processing operations for Blue Cross and Blue Shield in eleven states, including four of the five largest state Medicaid programs. Standard and Poor's corporations earnings reports show that this company had a profit margin of 48 per cent in 1969 and 31 per cent in 1970.[282] In Nevada Blue Shield profits directly from the administration of Medicaid, because the state pays a "fee unrelated to costs" of ten cents per claim processed.[283]

Maladministration has been a serious problem for Medicaid.[284] HEW does not have sufficient information to know whether the program has functioned more effectively in states using fiscal intermediaries or in states that administer the program directly. The HEW regional offices, which have prime responsibility for assuring that the categorical assistance and Medicaid programs are operated in accordance with federal requirements, have done little to monitor the intermediaries.[285] In recent years the most effective policing of state Medicaid and welfare programs has been initiated by the beneficiaries of these programs. Where states have failed to provide the benefits required under the Social Security Act, beneficiaries have enforced federal requirements, either through the courts [286] or by bringing pressure on HEW.[287] However, the actual administration of Medicaid has not been a subject of public or beneficiary concern. The function of Blue Cross in Medicaid administration is not widely understood. It is difficult to obtain information about Blue Cross/Medicaid operations. The effects of maladministration are diffuse, and often correction of problems would not produce any tangible gain to any particular class of beneficiaries. Lack of public and beneficiary interest, while understandable, is unfortunate, since when hospital books go unaudited excessive payments are made to fiscal agents, duplicate payments are made to doctors and hospitals, total program costs soar, benefits are reduced, and the needy beneficiaries suffer. Until 1972 the Social Security Act provided that a state could not reduce the scope of benefits available under Medicaid unless it could demonstrate that it had instituted a program to control unnecessary utilization of services.[288] The 1972 amendments eliminated this requirement, and states are now free to reduce Medicaid benefits as they choose.[289]

BLUE CROSS AND FEDERAL EMPLOYEES BENEFITS

The Federal Employees Health Benefits Act of 1959 was the first governmental health program to make substantial use of Blue Cross.[290] The act provides government contributions toward prepaid health service benefits for federal employees, annuitants, and their dependents. It authorizes the Civil Service Commission to contract for or approve four types of health benefit plans: a service benefit plan, an indemnity benefit plan, employee organization plans, and comprehensive medical plans.[291] It was passed to make government employment competitive with employment in the private sector.[292]

Blue Cross was a vigorous advocate of health insurance for federal employees, and the act bears the mark of Blue Cross influence. Unlike Medicare, the Federal Employee Benefit Program (FEBP) is an underwriting program in which the government purchases insurance for its employees from private insurance companies. During the legislative debate, Blue Cross and Blue Shield convinced Congress of the superiority of hospital service benefit coverage and of their exclusive superiority in the field.[293] The act requires that there be one government-wide service benefit plan, and Blue Cross/Blue Shield are the only existing organizations that meet the statutory specifications.[294] To assure their hegemony against potential competition, Blue Cross/Blue Shield obtained a provision allowing the Civil Service Commission to contract without competitive bidding.[295]

The FEBP is the largest voluntary employee group health insurance program in the world, insuring more than 8 million people in 1970: 61.5 per cent of these have selected the service benefit plan of Blue Cross/Blue Shield.[296] Subscription income to Blue Cross and Blue Shield totaled more than $700 million in 1971 and was projected to reach over $1 billion in 1972.[297] FEBP accounts for about 6 per cent of the total business done by Blue Cross and 8 per cent of its total premium income.[298] Under the act federal employees must be offered both a high option and low option service benefit contract.[299] The options differ in the range of covered services, coinsurance, deductibles and dollar maximums, and subscription rate. Eighty-five per cent of federal employees electing the service benefit coverage have chosen the high option plan.

Responsibility for the administration of FEBP is assigned to the Civil Service Commission (CSC), which in turn delegates contracting and supervisory duties to the Bureau of Retirement Insurance.[300] The BCA and the National Association of Blue Shield Plans (NABSP) serve as contracting agency for 147 local plans around the country.[301] Under the contract with the national associations, the local plans are required to provide all benefits enumerated to eligible subscribers in the areas they serve.

The statute gives the CSC great discretion in determining the scope of benefits offered, premium rates charged, reserve levels, and administrative procedures. Theoretically, the role of the CSC is that of a large employer negotiating on behalf of itself and its employees for the best possible health insurance package obtainable. As will be shown, the CSC has in fact used the discretion given it under the statute to create a program in which the premium levels and reserves are set at inflationary levels, which assure that Blue Cross and Blue Shield bear absolutely no risk and are guaranteed generous administrative expenses and profits.

Premium rates are determined, on the basis of the experience of those insured under the FEBP, by negotiations between the CSC and the BCA/NABSP.[302] The CSC is supposed to be guided by the general practices of other large employers. The initial rates determined in 1960 remained stable until 1964, when rates began to increase.[303] From 1960 to 1970, the cumulative overall Blue Cross rate increase was 202 per cent.[304] Costs of the program are shared by the government, which contributes an annually adjusted amount of about 40 per cent of the average premiums, and the federal employees, whose contributions are deducted from pay or annuity.[305] The CSC may use up to 1 per cent of premium income per annum for the costs of administering the program and may set aside up to 3 per cent per annum of premium income for a contingency reserve.[306] The net subscription charges and government contributions, exclusive of the administrative and contingency reserves, are paid to Blue Cross/Blue Shield for subscriber health benefits.[307]

The act provides that the contingency reserve may be used to defray increases in future rates, to reduce the contributions of employees and the government, or to increase benefits.[308] The contingency reserve has not been used for these purposes but rather has been kept at a high level and accumulated from year to year. The CSC regulations specify one month's premium income, or approximately $45 million, as the preferred minimum balance to be held in the reserve.[309] The actual contingency reserve fluctuates between one and two months' premium.[310] As the contingency reserve builds up above this level, the excess is paid to Blue Cross/Blue Shield.

In addition to the contingency reserve, special reserves are also held by the BCA and NABSP. The special reserve is the net gain as calculated from the inception of the program. Each year, all premiums paid are added together, and from this amount are subtracted all claims paid, administrative expenses, taxes, *state mandatory reserves,* and risk charges, or profits. The money remaining, if any, is credited to the special reserve.[311] By the end of 1969 the level of the cumulative special reserve had reached approximately $20 million.[312] In 1970 the plan sustained an operating loss of approximately $57 million; since the previous year's surplus in the special reserve and investment income of approximately $6 million were used, the deficit in the special reserve was $30 million at the end of 1970.[313] The special reserve is supposed to serve as a cushion against future experience. If the premium in any year is not sufficient to cover the cost of benefits and other liabilities, as it was not in 1970, the necessary money is taken out of the special reserve. If there is not enough money in the special reserve to cover losses in any one year, the deficit is carried over and is a proper charge against the special reserve that may be recovered in subsequent years by rate increases.

Blue Cross/Blue Shield also holds a claims reserve for expenses incurred by subscribers but not yet presented for payment. CSC regulations require that the total of the special and claims reserves be equal to the prior five months' subscription charges. If, at the end of the contract year, the total claims reserves are below this level, they are brought up to the required minimum with payments from the CSC's contingency reserve.[314] Since funds in the contingency reserve have always been well above the required one month's premiums, these transfers keep it from accumulating to even more astronomical levels.[315]

This generous three-part reserve structure has been severely criticized as inflationary. The CSC has attempted to set rates so that there would be one month's premium income in the contingency reserve and two month's premium income in the special reserve.[316] This amounts to 25 per cent of the annual premium income in reserve. In 1972 the comptroller general studied the FEBP and found that traditional insurance theory would not justify cumulative and special reserves in excess of 5 per cent.[317] The CSC justifies the high reserve levels on grounds that it promotes rate stability and avoids the necessity of readjusting rates every year.[318] But if large sums of money are accumulated in reserves it is likely that costs will go up. The Wyatt Company report notes:

> subscription rates for the government-wide service benefit plan may be instituted so far in advance of its effective date that increase in hospital and surgical charges can be planned to use up the extra money. In short, there may be a kind of Parkinson's law operating here, such that health costs tend to rise to the level of contemplated subscription income.[319]

Special and claims reserves held by Blue Cross and Blue Shield must be invested,[320] and the investments must be supervised. Investment policy is determined by the Joint Contract Administration Committee (JCAC) composed of four representatives from Blue Cross and four from Blue Shield.[321] In 1970 the income from the investment of these reserves was over $6 million.[322] Despite the obvious possibilities for abuse in the management of such large sums of money, the CSC exercises no active control.

For example in 1960 the JCAC established a policy to hold three-quarters of a month's subscription income in cash to meet current obligations. On December 13, 1962, this policy was changed to require the holding of one-half month's income in cash. This amounted to over $10 million. The JCAC delegated management of the cash balance to Group Hospitalization, Inc. (GHI), which holds a contract with the national plans to perform FEBP administration. GHI placed the money in noninterest-bearing accounts in banks that had officers who also served as GHI directors.[323] The CSC did not notice these conflicts of interest and violation of fiduciary responsibility until 1964. In 1963 and 1964 the CSC audited GHI and the BCA and merely suggested that Blue Cross and Blue Shield "reexamine" their investment policy. In 1964, Blue Cross/Blue Shield adopted a policy requiring GHI "to maintain in its cash accounts only such funds as are required to promptly satisfy FEBP obligations, and to make all other FEBP funds available for investment."

But in 1967 a General Accounting Office audit of GHI revealed that funds in excess of $10 million were still being held in noninterest-bearing savings accounts. GHI initially resisted GAO recommendations to alter this policy and reduce the cash balance. On December 31, 1967, arrangements were finally made to open an interest-bearing savings account for these funds.[324]

Federal employees' premiums and government contributions are inflated by high administrative costs and profits to Blue Cross/Blue Shield. The CSC makes no effort to establish standards or to monitor the legitimacy of administration costs. Blue Cross and Blue Shield are paid actual administrative expenses incurred, not exceeding a total of 4.5 per cent of the annual subscriptions charged.[325] The contract provides that determination of the "actual and necessary expenses incurred" is to be made by Blue Cross and Blue Shield.[326] In 1971 they used 4.38 per cent of subscription income for administrative expenses.[327] In 1970 and 1971 enrollment increased by 11 per cent, subscription charges increased by 48 per cent, and administrative expenses grew by 45 per cent.[328] Aetna, which underwrites the FEBP government-wide indemnity benefit plan, has a contractual ceiling on administrative expenses of 4 per cent of subscription income. Its actual expenses are 2.5 per cent of subscription income.[329] The Wyatt Company report recommended a careful CSC examination of the Blue Cross/Blue Shield administrative expenses. The commission has conducted no such review [330] and simply accepts the explanation that the service benefit plan is inherently more costly to run than the indemnity benefit plan.[331] In response to congressional questioning about high entertainment costs and first class air fare, a Blue Cross official drew a distinction between Blue Cross as an intermediary for Medicare and Medicaid, which are considered government accounts, and as an underwriter for the FEBP, which is considered a private insurance arrangement.[332]

Blue Cross and Blue Shield are guaranteed a profit on the FEBP contract. Prior to 1972, the amount paid was based on a percentage of premium income. In 1960 they received profits of 1.5 per cent of premium income; by 1971 the rate had been reduced to 0.6 per cent.[333] Government contracts providing for the payment of costs plus a percentage of costs raise serious legal questions,[334] and in 1972 the basis for calculating profit was changed. Under the 1972 contract Blue Cross and Blue Shield receive a flat, negotiated sum of $5.1 million, which amounts to about one dollar for each person enrolled.[335] The amount of profit paid to Blue Cross has never depended upon its administrative efficiency or financial experience. In a year in which Blue

Cross and Blue Shield claimed a $68 million deficit, they received a $5 million profit.[336]

Even though Blue Cross and Blue Shield are nonprofit organizations, they receive this profit on the FEBP contract just as the commercial insurers do. The profit was originally paid to them because they insisted upon it,[337] although in the early years of the program it was called a "risk charge" and sometimes justified as a payment for some unidentifiable risk they took in administering the program.[338] In the 1972 contract the profit item is denominated a "public service charge." Blue Cross is not required to spend this money for "public service," however, and the CSC takes no responsibility or interest in its disposition.[339]

The greatest FEBP costs are not for reserves, administration, or profits but rather for payments to doctors and hospitals for services rendered to subscribers. The CSC does not examine the rates of hospital or physician reimbursement, and there is little public information available on this element of the program's cost. A recent suit by the National Association of Government Employees and others challenges as wasteful and unnecessary a provision of the current contract which requires that psychological services be supervised by a physician.[340] Further study is needed of cost control under the FEBP contract.

In 1972 the negotiation process between the CSC and Blue Cross/Blue Shield was for the first time subject to public scrutiny as a result of investigations by a special subcommittee of the House of Representatives. This examination illustrates some of the problems besetting the program.

In June 1971, BCA/NABSP submitted a request to the CSC for a 53.2 per cent rate increase based on a claimed 1970 deficit of $8 million and a projected 1971 operating loss of $68 million.[341] The increase was intended to recoup the entire 1971 cumulative deficit and reestablish a special reserve of one month's subscription charges.[342] The CSC did not question the accuracy of the BCA/NABSP data. It counterproposed a 39.9 per cent increase in the high option plan with no reduction in benefits.[343] This was based on a goal of zero balance in the special reserve rather than the building of a positive one month's special reserve. The commission offered a contract amendment pledging the contingency reserve to the credit of the BCA/NABSP for payment of incurred claims in the event the contract was ever terminated by either party.[344]

The CSC also proposed that the profit be paid as a flat rate of $5.1 million rather than as a percentage of premium and, as we have seen, be called a "public service charge" rather than a "risk charge." The flat rate "public service charge" meant a loss in profit of about $2 million. Blue Cross/Blue Shield first rejected the proposed change but later accepted it on condition that the CSC pledge that the contingency reserve would be available, upon discontinuance of the contract by either side, for the payment of all liabilities arising under the contract, including the administrative expenses related to contract discontinuance.[345] In September 1971 the parties agreed on a contract providing for the 39.9 per cent rate increase, a $5.1 million "public service charge," and the pledge of the contingency reserves for all expenses associated with discontinuance of the contract.

The CSC did not drive a hard bargain.[346] The pledge of the contingency reserve, an enormous gift to Blue Cross/Blue Shield, removes the last vestige of risk existing under the contract and provides the organizations a bonus for discontinuing the contract.[347] The CSC reached this agreement despite having engaged a firm of actuaries that studied the 1972 benefit structure and recommended that a 25 per cent increase in the high option plan and no increase in the low option plan would be ideal and that "a strong bargaining position is warranted in the matter." [348]

Subsequently the 1972 contract had to be renegotiated to comply with the guidelines for Phase II of the President's Economic Stabilization Program.[349] Blue Cross/Blue Shield adjusted its loss projections and proposed a 34.1 per cent high option increase, which was accepted by the CSC on October 28, 1971. In December 1971, the Price Commission reduced the proposed increase to 22 per cent, without elaborating on the factors upon which its decision was based.[350] Blue Cross/Blue Shield protested that the 22 per cent increase would jeopardize their existence and projected a loss of $60 million on the FEBP contract in 1972.[351] By April 1972 financial statements showed that the cumulative deficit actually incurred at the end of 1971 was $15 million rather than the $68 million forecast, and the projected loss for the end of 1972 was $6,752,000 rather than the $60 million projected three months before.[352]

One of the factors reducing the costs of the FEBP in 1972 was a restriction in the extent of benefits provided. On June 23, 1971, BCA/NABSP distributed an internal memo to participating plans direct- ing them to take immediate steps to "assure more precise benefit ad- ministration to the *letter* of the FEP Contract with the U.S. Civil Service Commission." (Emphasis in original.) It listed sixteen benefit areas that should receive "immediate executive and administrative attention" and stated, "We cannot overemphasize the *urgent* need to implement steps to provide the maximum relief from present incidence and cost trends." (Emphasis in original.) [353] The practical effect of this new policy was to reduce the scope of benefits provided by initiating a tightened system of claims review in which payments were denied for services that pre- viously were covered.[354] Blue Cross/Blue Shield did not give notice to federal employees of this change in coverage and did not inform the CSC or the Price Commission of the reduction in services even though it was intended to and, in fact, had an immediate and sizable impact on cost and utilization trends in 1972.[355]

When the CSC finally learned of the new policy, it determined that only one of the sixteen cost control measures was a direct breach of the contract, but it refused to take any action except to try to persuade Blue Cross/Blue Shield to abide by the contract.[356] Aggrieved federal employees instituted legal action to enforce the contract,[357] and an out- of-court settlement favorable to the employees was subsequently reached.[358] Representative Jerome Waldie, chairman of the House Sub- committee on Retirement, Insurance, and Health Benefits, filed an ap- peal with the Price Commission calling for an immediate reduction of the 1972 rate increase.[359]

The CSC failure to react to the unilateral reduction in the scope of benefits is typical of the approach the agency has taken. Under the FEBP, the CSC has broad discretion to negotiate the scope of benefits to be provided.[360] The benefits now provided are oriented toward the coverage of inpatient hospital care for catastrophic medical problems. Federal employees who choose Blue Cross do not enjoy the benefits of comprehensive or preventive care and tend to use more and costlier hospital services than federal employees who are enrolled in group practice plans.[361]

Because of the rate structure, workers who choose low option Blue Cross coverage subsidize those who take high option coverage.[362] Em- ployees are not given clear information on the scope of benefits provided. They often obtain services which they believe the insurance will pay, only to discover after the fact that Blue Cross and Blue Shield have denied payment. The employee has no effective means of challenging this sometimes arbitrary, ex post facto denial of coverage.[363] The CSC has shown no interest in any of these problems and has not acted on behalf of employees to find equitable solutions.[364]

The CSC is wholly dependent upon Blue Cross and Blue Shield for the actuarial estimates upon which rates are based.[365] The act provides that the CSC may request an annual budget in which the expenses of administering and supervising the FEBP do not exceed 1 per cent of the premium income.[366] In 1972 $13 million was available to the CSC, but it requested an appropriation of only $1,641,000.[367]

The FEBP statute gives the Civil Service Commission great discretion and places upon it the responsibility of negotiating the best possible health insurance coverage obtainable. It requires that the commission actively work to protect the interests of the employees and the government. It is not easy, however, to devise a statutory framework that will promote and assure an aggressive administrative attitude. The act attempts to insure that the CSC will be accountable to federal employees by providing for an employee advisory committee,[368] but this committee is purely advisory, is controlled by the CSC, and has been ineffectual.[369] A recent suit by the National Association of Government Employees alleges that they are not "permitted to, nor do they, participate in any manner in the negotiations as to the import, purpose or meaning of the contract [which] . . . is presented to the subscribers and the general public as an accomplished fact." [370] Furthermore, the present CSC staff is probably inadequate to negotiate effectively on behalf of federal employees for the best possible coverage and lowest possible premiums. The experience of the FEBP service benefit plan shows the dangers of a flexible program involving private insurance companies without strict regulatory control by a vigorous and independent agency. The issue of how such an agency can be created will be considered after more detailed examination of Blue Cross administration of payments to hospitals and claims and utilization review.

4. BLUE CROSS AND THE COST OF HOSPITAL SERVICES

The method and amount of payment to providers of services are probably the most important issues in any public health service program. Not only is the cost of the program critical in itself, but, since hospital service is not a fixed identifiable commodity, payment patterns can have a large effect on the character and quality of services, utilization patterns, and institutional and community planning. The Social Security Act requires that hospitals be paid their full "reasonable costs" for services provided to poor people eligible for Medicaid and the aged eligible for Medicare. In programs such as these, which rely upon the voluntary cooperation of providers of services, payment levels are a key factor in determining whether services will be available. Methods of reimbursement under Medicare and Medicaid significantly influence payment standards under private hospitalization programs and the entire fiscal structure of the hospital industry.

GENESIS OF THE REASONABLE COST CONCEPT [371]

As has been noted, Blue Cross has been committed from its inception to the payment of service benefits to hospitals as opposed to a fixed cash indemnity to subscribers. In its early years, payments were made to hospitals on the basis of charges or a percentage of charges. Payments were made essentially on an arbitrary basis, depending on the relative negotiating strength and wishes of both hospitals and Blue Cross. Precise measurement of the fair costs of services was impossible because of the unwillingness or inability of hospitals to make available actual costs of service and because of the lack of uniformity in hospital accounting. [372]

The first major service-benefit, cost-based reimbursement program in the nation was the Emergency Maternity and Infant Care Program (EMIC), established in April 1943 on a temporary wartime basis by the U.S. Children's Bureau. A memo in that year from the bureau to the state health agencies administering the program instructed them that payment for hospital services was to be based on

> the actual per diem cost of operating the hospital, to embrace all costs of care while mother and newborn infant are in the hospital, including delivery room, laboratory service, drugs, and so forth, except the medical services of the attending physician.

The definition was refined in subsequent memos to exclude the costs of research and education and include the salaries and expenses of house staff and "other" physicians. Depreciation was not allowed as a cost, but an overall allowance of 10 per cent of the per diem costs was paid to cover this item, bad debts, and other unspecified costs.[373] This reasonable cost reimbursement system was popular with the hospitals.[374] By the late fifties, there was a definite trend toward "reasonable cost" reimbursement by Blue Cross plans.[375]

Reasonable cost reimbursement had, and has, little to do with reasonableness. The method as utilized by Blue Cross simply meant that an average daily cost of hospital care was determined by dividing the hospital's total allowable expenses by the total number of patient days. An adjustment was then made for private, semi-private and ward service, with semi-private costs at 100 per cent, private at 115 per cent, and ward at 90 per cent. These figures were recognized to be essentially arbitrary.[376] No effort was made to determine whether total hospital costs or any component thereof were reasonable according to some market or other standard. Rather, Blue Cross use of the concept focused solely on what costs were "allowable." Even the standards governing what was "allowable" were rather limited and arbitrary.

In 1953 the American Hospital Association first published its Principles of Payment for Hospital Care setting forth, in the most general terms, standards for the determination of allowable costs. In 1963 an AHA-Blue Cross task force produced a slightly revised edition of the Principles of Payment. This 16-page document had great influence on the development of the Medicare program. In general it required that Blue Cross payments to hospitals should be such as to "pay fairly and adequately for services purchased, maintain essential services, and encourage the development of higher standards of service to meet the needs of the community." Total costs should not exceed total charges. "Rates of payment should reflect current hospital costs." "Payments to different hospitals for the same service may differ.'' [377] The principles provided general guidance for determining reasonable costs and stated how certain specific items, such as education costs, bad debts, and depreciation, were to be treated. [378]

Within the federal government, there was some additional experience with payment for hospital services on a reasonable cost basis. The Vocational Rehabilitation Act of 1943 made grants available to the states to provide services to disabled individuals with employment potential and called for payments to hospitals on the basis of a reasonable cost formula. [379] Under Title V of the Social Security Act, beginning in 1940, grants were provided to the states for payments for medical care for crippled children. States were to pay hospitals on the basis of a reasonable cost formula. [380] The Department of Defense program of Medicare for military dependents, which began in 1956, utilized private insurance companies in administration (Blue Cross on the coasts and Mutual of Omaha in central states) and paid hospitals according to the customary method of reimbursement utilized by the insurance company involved. [381] None of these programs was very large. [382] Further, there seems to have been virtually no study or analysis of the effect of this method of reimbursement, as opposed to another, in any of these programs.

The AHA principles were heavily relied upon in congressional consideration of the payments to be made to hospitals under Medicare. [383] Given the growing popularity of ''reasonable costs'' as a basis for Blue Cross reimbursement, and the AHA's commitment to this method of payment, there was never any doubt that Congress would declare that providers should be paid their ''reasonable costs.'' [384] During the legislative consideration, once the difference between costs and charges had been made clear, [385] the AHA principles were relied upon exclusively. The Ways and Means Committee was concerned—as part of a larger concern about noninterference with the medical profession—that the Medicare provision not affect the charges which hospitals made to non-Medicare patients. Wilbur Cohen, under secretary of HEW, assured the committee that what hospitals charge non-Medicare patients ''is of absolutely no concern to us under the bill.'' [386]

It was made quite clear that the reasonable cost principle would allow full reimbursement to a wide variety of hospitals. Robert Ball, HEW actuary, explained that the ''general point''—the ''main'' and ''overwhelming'' principle—was to ''figure costs according to nationally determined cost accounting principles. The resulting per diem costs will differ depending on the hospital and from place to place, and we will reimburse whatever it turns out to be.'' [387] The only exception to this rule was taken from the AHA principles, which state, ''If a hospital's costs depart substantially from other hospitals of similar size, scope of services, and utilization, maximum reimbursement may be established through agreement reached between third party purchasers.'' [388] However, as Mr. Ball explained, this exception would only apply where a hospital ''seems to be managed badly and very uneconomically. . . . But this would be extremely rare, and the usual situation would be whatever it costs, that would be paid.'' [389]

The basic statutory standard for payments to hospitals, nursing homes, and home health care agencies under Medicare, Part A, provides that ''the amount paid to any provider of services with respect to services for which payment may be made under this part shall . . . be the lesser of (A) the reasonable cost of such services, . . . or (B) the customary charges with respect to such services.'' [390] The secretary is to promulgate regulations defining ''reasonable costs or methods to be used, and the items to be included, in determining such costs for various types or classes of institutions, agencies, and services.'' He is given wide latitude and

> may provide for determination of the costs of services on a per diem, per unit, per capita, or other basis, may provide for using different methods in different circumstances, may provide for the use of estimates of costs of particular items or services, and may provide for the use of charges or a percentage of charges where this method reasonably reflects the costs. [391]

He should ''consider, among other things, the principles generally applied by national organizations or established prepayment organizations.'' [392] The statute provides two additional general mandates. First, regulations on reasonable cost shall

> take into account both direct and indirect costs of providers of services in order that . . . the costs with respect to individuals covered by the insurance programs established by this title will not be borne by individuals not so covered, and the costs with respect to individuals not so covered will not be borne by such insurance programs. [393]

Each group must pay its own way. Second, the secretary should provide for making suitable "retroactive corrective adjustment" where reimbursement proves "either inadequate or excessive." [394]

Apart from this general guidance, the statute mandates that inpatient care should normally be given in semi-private accommodations and requires that appropriate adjustments be made when services are given in private accommodations or on a ward. If private accommodations are medically indicated, they can be reimbursed on the reasonable cost basis. [395]

Development of Medicare Principles of Reimbursement

Before examining some of the major issues of reimbursement under the federal regulations, it is useful to look at the process by which the regulations were determined. When the Medicare program was enacted on July 30, 1965, the Social Security Administration began consultations with the American Hospital Association, the Blue Cross Association, local Blue Cross officials, and others to determine the details of the reasonable cost reimbursement formula. These negotiations were conducted entirely in private. Even Congress was denied access to information. During the year of negotiations, Senate Finance Committee staff requested, and were denied, the minutes and reports of the Health Insurance Benefits Advisory Council [396] which had been set up by HEW to work out the details.

On May 2, 1966, HEW announced its proposed Principles of Reimbursement. At this point, the regulations were not published in the *Federal Register,* but instead general principles were announced at a press conference. Congressional response to the announcement was extraordinary. On May 4, Russell Long, chairman of the Senate Finance Committee, issued a press release expressing "grave concern" over the principles and noting that, if adopted, the costs of Medicare would increase above the actuarial estimates previously given by some $750 million over the next 10 years. On May 16 the staff of the Senate Finance Committee issued a report entitled *Proposed Medicare Reimbursement Formula: Congressional Intent, Policy and Costs.* [397] This document laid out several specific areas in which the proposed Principles of Reimbursement departed from what had been the congressional understanding upon which original actuarial estimates had been made. The principles departed from previous congressional agreement by: allowing depreciation on assets paid for with public funds; allowing unfunded depreciation; allowing a 2 per cent plus factor; and permitting hospitals to be paid one month in advance for services to be rendered to Medicare beneficiaries.

On May 25, the Senate Finance Committee began hearings on the proposed principles.[398] The hearings were held in executive session because the chairman "was informed that if we didn't watch out we were going to have to invite all these hospital people to come in here and demand a lot more than this.[399] Dr. Herman Somers, a leading analyst of the Medicare program, commented, "Many congressmen may not have realized how elastic the concept of 'reasonable costs' could be, that it was as much an issue to be resolved by bargaining as by the data, complicated by the generally backward state of cost accounting in most hospitals." [400] Although congressional naïveté was certainly a factor in the development of the Medicare program, the main issues disputed in the proposed HEW cost guidelines *had* been addressed by Congress. Senator Anderson's description of the process seems more accurate. He said, in discussing the allowance of a 2 per cent plus factor,

> The decision [not to allow the plus factor] was reached a long time ago. Now you resurrect it and say, all the time we planned to do it, when all the time you didn't plan to do it. . . . There is nothing anywhere in the hearings that indicates the allowance of the 2 percent would ever be considered. . . . Yet you have agreed to it because the hospitals put pressure on you.[401]

The Social Security Administration, the AHA, and the BCA, all of which had previously characterized the AHA formula as "Governing Principles . . . which have attained a large measure of agreement," now relied upon the "fuzziness" inherent in the "reasonable cost" concept.[402] Robert Ball stated that the words "reasonable cost" were subject to interpretations that would increase the cost of the program by 19 per cent over original actuarial estimates.

While it is certainly true, as Dr. Somers states, that the AHA Principles of Reimbursement are quite "elastic," the problem in the initial formulation of the Medicare payment standards did not arise primarily from their vagueness. Rather, immediately after Medicare was enacted, the AHA amended its principles in several critical respects.[403] For example, where the principles had previously called for depreciation to be paid on an historic (original cost) basis, and then only if the depreciation was funded, the 1965 revision called for depreciation payments on the basis of "replacement cost" and eliminated the funding requirement.[404]

In the May Senate Finance Committee hearings, HEW urged the committee to act quickly, since Medicare was to start in 36 days, most of the hospitals had not signed formal agreements pending the final promulgation of regulations, and HEW was anxious to publish the proposed regulations in the *Federal Register,* as required by law, to "give other people throughout the country the opportunity to make their comments and criticisms in the 30-day period." [405] At this point, it was, of course, too late for public involvement. By the time information was made available to the public and to Congress, it was so late that even those congressmen who were very critical of the reimbursement principles felt that it was impossible to do anything but go along with them, at least for the time being.[406] Different results might have been achieved if Congress and the public had had access earlier to information on the issues involved and if there had been public debate. It is easy to imagine how the interests of the aged and of the general public could have gotten lost in discussions among federal administrators attempting to put together a functioning program and the hospitals and Blue Cross seeking a stable and generous source of financing.

Major Issues of Reasonable Cost Reimbursement

There are four key issues in the determination of reasonable costs. First, which items are allowable costs? Second, how are costs to be allocated among different groups of patients and sources of payment? Third, at what point does the cost for an allowable item become so excessive as to be unreasonable? Fourth, how are the formulas, however defined, to be applied and implemented?

What items are allowable costs?

The major controversies over reasonable cost reimbursement have centered on questions of what costs are allowable. These issues cannot be resolved by reference to accounting principles or any other technical discipline. Rather, they raise fundamental social policy questions. For example, to what extent and in what manner should medical education be publicly subsidized through hospital insurance for the poor and aged? What are the needs for more hospital beds, new equipment, expanded services? Who should be making these judgments—Blue Cross, the hospitals, HEW, or state or regional planning bodies? Three items of allowable costs will be discussed here: depreciation, profits, and public relations costs. They were selected because each has been the subject of congressional concern. The extent to which the costs of medical education and research are, and should be, allowed in third-party reimbursement raises issues that deserve comprehensive analysis and study but are beyond the scope of this discussion.

The determination of allowable items is also closely related to the issue of allocating costs among programs. Since 87 per cent of hospital revenues are received from third-party payers,[407] it is obvious that if a particular item is "allowable" under Medicare formulas and not allowed in payments for private Blue Cross subscribers, the Medicare program will, to that extent, be bearing a disproportionate share of total "costs."

Depreciation. Depreciation is the gradual using up of a durable asset over the period of time during which the asset is expected to be usable. Because the depreciating asset is being used over time, the costs of depreciation can be included as an operating cost. Under normal accounting principles and the AHA/BCA principles of 1963, depreciation is based on the original ("historic") cost of the asset. After the passage of Medicare, the AHA/BCA Principles of Payment were amended to require depreciation on the basis of "current replacement costs." The difference is substantial; depreciation on the historic cost basis is assumed to represent about 6 per cent of total reimbursement to hospitals under Medicare and Medicaid, while depreciation on the replacement basis would be between 50 and 90 per cent higher.[408] Paying depreciation on a replacement basis assumes the perpetual existence of every hospital and every asset for which payment is made. This was one of the few points on which the Social Security Administration did not give in to the demands of Blue Cross and the AHA; the Principles of Reimbursement for Medicare call for depreciation based on historic cost.[409]

Despite this, the depreciation guidelines under Medicare are very liberal. The hospitals won a major concession—the use of accelerated depreciation—even though this had not been included in the actuarial assumptions of the program.[410] Hospitals were permitted to use one method of depreciation for one asset or group of assets and another for others, in whatever combination was most advantageous, and to switch from one method of computation to another.[411] Depreciation was allowed upon all of the assets being used by a hospital at the time it entered the Medicare program, even though such assets had already been fully or partially depreciated on the hospital's books.[412] Depreciation was allowed upon assets purchased with public funds, such as construction financed with federal grants under the Hospital Survey and Construction Act (Hill-Burton).[413] Finally, there was no requirement that depreciation allowances be placed in a specially designated fund, even though the entire justification for the depreciation allowance is to provide a fund out of which assets can be replaced when they are used up. As a result, hospitals have commonly utilized these funds for operating expenses.

> The depreciation money becomes inflationary for Medicare and for all other consumers. When the need for replacement or modernization arises, the hospital will turn to traditional fund raising sources, philanthropy and government, and they will get the money.[414]

Hospitals and extended care facilities have not in fact generally funded their depreciation costs.[415] Apart from the general inflationary impact of utilizing depreciation allowances as operating funds, the availability of this large source of unrestricted funds undercuts and makes futile efforts to rationalize planning.

Since 1946, under the Hill-Burton Act, the federal government has made funds for hospital construction available to the states on the condition, among others, that the state establish a planning agency and a plan to inventory all existing health facilities and deficiencies and to develop a statewide plan for expansion, giving priority to areas of greatest need.[416] In 1966, the Comprehensive Health Planning and Public Health Services Act was adopted to make funds available to states for the purpose of coordinating planning and strengthening planning mechanisms at all levels.[417] The impact of these planning efforts has been minimal. The planning agencies do not coordinate with each other or, more significantly, with the primary sources of federal funds.[418] Simply in terms of money, the Hill-Burton and Comprehensive Health Planning agencies can do little more than play at the fringes of the health delivery system. The bulk of the federal monies are provided, without conditions or controls, through Medicare and Medicaid. For example, by conservative estimate depreciation alone accounts for about 6 per cent of the total reimbursement to hospitals under Medicaid and Medicare.[419] This means that in 1970 the federal government paid hospitals approximately $611 million in depreciation under Medicaid and Medicare, while $150 million was made available under the Hill-Burton Act, and $214 million was spent for comprehensive health planning.[420]

The 1966 Senate Finance Committee staff report had recommended that, "Depreciation should be allowed on publicly-financed assets only if all depreciation allowances (including those for non-publicly financed assets) are funded in accordance with a plan approved by the State or an agency or agencies designated by the State." [421] The Office of General Counsel took the view at that time that the secretary of HEW did not have the authority to require that hospitals use depreciation allowances for replacement purposes, much less that the funds be subjected to some sort of public planning process.[422] He stated that

> the statute directs him, unconditionally, to pay providers the reasonable cost of services to beneficiaries and confers no authority to control the use that the providers may make of the proceeds. Section 1801, indeed, specifically forbids him to excercise any supervision or control over the administration or operation of a provider.

The argument ignores the fact that in requiring the secretary to pay only "reasonable" costs, Congress provided a large measure of administrative discretion to determine under what circumstances costs would be considered "reasonable." The statute also gave the secretary broad authority to promulgate standards and conditions for hospitals participating in Medicare.[423] With respect to Hill-Burton funds, the administration's justification for inaction was internally inconsistent in that payment of depreciation on federally funded assets is supportable only by looking toward future replacement costs, while the general counsel's objection treated depreciation as payment for an expense already incurred. The Senate Finance Committee report in 1965, prior to the enactment of Medicare, assumed that Medicare depreciation payments would be coordinated with the Hill-Burton planning structure. It stated, "reasonable cost should include appropriate treatment of depreciation on buildings and equipment (taking into account such factors as the effect of Hill-Burton construction grants and practices with respect to funding of depreciation)." [424] Although all the members of the Senate Finance Committee who expressed themselves on the subject believed that HEW had the authority to require hospitals to fund depreciation (that is, to earmark depreciation allowances for replacement purposes) and to coordinate depreciation policy with official planning agencies, HEW did not require such coordination.

The depreciation allowances proved, in the words of the 1970 report of the staff of the Senate Finance Committee, to be a "bonanza" for hospitals. [425] The provisions subject to most flagrant abuse were those allowing accelerated depreciation and the option to choose the most profitable method of calculating depreciation costs.

> These provisions served as an incentive to the sale and resale of proprietary facilities at inflated prices. The objective in such situations would be to repeat the write off of the facility and its equipment once again on the basis of accelerated depreciation and thereby realize inordinately high and duplicative cash payments from the government. [426]

In response to congressional criticism, HEW finally promulgated regulations, effective August 1, 1970, requiring that the basis for computing depreciation for any asset acquired after that date by the lowest of its: (1) historic cost, (2) fair market value, or (3) current reproduction cost less straight-line depreciation. Assets acquired after August 1, 1970, must be depreciated on a straight-line basis, except that the hospital may compute accelerated depreciation, not to exceed 150 per cent of the straight-line rate, if it can demonstrate to the intermediary that depreciation funds recieved are insufficient to meet the amortization of a reasonable amount of principle on debts related to the total depreciable assets. [427] While these regulations curbed some of the most flagrant abuses, they did not touch fundamental issues of whether capital requirements of hospitals should be borne by insurance programs for the poor and the aged and whether depreciation funds provided under these programs should be given over to the unfettered discretion of individual hospitals.

In 1972 Congress considered the problem of coordinating capital funds provided under Medicare and other federal programs with the official planning agencies [428] and amended the Social Security Act to make plain that the secretary has the authority to require such coordination and to deny Medicare reimbursement for expansion inconsistent with overall planning objectives.[429] It remains to be seen whether this explicit grant of authority and strong congressional urging affect the policies of HEW and the intermediaries.

It is difficult to compare Medicare depreciation reimbursement policies with Blue Cross depreciation allowance practices with respect to payments for services to private subscribers. Some plans have attempted to coordinate their reimbursement with local planning agencies,[430] and some insurance commissioners have required such cooperation.[431] However, because of deficiencies in hospital accounting, calculation of payments for depreciation often bears little relationship to the cost of assets or to the principles of HEW or the AHA. For example, in 1960 the insurance commissioner in New York allowed Blue Cross to pay a "depreciation allowance" of 5 per cent of the semi-private per diem rate, on condition that the allowance be designated only for replacement of existing equipment and buildings. In granting a flat rate not related to the cost structure of any particular hospital or asset, he noted that more accurate determination was impossible, because many hospitals did not have adequate records.[432] In 1970, twenty-four Blue Cross plans continued to reimburse hospitals on the arbitrary basis of charges or a percentage of charges, and an unknown number of those plans paying on the basis of costs are not able to calculate the amount properly attributable to depreciation.[433]

The Plus Factor. A second major concession that the Social Security Administration made to the AHA and Blue Cross was the inclusion in the reimbursement formula of an allowance of 2 per cent of all other allowable costs, except interest expenses, to be paid to voluntary hospitals.[434] This plus factor was originally characterized as payment "in lieu of specific interest on equity capital, as well as other factors not given specific recognition." In the final version of the regulations, it is labeled "in lieu of specific recognition of other costs in providing and improving services." Before the Senate Finance Committee in 1966, HEW explained that the plus factor was given because of "difficulty in measurement, lack of data," and other elements of imprecision in the determination of reasonable costs.[435]

The plus factor was criticized on many grounds. Since the reimbursement formula was both comprehensive and generous, it has never been clear what "other costs" were covered by the plus factor. It was not supported by the legislative history and had not been included in actuarial estimates. Imprecision could just as well result in overpayments as underpayments. Since hospitals that spend most would get most, payment of a percentage of other costs would encourage hospitals to increase the base upon which the plus factor was computed. Most fundamentally, it provided funds for expansion and growth that would not be subject to any planning process and thereby further undermined planning efforts through Hill-Burton, Comprehensive Health Planning, and other programs.

The Medicare statute as enacted in 1965 made no specific provision for payment of a reasonable profit to proprietary, that is, profit-making, institutions. The plus factor was one way of providing a return on equity capital for the proprietaries. (Another method of assuring profits, which was not expressly authorized by regulations but is certainly allowed, is simply to pay administrators very high salaries.) [436] However, the plus factor was a very poor device for paying profits to proprietary institutions. It was payable on allowable costs only after deduction of interest expense. Proprietary institutions, because of their greater debt structure, would have to deduct larger payments of interest than would the nonprofits, thus reducing the cost base on which the 2 per cent would be calculated. Further, the plus factor payment could not exceed 4.75 per cent (then the current rate) of equity capital. The smaller equity of proprietary institutions relative to the nonprofits meant that the nonprofits would get the 2 per cent while the proprietaries would be limited to 4.75 per cent on their smaller equities. The nonprofits had a further advantage in that Hill-Burton and other publicly financed and donated assets would not be subtracted from their equity capital for the purpose of calculating the 4.75 per cent limit. [437] In short, the plus factor was a particular boon to the nonprofit institutions that dominate the American Hospital Association and Blue Cross.

The inequity to the proprietaries was corrected in 1966 with an amendment providing that for proprietary institutions the reimbursement formula should include "a reasonable return on equity capital." [438] The rate of return was not to exceed one and one half times the average of the rates of interest on obligations issued for purchase by the Federal Hospital Insurance Trust Funds. At the same time, the plus factor for proprietary providers was reduced to 1.5 per cent.

The plus factor was simply profit. It, as well as the other liberal principles of reimbursement, had a predictable inflationary effect. The plus factor especially was the subject of criticism, and in 1969 HEW deleted it from the Medicare regulations,[439] substituting an allowance of 8.5 per cent of the costs of nursing services for Medicare patients.[440]

Public Relations Costs. Generous allowances for depreciation and the plus factor were disturbing because they substantially increased the costs of the Medicare program and provided hospitals with a large and stable source of public money not subject to any public control. Public relations costs are disturbing, not because of the magnitude of the monies involved, but rather because relatively small amounts of money can shape public policies to serve the narrowly defined self-interest of the hospitals and Blue Cross in ways that may be inimical to the interests of the subscribers and beneficiaries who provide the funds.

Medicare regulations allow both the hospitals and Blue Cross to make open-ended claims for administrative expenses. There are no specific principles on allowable administrative costs, but in general

> reasonable cost includes all necessary and proper expenses incurred in rendering services, such as administrative costs, maintenance costs, and premium payments for employee health and pension plans. It includes both direct and indirect costs, and normal standby costs.[441]

In addition to open reimbursement for administrative costs, the Medicare principles specifically allow payments to providers for advertising costs "if the advertising is primarily concerned with the presentation of a good public image and directly or indirectly related to patient care." [442] Medicare also pays the costs of initiation fees, dues, and subscriptions in professional, technical, or business-related organizations, as well as civic groups. Costs of attending conferences, travel, etc., are allowable so long as the meeting relates to the "advancement of patient care or efficient operation of the facility" or to "the promotion of civic objectives." [443] The fiscal intermediary is also reimbursed on a cost basis for services performed under the Medicare program, and the principles of reimbursement are similarly broad.[444]

Under these catchall administrative headings, hospitals can, for example, write off the substantial costs of conducting antiunionization campaigns. Antiunion costs can, and in some cases have, taken the form of legal fees, personnel costs, and strategic pay increases to convince employees that the union is not needed. Officials of Blue Cross and HEW who were asked how antiunion expenses would be treated under the reimbursement formulas agreed that it was unlikely that such expenses would be identifiable in hospital cost records.[445] Auditors are concerned only with verifying that the expenses were in fact paid to legitimate firms. There is certainly no policy prohibiting reimbursement for the costs of antiunion campaigns. An official of the New York State Insurance Department indicated that antiunion administrative expenses would not be questioned by that office, and there is little reason to believe that the policy in the insurance departments of other states is different.[446] Where a hospital finances a lengthy and expensive appeal from a finding of unfair labor practices, the reimbursement formula therefore allows the payment of costs that run flatly counter to public policy as well as the interests of many subscribers and beneficiaries.

Another example of the use of public funds to promote Blue Cross and hospital self-interest came to light in November 1971 with the publication of memos from BCA officials to plan executives describing a task force aimed at persuading key members of Congress that Blue Cross should have a prominent role in any national health insurance program. Memos urging Blue Cross executives to contact congressmen "in the home surroundings where [they were] relaxed and receptive" were marked confidential and stated that there should be "no out-of-Plan publicity whatsoever." [447] A Blue Cross official testifying before a Senate subcommittee stated that funds for the program had come from the local Blue Cross associations "from premium income." [448] Senator Edward Kennedy sharply criticized the Blue Cross lobbying effort, pointing out that many Blue Cross subscribers, notably members of labor unions, were supporting national health insurance plans that would not utilize Blue Cross. Open-ended reimbursement of administrative costs under vague and general principles also invites abuses and excessive costs not related to the promotion of any particular social or political objective.[449]

There is no easy answer to this situation. It seems obviously improper to allow Blue Cross to utilize funds provided by subscribers and the public to lobby for policies flatly contrary to the interests of at least some of those providing the funds. However, it is difficult to draw lines between expenses in the public interest—for example, the expenses a hospital would incur in transferring patients in the event of a strike or the expenses of preparing technical information on the operation of the Medicare program for congressional committees—and expenses directed toward lobbying or the promotion of narrow self-interest. Given the present structures, it would be difficult to apply distinctions even if they could be defined. The auditing capacity of the Social Security Administration over the BCA or of Blue Cross plans over the hospitals is simply not sufficient to uncover illegitimate expenses. Subscribers and beneficiaries could play an important role in assuring that Blue Cross or hospital efforts to shape social and public policy reflected their wishes but only if they had full access to information and some mechanism for influencing the organizations' policies.

How are costs allocated among different groups of patients and sources of payment?

The experience of Blue Cross in paying hospitals for services rendered to subscribers was a major strength upon which the organization relied in securing the responsibility for the administration of Medicare. But the fact that the organization functions in a dual role, as intermediary for the public programs and as a private insurance organization paying for services to private subscribers, is also a major weakness in the use of Blue Cross as fiscal intermediary. Given the open-ended public funds available for hospital care under Medicaid and Medicare, it would be natural to expect that where there are ambiguities, or where a reasonable person could attribute a cost either to the private business or to the public programs, costs would be loaded onto the public programs. This tendency has been exacerbated in recent years as subscribers and state insurance commissioners have pressed to control the rise of private Blue Cross subscription rates. There is little corresponding pressure to control the rates at which hospitals are reimbursed for publicly financed services rendered Medicare and Medicaid beneficiaries. Given this inherent potentiality and pressure to overload costs onto the public programs, an effective, accurate formula for allocation of costs between public and private funds is essential.

It is well known that the costs of hospital care tend to be substantially higher in the initial days of hospitalization and tend to decrease as the hospital stay continues. The aged generally take a longer time to recover from serious illness or injury requiring hospitalization; the national average length of stay for patients 65 years or over is 13.65 as compared with 6.64 days for those under 65, excluding the newborns.[450] Congress was aware of the utilization patterns of the aged in 1965,[451] and the Medicare statute specifically requires that "costs with respect to individuals covered by the insurance programs . . . will not be borne by individuals not so covered, and the costs with respect to individuals not so covered, will not be borne by such insurance programs." [452] Blue Cross commonly pays hospitals on an average per diem basis; payment on this basis would grossly inflate costs if the same rate were applied to the aged population as to the nonaged. As the regulations explain:

> In considering the average per diem method of apportioning costs for use under the program, the difficulty encountered is that the preponderance of presently available evidence strongly indicates that the over-65 patient is not typical from the standpoint of average per diem cost. On the average he stays in the hospital twice as long and therefore the ancillary services that he uses are averaged over the longer period of time, resulting in an average per diem cost for the aged alone, significantly below the average per diem for all patients.[453]

Although the regulations cite the decreasing number of ancillary services (for example X rays, laboratory work) needed in long-term cases, the amount of routine service (for example dietary and nursing) also decreases as the patient passes from a period of acute illness to convalescence.

Both the AHA and Blue Cross acknowledged the special utilization patterns of the aged during congressional consideration of Medicare. HEW had estimated that in order to determine the actual daily hospital costs for the aged, a 13 per cent reduction should be applied to the per diem rate based on total hospital costs for all patients. Blue Cross questioned this figure and estimated that the daily cost for the aged was an average of 12.5 per cent less. The AHA set the differential at 7 per cent.[454] Despite their previous acknowledgement that care of the aged costs less per day than average, during the 1966 negotiations with HEW both organizations argued strongly for average per diem reimbursement for Medicare.[455] However, given the plain evidence that costs decrease rapidly after the initial days of hospitalization, the legislative history, and the statutory mandate, HEW rejected the average per diem approach and sought a formula that would more accurately apportion costs.

The initial HEW regulations set forth two basic methods of apportionment: the departmental RCCAC method and the combination method.[456] Under the departmental RCCAC method, first, the direct costs of providing service to all patients were computed by all revenue-producing departments (that is, all departments for whose services a separate charge is customarily made). Some revenue-producing departments are: operating room, anesthesiology, radiology, laboratory, physical therapy, pharmacy, and delivery room. Second, the costs of all nonrevenue-producing departments were prorated to each revenue-producing department. Typical nonrevenue-producing departments are: administration, maintenance, housekeeping, medical records, social service, physical plant. Third, Medicare then paid a percentage of the total costs of each revenue-producing department. The percentage was calculated by dividing the total charges made to Medicare patients by that department by the total charges made to all patients (including Medicare beneficiaries) by that department. This ratio was multiplied by the department's total costs to arrive at Medicare's total dollar reimbursement for that department.[457]

Under the combination method of apportionment, the total costs (direct and indirect) for routine services (regular room, dietary, and nursing services) were divided by total inpatient days for all inpatients (including Medicare beneficiaries) to arrive at an average per diem rate (cost per inpatient day). This average per diem rate was multiplied by the total number of inpatient days for Medicare inpatients to arrive at the total amount to be reimbursed for the costs of routine services. The total costs, indirect as well as direct, for all ancillary services (those services for which a separate charge is customarily made) were added together (all ancillary departments contributed to this one total ancillary cost figure). Medicare then paid a percentage of this total ancillary cost figure. The percentage was computed by dividing the total Medicare inpatient charges for ancillary services by the total inpatient ancillary charges including Medicare charges. The ratio or percentage was multiplied by the total cost of all ancillary services. Total Medicare reimbursement for all routine services and all ancillary services were added to produce the total amount reimbursable to the hospital for the "reasonable cost" of providing services to Medicare beneficiaries.[458]

There have been four fundamental defects in the allocation formulas as originally written and as later revised. Some have been corrected, as we shall see; some have not. First, the formulas use "charges" that are simply arbitrary figures set wholly at the discretion of the hospitals. Second, Medicare payments subsidized expensive services not generally utilized by the aged, for example maternity room costs and private rooms. Third, hospitals were allowed to choose the method of reimbursement that resulted in greatest reimbursement. Fourth, Medicare now pays an additional allowance for routine nursing costs, which is not justified by the available evidence. We shall take these points up one by one.

Hospital charges. The figures called "hospital charges" are simply arbitrary statistics devised by the hospital itself. In mandating the payment of reasonable "costs," Congress explicitly repudiated payment on the basis of charges. Robert Ball, explaining the reasonable cost formula to the House Ways and Means Committee, stated:

> We would not want to do it on a charge basis [because] I think it then puts you at the mercy of the individual hospital. They can just put up a charge, and then you have to pay it, because your patient went in there. There is no control. If you were to have us go on just whatever they charge I would be afraid even of a hospital maybe setting up a wing for older people, arranging it somehow specially, and if we are going to pay the whole bill, I do not see what is to prevent them from making a charge that is significantly more than cost.[459]

Charges as a basis of payment were firmly rejected by Congress. Chairman Mills summarized:

> First of all, you are not concerned with the charge which is published for the use of a hospital. What you are concerned with is the reasonableness of the cost to which you are being subjected, and in trying to determine for the benefit of these funds what reasonable costs are. . . . What you are seeking to do is to pay reasonable costs. You are not seeking to pay reasonable charges.[460]

In any noncompetitive market, charges are essentially arbitrary. With respect to hospital services, neither supply and demand nor competition have any significant impact on them. Hospital services are an undesired necessity rather than a service sought by consumers,[461] who have little control over the decision to be hospitalized or where. Apart from these peculiarities in demand, hospital charges are arbitrary because hospitals do not compete for the business of many purchasers but rather sell most of their services to one major purchaser: Blue Cross. The essentially arbitrary nature of charges in a noncompetitive market is accentuated by hospitals' common policy of expressing social judgments and preferences through the charge structure. For example, the operating room typically subsidizes obstetrics, because it is thought that young couples just beginning a family are deserving of support through the charge structure.[462] During the long years that Medicare was debated, the skewing of charges was further and acutely distorted by hospitals recalculating their charge structures to take advantage of the allocation formula. As one hospital administrator noted, "RCC is based on certain hospital statistics but the key statistic is controllable by the hospital." [463]

The following example demonstrates how a hospital may manipulate its charge structure in order to maximize Medicare reimbursement. The basic technique involves making disproportionately high markups (ratio of charge minus cost to cost) in those departments or procedures that are heavily utilized by the aged.

YEAR I

1. Department X, Charge-Cost List

Procedure	Charge	Cost	Markup
a	$1.00	$ .75	33%
b	2.00	1.50	33%
c	3.00	2.25	33%
d	4.00	3.00	33%
e	5.00	3.75	33%
f	6.00	4.50	33%
g	7.00	5.25	33%
h	8.00	6.00	33%
i	9.00	6.75	33%
j	10.00	7.50	33%

Note that all charges are marked up uniformly one-third over costs.

2. Medicare-Medicaid eligibles buy only procedures a–e, other patients buy only f–j.

3. All procedures are sold ten times each, resulting in Department X Income Report as follows:

No. of Procedures		Total charge	Total cost
	CHARGES		*COSTS*
10	a	$10.00	$ 7.50
10	b	20.00	15.00
10	c	30.00	22.50
10	d	40.00	30.00
10	e	50.00	37.50
	Subtotal	$150.00	$112.50
10	f	60.00	45.00
10	g	70.00	52.00
10	h	80.00	60.00
10	i	90.00	67.50
10	j	100.00	75.00
	Subtotal	$400.00	$299.50
	Total charges	$550.00	Total costs $412.00

4. Apply the department RCC formula:

$$\frac{\text{Total Medicare charges} = \$150}{\text{Total patient charges} = \$550} \times \text{Total costs } \$412.00 = \text{Medicare total reimbursement } \$112.50$$

5. $112.50 by use of the departmental RCC formula equals exactly what the income report says its cost to eligibles should be.

YEAR II

Assume:

1. Costs have gone up one-third for all procedures, but the charges have been altered (marked up at different rates).

Department X, Charge-Cost List

Procedure	Charge	Cost	Markup
a	$2.00	$1.00	50%
b	4.00	2.00	50%
c	6.00	3.00	50%
d	8.00	4.00	50%
e	10.00	5.00	50%
f	7.00	6.00	17%
g	8.00	7.00	14%
h	9.00	8.00	12%
i	10.00	9.00	11%
j	11.00	10.00	10%

Eligibles still "buy" only a–e.
Other patients still "buy" only f–j.

2. Year-End Income Report, Department X
   Each procedure is still sold ten times.

		CHARGES			COSTS	
No. of procedures		Total charge	% increase Year I to Year II		Total costs	% increase Year I to Year II
10	a	$20.00	100%		$10.00	33%
10	b	40.00	100%		20.00	33%
10	c	60.00	100%		30.00	33%
10	d	80.00	100%		40.00	33%
10	e	100.00	100%		50.00	33%
Subtotal		$300.00			$150.00	
10	f	70.00	16.6%		60.00	33%
10	g	80.00	14.3%		70.00	33%
10	h	90.00	12.5%		80.00	33%
10	i	100.00	11.1%		90.00	33%
10	j	110.00	10.0%		100.00	33%
Subtotal		$450.00	12.5%		$400.00	33%
Total charges		$750.00	36.36%	Total costs	$550.00	33%

3. Apply departmental RCC formula:

$$\frac{\text{Total Medicare charges} = \$300.00}{\text{Total patient charges} = \$750.00} \times \frac{\text{Total costs}}{} \quad \$550.00 = \frac{\text{Total Medicare reimbursement} \ \$220.00}{}$$

4. Now compare with the first year.
   a. Utilization stays exactly the same: half of the department's 100 procedures "sold" went to the covered patient population; half did not.
   b. Total departmental costs went up one-third ($412.00 to $550.00), but because of the selective charge increases total program reimbursement for this department has increased more than 95%.

<table>
<tr><td>Year I reimbursement</td><td>Year II reimbursement</td></tr>
<tr><td>$112.50</td><td>$220.00</td></tr>
</table>

Under the combination method procedures a through e and f through j could represent departments, and the same result would be applicable to the whole hospital, rather than just one department.

Hospitals—particularly those with sophisticated understanding of the reimbursement formula and accounting capacity—have utilized this technique to load costs onto the Medicare program. The AHA and Blue Cross have disseminated information on techniques of cost loading.[464] A General Accounting Office study of one hospital revealed a pattern of differential markups among different ancillary services. The three departments utilized most heavily by Medicare beneficiaries had the highest markups. In the X-ray and laboratory services the percentage of Medicare charges to total charges was 35 per cent, and the markup in these two departments was 67 per cent. Medicare patients accounted for 40 per cent of the drugs sold, and the cost-to-charge ratio was 50 per cent. The markup in services not utilized extensively by the aged was substantially less. For example, only 25 per cent of the operating room charges were attributable to Medicare patients, and the cost-to-charge ratio for that service was 25 per cent. Medicare patients utilized no maternity room services, and the cost-to-charge ratio was a *minus* 50 per cent.[465]

Since charges were rejected as a basis for payment under Medicare, the legislative history makes plain that the secretary is not to regulate hospital charges.[466] The current regulations do not prescribe how charges are to be determined.[467] Determination of charge structures is left to the sole discretion of the hospitals. Under existing regulations, it is not illegal to manipulate the charge structure to maximize Medicare reimbursement. It is not even shady practice to do so but sensible business behavior. As an article in *Hospitals, Journal of the American Hospital Association,* explained,

> Suppose an administrator is interested in manipulating the amount of his Medicare reimbursement. Nothing can prevent him from reducing by $4 per day the current room and board charge and increasing the delivery room charge by $20 per delivery. Such action on the part of an administrator interested in manipulating his Medicare reimbursement rate cannot be prevented under existing regulations. . . . This is not to infer that such action has an immoral or even an illegal taint to it. On the contrary, it is a well-established principle that a taxpayer may take advantage of loopholes in the tax law without any fear of criticism.[468]

Utilization patterns of the aged. As has been noted, the reason the RCCAC methods were adopted was that old people tend to take a longer time to convalesce than the young, and Medicare payments based on an average per diem rate would require Medicare to pay at an unjustifiably high rate for the later days of hospitalization in which care is less intensive. However both the combination and departmental methods apportioned routine costs by applying the ratio of Medicare patient days to total routine costs. The result was an average per diem cost for routine services. Utilization patterns of the aged are also atypical in that Medicare beneficiaries normally occupy semi-private accommodations. The average per diem rate under both combination and departmental methods included the higher costs of private rooms in the total cost of routine services. Thus, with respect to routine services, both the combination and departmental methods failed to take account of the unusual patterns of the aged.

The combination method also failed to take account of the special utilization patterns of the aged with respect to ancillary services. The second step in the computation of Medicare costs under this method required the hospital to total all the costs of ancillary services into one figure and apply a percentage to that figure equal to the ratio of total ancillary charges for Medicare beneficiaries over total ancillary charges for the entire inpatient population. The inclusion into one total of all ancillary costs allowed the hospital to be reimbursed for the costs associated with delivery rooms even though Medicare patients do not use delivery rooms. This was possible because delivery rooms, which are often operated at a loss, have a significantly different ratio of costs to charges than do all other ancillary departments. Similarly, costs associated with expensive special care units such as intensive care, coronary care, and burn treatment could be included in either the routine total costs or the ancillary total costs component of the hospital's total allowable costs. The inclusion could occur even though few or no Medicare beneficiaries used these units. The costs associated with the unit would then be apportioned according to the ratio of beneficiary charges to all inpatient charges or as part of the routine average per diem rate.

As early as 1967 the general counsel of HEW questioned the legality of the combination method of reimbursement, because it allowed inclusion of costs for services not rendered Medicare beneficiaries.[469] In 1969, the HEW Audit Agency recommended that the Combination Method be eliminated.

> If a hospital has a number of non-Medicare private room patients and its routine service costs applicable to these patients are greater than similar costs for semi-private room patients, then reimbursement from Medicare under this method may include private room costs. This is because the average cost per diem—and ultimately the Medicare reimbursement—includes the cost of private room accommodations since it is arrived at by dividing total costs of all routine services by total inpatient days for all patients.
>
> Delivery room costs are included in Medicare reimbursement for similar reasons when a hospital uses the Combination Method.[470]

The General Accounting Office estimated that the inclusion of the costs of private rooms and delivery rooms in Medicare reimbursement under the combination method produced an overpayment by Medicare to hospitals by as much as $200 million annually.[471] The HEW Audit Agency stated, "While the total dollar effect nationwide of the inclusion of delivery room costs in hospital reimbursement is not available, information developed by one intermediary shows that for the largest cost hospitals these costs can range as high as a million dollars annually.'' [472]

Despite this widespread criticism of the costly inequity in the apportionment formulas, for several years HEW refused to amend the regulations. In 1969, HEW argued that the whole area of Medicare reimbursement was under intensive study, and any reform in the allocation regulations must await the outcome of this examination.[473] The combination method had been subject to particularly sharp attack; HEW defended it by pointing out that the departmental method was also defective.

> It is assumed in the Departmental RCCAC Method that costs follow charges. Since the actual costs of each type of accommodation (private, semi-private, ward) are not determined as in the case of the Combination Method, the statistics or charges used to apportion such routine costs to the Medicare program do not guarantee that the difference between costs and charges for each accommodation area is the same . . . Therefore, *in the routine service cost area, the basic problem present in the Combination Method is also present in the Departmental RCCAC Method.*[474] (Emphasis added.)

Pressure from Blue Cross contributed to the HEW decision to retain these apportionment methods,[475] but new regulations drawn up in 1971 were designed to exclude payments for services not used by the aged, as we shall see shortly.

Hospital choice of apportionment method. A third criticism of the apportionment methods selected was that the regulations allowed hospitals to choose whether to utilize the combination method or the departmental method. The combination method is less accurate and produces a generally higher rate of reimbursement. During the first two years of the Medicare program only about 10 per cent of the hospitals utilized the departmental method.[476] In terms of hospital record-keeping the two methods are essentially similar. Under the departmental method the Medicare and non-Medicare charge data must be maintained for *each* ancillary department, whereas under the combination method the Medicare and non-Medicare charge data must be maintained only for *total* ancillary charges. In 1971 the General Accounting office noted, ''We believe that it is reasonable to assume that those hospitals that use the Combination Method with cost finding elected to do so because its use resulted in higher Medicare reimbursements.'' [477]

The weakness in the regulatory policy allowing hospitals to select their method of reimbursement was exacerbated by Blue Cross practices. The HEW Audit Agency studied the cost reports of 103 hospitals and found that many hospitals were utilizing the combination method simply because it produced a higher rate of reimbursement. Further,

> In a number of instances hospitals had initially filed cost reports based on the Departmental Method only to be later advised by their intermediary or the intermediary's accounting firm to use the Combination Method instead. In one case studied, the hospital submitted a cost report based on the Departmental Method and the intermediary voluntarily recomputed the hospital's cost using the Combination Method to produce a higher reimbursement. [478]

Some more conscientious intermediaries questioned whether hospitals that were able to utilize the departmental method should be allowed to claim more lucrative reimbursement under the combination method. [479] The BCA recommended that local plans continue to approve reimbursement under the combination method. ''As a general operating principle, we should not deduct cost from a provider's cost report which the existing rules and regulations allow.'' [480]

In 1971 HEW promulgated new regulations that eliminated the choice previously offered to providers between the combination and departmental methods of apportionment. The new regulations require all hospitals having less than 100 beds to utilize a revised combination method and hospitals having 100 or more beds to utilize a revised departmental method. All extended care facilities must use the revised combination method, except those that are part of a hospital–extended-care-facility complex having 100 or more beds; this group must use the revised departmental method. [481] This regulation came, not as a result of the completion of the ''intense study'' of reasonable cost reimbursement which HEW had promised but rather because a series of government agencies and congressional committees had severely criticized the inequity of the combination method and particularly the abuses of the method fostered by the fiscal intermediaries. [482]

Under the revised departmental method of reimbursement only the cost of each ancillary department is determined by a ratio of beneficiary charges to total patient charges applied to cost (RCCAC). The cost of routine services under the new definition is determined on the basis of a separate average cost per diem for "general" routine patient care areas, plus a separate average cost per diem for each intensive care unit, coronary care unit, and other special care inpatient hospital unit.[483]

The new regulations are an improvement in that they exclude the costs of delivery rooms and other expensive specialty services not utilized by Medicare beneficiaries and eliminate the option that allowed the hospital to utilize the most lucrative method of reimbursement. They are deficient in that they retain the arbitrary charge figures as the basic means of allocating costs and allow hospitals to continue loading private room costs onto the Medicare bill. The General Accounting Office criticized the regulations for their reliance on room charges in allocation of routine costs. The GAO proposed a means of making apportionment of routine costs more accurate that would have saved an estimated 1 per cent in the routine service costs reimbursable by Medicare, without adding appreciably to the administrative difficulty of cost finding.[484] These proposals were rejected by HEW.

The nursing cost differential. A fourth defect in the Medicare allocation formula producing disproportionately large payments for services rendered to Medicare beneficiaries is the 8.5 per cent nursing cost differential.[485] As has been noted, from the time Medicare was first established, there was congressional criticism of the HEW decision to pay hospitals a 2 per cent plus factor for unspecified costs. In response to this criticism, the 2 per cent plus factor was eliminated as of June 30, 1969. However, it was replaced by a new element in the reimbursement formula, retroactive to the same date, which pays hospitals a bonus of 8.5 per cent of the costs of routine nursing services rendered to Medicare beneficiaries.

The regulation announcing the nursing differential recites that it is being given in recognition of "the above average cost of inpatient routine nursing care furnished to aged patients." There is no evidence that the aged receive more nursing care—and certainly no evidence that would justify payment of an additional 8.5 per cent of total nursing costs. The author asked the American Hospital Association and HEW to cite studies showing that the nursing costs for the aged are greater than for the general population. Both cited the *American Hospital Associa-*

tion Nursing Activity Study Project as the principle source of data upon which the 8.5 per cent reimbursement bonus is based.[486] The AHA study was conducted in the fall of 1966, just after the implementation of Medicare. It concludes that, ''depending on the manner in which the non-assignable tasks are pro-rated, it can be stated that patients 65 and over received 14.39 per cent or 22.40 per cent more hours of nursing care per patient than did patients under 65 years of age.''

There are serious methodological defects in the study. First those responsible for the conduct of the study were neither disinterested nor professionally qualified. Three of the four authors were employees of the American Hospital Association, and the fourth was a registered nurse. None were professional sociologists. Second, the actual observers gathering data were selected by the hospitals being studied. Third, ''nursing personnel in the units selected for study were briefed as to the purposes of the study in order to allay any fears that this was to be a study of staffing patterns, quality of care, efficiency of personnel, or salary level.'' The observers were told that the purpose of the study was to show that the aged receive more nursing care.

Conventional sociological methodology requires that observers be double-blinded. It has been demonstrated, and is well known in the profession, that when observers are told the purpose for which they are making observations, they are likely to produce biased information.[487] This bias could have been controlled by splitting the sample of hospitals into two halves and telling the observers in each half a nonage-related hypothesis. For example, in half of the hospitals the observers could have been told that the study was being conducted to show that X causes T, and in the other half they could be told that the study was to show that T causes X. This procedure would have provided an effective check on bias, especially if X and T were not related to age.

Apart from the lack of evidence for the basic proposition that the aged receive more nursing services,[488] even the AHA study does not provide any basis for the 8.5 per cent figure. Further, the nursing cost differential, like the 2 per cent plus factor which it replaces, tends to be inflationary and to encourage an increase in the base cost to which the percentage is applied.[489] The nursing cost differential is provided to all hospitals, whether or not they provide more or less nursing services to the aged. For example, the AHA study showed that in 7 of the 53 hospitals for which data were compiled, younger patients received more nursing care than did the elderly; under the regulations, the bonus is paid to these hospitals as well.

It is apparent that fair allocation of hospital costs among different sources of payment and programs is a difficult task and that HEW's allocation formulas do not assure that costs will be equitably distributed. The allocation problem has also vexed government attempts to curb inflation under the Economic Stabilization Act of 1970.[490] Those institutions with some accounting sophistication or with a fiscal intermediary willing to assure the largest possible public reimbursement are provided large opportunities for loading costs onto the publicly financed programs. What difference does it make if Medicare and Medicaid pay more than their "fair share" of hospital costs? Private Blue Cross rates are rising dramatically, and it could be argued that it is socially useful to subsidize hospital care for those who are not poor or aged through a skewing of the allocation formula.

The basic objection to this sort of back-door public subsidy for the patient with private insurance or funds is that it completely eliminates any measure of public accountability. The judgment whether Medicare and Medicaid funds should subsidize services to private patients, and to what extent, are made entirely by the hospitals and the fiscal intermediaries. The judgments are made in the course of the highly confidential auditing process, and hence it is not possible for the public or Congress to know the extent to which public funds are subsidizing private patients. This information is critical in determining both the need for some form of national health insurance and the costs of such a program. If the need for expanded national health insurance is determined on the assumption that patients with private insurance now pay their own costs, need will be underestimated. If cost estimates of proposed national health insurance programs are based on an assumption that past Medicare and Medicaid costs covered only services to beneficiaries of those programs, they will be overstated to the extent that the public programs have actually provided a subsidy to private patients. The most direct and demonstrable effect of overloading hospital costs onto the public programs is the effect on the beneficiaries of the program. As program costs have gone up, the response of HEW, the states, and Blue Cross has been to restrict the scope of services provided, as we will see in chapter 5.

One final point is worth noting. Allocation of costs on a fair and equitable basis requires a better formula than HEW has yet devised, more sophisticated cost accounting than the hospitals have yet been able or willing to perform, and careful and continuing audits. Even with a better formula, there will almost inevitably be room for juggling costs one way or another. These factors may, in and of themselves, support the need for public administration of any national health or hospital insurance program. Misallocation could be minimized by a more precise allocation formula and by using an administrator having no direct pecuniary advantage to gain through misallocating costs to the public programs. Even with HEW as administrator, there would likely be some overloading of costs onto the public programs, since the hospitals would have a financial incentive to do so. But at the very least HEW would have no incentive to encourage such misallocation.

At what level are costs reimbursable?

The Principles of Payment of the American Hospital Association define "reasonable costs" as those costs that are attributable to "allowable" items. The AHA principles do not call for any inquiry as to whether an allowable item was purchased at a reasonable price. Thus if a salary is "allowable" for a particular position, it is a reasonable cost whether the amount paid is $10,000 a year, $50,000 a year, or $200,000 a year. This concept of reasonableness, under which most of the income of American hospitals is received, has had a significant effect on hospital suppliers. Exploration of the economics of hospital supply is beyond the scope of this book, but it is sufficient to note that, since the establishment of Medicare, the surplus of revenues over expenses in voluntary hospitals has grown enormously,[491] as have the profits of hospital supply and drug companies.[492] Investment analysts believe that hospital suppliers and drug companies are operating in a sector of the economy that is virtually recession-proof.[493]

Only one instance can be found in which a local Blue Cross plan, or state official supervising such a plan, has attempted to limit hospital reimbursement to a reasonable level for allowable items. Pennsylvania's Insurance Commissioner Herbert Denenberg noted that

> Evidence at the Blue Cross hearings indicated hospitals may buy such items as scissors, tape measures and furniture through hospital supply companies at many times the cost of identical equipment

through conventional channels. For example, one witness at our hearings indicated "hospital" tape measures might sell for $2.50 and "hospital" scissors for $7.50, but identical products could be bought elsewhere for $.25 and $2.49, respectively.[494]

Commissioner Denenberg asked that the contract between Blue Cross and the Philadelphia hospitals include provisions to assure that hospitals would not be reimbursed for merchandise purchased at inflated prices. The provision finally adopted states:

> Sec. 19. *Purchasing Procedures.* Provider's governing board, or a committee thereof, shall review the practice and procedures of its purchasing officers and agents to insure that the "Prudent Buyer Concept" is employed when making purchases of equipment, supplies and services. The reports and statistical data used by the purchasing officers and agents shall be made available to Blue Cross for review.[495]

It is still too soon to know what impact, if any, this provision will have on the purchasing practices of Philadelphia hospitals.

The "Prudent Buyer Concept" referred to is adopted from a Social Security Administration Intermediary Letter of the same name.[496] The letter consists of two pages of typewritten text and represents the only federal regulation demanding that allowable costs be reasonable. It does not require that hospitals purchase on the basis of competitive bidding or pay no more than a defined market price for products and services. Rather, the prudent buyer concept is addressed to special problem situations. It provides:

> *On bulk purchases and discounts.* It is not expected, for example, that reimbursement will be based on costs arising from a provider paying at individual rates for physical therapy which is provided by a single therapist to groups of patients simultaneously. Nor is it expected that reimbursement be based on costs arising from the purchase of drugs at prices above the prices commonly charged in the area.

> *On premiums.* Any premium which a provider chooses to pay above the going price for a supply or service, where there is not clear program justification for the premium, must be excluded in determining allowable costs under Medicare.

On self dealing. Wherever there are dealings between ostensibly unrelated providers and suppliers, but there is reason to suspect that there is, in fact, a financial relationship between the two, intermediaries should examine costs purportedly incurred with special care to assure that all direct and indirect discounts were reflected in determining costs.

On services to Medicare patients. When most or all of the recipients of a service are Medicare beneficiaries, costs incurred should be examined with particular care.

Thus the SSA's "prudent buyer" is not so much a reasonable, cost-conscious purchaser as one who does not directly defraud the Medicare program.

The major part of the costs of hospital care are personnel costs. Lower echelon hospital workers—maintenance workers, orderlies, aides, and even nurses—have traditionally been paid substandard wages. In recent years, with unionization and the threat of unionization, there have been improvements in their salary levels.[497] Spokesmen for the hospital industry often attribute the astronomical rise in hospital costs of the past decade to these salary increases. However, nonlabor costs have increased more rapidly than labor costs.[498] Also, personnel costs include the salaries of administrators, radiologists, pathologists, and other professionals whose salaries are anything but substandard.

It is impossible to evaluate what portion of rising hospital personnel costs is attributable to wage increases for lower paid workers and what portion goes toward high salaries for administrators and professionals. Although Blue Cross and the American Hospital Association gather a wide range of statistical information on hospital growth and operations, since 1958 they have not collected statistical information on increases in personnel costs or the distribution of personnel cost increases.[499]

The compensation of pathologists and radiologists has been particularly problematic. Private voluntary hospitals normally contract with professional organizations for these services. The hospitals provide space, equipment, and business to pathologists and radiologists, who unilaterally set their charges and are compensated on the basis of a percentage of their profits or total charges.[500] The charges of hospital-based pathologists and radiologists are high and substantially above those of independent laboratories used by private physicians.[501] The power of these professionals is preserved through a variety of devices. The standards of the Joint Commission on Accreditation of Hospitals require that accredited hospitals have a laboratory and that a pathologist be in charge.[502] Until 1969 one of the Canons of Ethics of the College of American Pathologists provided that, "I shall not accept a position with a fixed stipend in any hospital." This canon was deleted in response to antitrust litigation instituted by the Justice Department alleging that pathologists had forced patients to pay excessively high fees by conspiring to: boycott hospitals that refused to pay pathologists a percentage of profits, refuse to accept a hospital position unless the pathologist already occupying the job had been consulted, boycott commercial laboratories not owned by a pathologist, and agree not to compete by lowering prices.[503] The antitrust litigation was settled when the pathologists agreed to stop these practices without admitting the allegations. However, hospital administrators say little has changed as a result of the litigation.[504] Even if an individual hospital or Blue Cross plan wants to curb the high costs of monopolistic goods and services, it is extremely difficult to take effective action on an individual basis. For example, one experimental Blue Cross cost control program found that the radiologist in a small rural hospital was paid $50,000 a year for working approximately fifteen hours a week. The salary was not challenged, because the rate was comparable to that paid by other area hospitals.[505]

There are palliative measures that Blue Cross, state insurance commissioners, and HEW could require in order to reimburse only at a reasonable level of costs. The law is rich with concepts and experience that could be utilized to define fair market price or require competitive bidding in situations in which there is a free market for goods or services. Blue Cross, the state and federal agencies, and Congress have been derelict in failing to impose such standards.[506] These techniques could solve the problem cited by Commissioner Denenberg of hospitals paying inflated prices for "hospital" scissors or tape measures.

Unfortunately, however, definitions and requirements tied to fair market price or utilizing competitive bidding will meet only a small part of the problem of inflated hospital costs. The basic problem lies in the hospital supply market itself. Many of the goods and services purchased by hospitals—particularly specialists' services and technical hardware—are produced solely for the hospital market. While there is a free competitive market for scissors and tape measures, and hence a market standard against which to judge hospital purchases, there is little competitive market for electronic thermometers or blood counters, hyperbaric chambers, scalpels, syringes, and catheters, or for the services of hospital administrators, radiologists, pathologists, anesthesiologists, etc. All of these products and services are consumed only by hospitals. One approach to cost control is to impose a fixed limit on allowable increases in reimbursement. Though this would do nothing to correct the present excessive prices and generous profits of hospital suppliers and professionals, it would help to prevent a bad situation from becoming worse.

Neither a freeze nor the more vigorous definition and application of the prudent buyer concept is likely to assure adequately that hospitals purchase goods and services at reasonable prices. These measures do not address the magnitude of the problem. After many years of open-ended Blue Cross reimbursement, without attention to the reasonableness of amounts paid, the entire hospital industry and related professions have become geared to demand and receive inflated prices for goods and services. The national health insurance proposal of the Medical Committee for Human Rights would prohibit hospitals (or comprehensive health centers) from contracting with profit-making institutions.[507] This is a radical remedy. But it is the only remedy thus far proposed that speaks to the problem of hospitals' dependency on high-profit industries and professions. Given the present situation, it is difficult to conceive of what an individual hospital, or even an individual Blue Cross plan, could do to force down prices in the drug and hospital supply industries and hospital-based professions. None of the current national health insurance proposals deals with this problem. The bills proposed by Senator Edward Kennedy and by the administration for changes in Medicare reimbursement would place limits on the amount available for hospital services and would provide hospitals incentives to cost-conscious purchasing. But unless the industries and professions upon which the hospitals depend are also fundamentally restructured, the result is likely to be chronic underfinancing of hospital service and a diminution of quality.

Implementation of reasonable cost concepts

Whatever standards are utilized for payment of hospital costs, many issues are settled by the manner in which they are applied and implemented. The ambiguity of the reasonable cost standard calls for close scrutiny of component items and of amounts claimed. The third party payer should make reasoned and timely challenges to particular items, either through the prospective review of budgets or through clear notice on an item-by-item basis of what expenses are to be covered in future years.[508] Timely audits are essential, so that payments may be made promptly and providers may know what expenses are allowable and make plans accordingly. Most hospital revenues are derived from third party payers on a cost basis, and there are no inherent economic incentives to control costs, plan intelligently, or confirm the need and utility of a particular item of capital, equipment, or personnel cost.[509] Thus it is absolutely essential that Blue Cross provide such incentives by raising questions as a prudent buyer or intelligent adversary.[510] Given the magnitude of Blue Cross purchasing power, and given the tendency to fill all hospital beds that exist,[511] public planning is doomed to fail unless Blue Cross coordinates reimbursement with the public planning processes.

Blue Cross has, with few exceptions, failed on each of these points. Under Medicare, interim payments are made, "on the most expeditious basis administratively feasible but not less often than monthly," in response to summary and unaudited information submitted by the hospitals.[512] The secretary of HEW provides advance funds to each intermediary on the basis of these cost reports filed by the providers and approved by the intermediaries.[513] Real checks on the reasonableness of cost claims must be imposed, if at all, when the cost reports are subsequently audited and adjusted. The contract with Blue Cross provides that the plans shall "make such audits of records of providers of services . . . as is necessary to insure that such providers of services . . . are being reimbursed in accordance with the provision of the Act and the Regulations."[514]

Most Blue Cross plans have subcontracted with independent public accounting firms for the purpose of auditing hospitals' annual Medicare cost reports.[515] The Social Security Administration Audit Agency notes "serious inadequacies in [intermediaries'] overall reviews and management of provider cost reports and audits. To all intents and purposes the intermediaries had abdicated this responsibility and had, in effect, transferred them to the accounting firms engaged to audit providers."[516] Blue Cross delegation of the authority delegated to it by the secretary further dilutes administrative accountability and increases the likelihood that responsibility will be shirked.

The use of private auditors has created large problems. Intermediaries have contracted with an estimated 200 private auditing firms, giving the bulk of the work to the "so-called big eight outfits, Price, Waterhouse and the like." [517] In many cases the firm auditing the Medicare cost reports also audits the cost reports for the provider's Blue Cross business. Use of private auditors has been expensive.[518] One SSA study showed that 134 audit subcontracts rose 26 per cent over their original estimated costs from $6,737,154 to $8,479,336.[519] A Contract Performance Review of the St. Louis plan revealed that audit costs paid to Price, Waterhouse and Co. increased almost 100 per cent from 1969 to 1970, even though the firm had been doing the plan's private audit work for 15 or 20 years and auditing the Medicare payments for three years. The Contract Performance Review commented that "it seems reasonable to assume that this working knowledge would assist the audit firm in the completion of audits on a more realistic cost basis." [520]

While the problem of costly auditing services is serious, monies spent on auditing would be well spent if the auditors were doing an effective job. The evidence is that they are not. There has been a program-wide failure among the intermediaries and auditors to complete audits within a reasonable time. As of January 1, 1970, cost reports for 1967 had not been settled for about 2,500 hospitals, or one-third of those participating in Medicare.[521] In Massachusetts as of 1970 there had been no fiscal audits by Blue Cross of hospitals for any year since Medicare began.[522] In 1970 Blue Cross of Southern California had received less than half of the provider cost statements due in June 1968.[523] Failure to make timely audits is the responsibility of both Blue Cross and the auditing firms. The intermediary retains basic responsibility for seeing that cost reports are filed on time, that audits are promptly started and completed, and that the settlement is based on the providers' reasonable, audited costs.

Although the intermediaries have the basic responsibility for seeing that audits are completed on time, long delays have also been caused by the failures of the Social Security Administration and the hospitals. During the first years of the Medicare program, SSA failed to provide statistical and financial data that had been promised to facilitate the auditing operation.[524] Hospitals are often late in filing year-end cost reports. Until 1969 no penalties were imposed upon hospitals that failed to submit their cost reports within the 90-day period specified in the regulations. Where the interim payments to hospitals are too high, and the hospital will be required to refund money after the final cost settlement, hospitals have a positive incentive to submit the cost reports late.[525]

After audits are completed and cost reports received, another problem arises. Blue Cross is often unable to make final settlement with providers who refuse to give in on disputed issues. For example, as of July 1970 St. Louis Blue Cross had not made final settlements with about 23 per cent of the hospitals for the first Medicare fiscal year and about 25 per cent for the second year. The Contract Performance Review team found that the plan "lacks aggressiveness in resolving some of the issues holding up final settlements and is apathetic toward providers who do not cooperate." [526] In 1971 the General Accounting Office recommended that SSA require the national Blue Cross Association to take a more active role in the final settlement process by assisting those local plans having the most serious backlogs of audited cost reports for which settlements had not been made. The SSA and BCA rejected this recommendation on grounds that the BCA did not have sufficient staff and that the role of BCA in the Medicare program was an "administrative, rather than an operative, one." [527] The meaning of this distinction is not immediately apparent.

When the local Blue Cross plan makes a final reimbursement determination, the provider may appeal to a BCA Provider Appeals Committee. Prior to June 30, 1973, the decisions of this committee were final; HEW was not involved in the settlement of specific reimbursement disputes.[528] The 1972 amendments to the Social Security Act establish a review board within HEW.[529]

The picture that emerges is one of total unaccountability. Hospitals are paid in advance for whatever they claim. Books are audited, often years later, by commercial auditors with no particular expertise in health services and no capacity to judge whether or not a cost is reasonable; they note only whether it was properly catalogued in the books and represents a payment actually made. This procedure makes application of the prudent buyer concept impossible. Whatever educational potential inheres in the auditing function is lost, or at least lost for a period of years. When particular items are caught and questioned, the hospital can engage in an extended dispute with the intermediary, confident that the intermediary will not be excessively "aggressive" in pursuing the matter.

Another major problem with the administration of reasonable cost formulas lies in the process by which the provider reimbursement contract between local Blue Cross plans and the hospitals is "negotiated." This process is deficient in several major respects. First, significant hospital influence in Blue Cross governance means that the two parties will not negotiate at arm's length.[530] Second, the Blue Cross plan often negotiates with the hospital's local trade association, which has obtained negotiating authority from member hospitals, rather than with the individual hospitals.[531] This leads to a situation in which the hospitals have enormous collective bargaining power, and contracts must be worked out by the association "to be acceptable to the least capable of its members." [532] Individual hospitals have significant bargaining power in their own right, since Blue Cross is interested in obtaining agreements, so that hospital services will be available to subscribers. Individual hospitals also have varying capacities for instituting reforms and saving costs. Even where Blue Cross negotiates with individual providers, the hospitals can, on a particularly critical issue, band together, threaten to withdraw, and sometimes force Blue Cross to abandon attempted reforms.[533] It is difficult to imagine what legitimate interests are served by determining reimbursement rates through negotiation with a monopolistic trade association.

A third problem arises from the lack of public or state involvement in the negotiation process. Two recent exceptions to the normal pattern of closed-door, unsupervised negotiation illustrate the difficulty and importance of making this process public. In 1968 Massachusetts enacted legislation requiring that provider reimbursement contracts be approved by a five-person rate commission.[534] In the spring of 1970 Blue Cross began negotiations with the Massachusetts Hospital Association. An impasse was reached in the negotiations, and MHA urged member hospitals "to make appropriate preparations for the possibility that no reimbursement agreement . . . will exist after September 30, 1970." [535] In response to concerted pressure from the hospitals, Blue Cross retreated, and an agreement was reached. It was only at this point that the Rate Setting Commission became involved. It held four days of public hearings, which "were the first in recent memory to be held on proposed

Blue Cross payments to hospitals.'' [536] Public regulatory involvement at this late stage was ineffectual. The chairman of the Rate Commission stated:

> Both Blue Cross and the hospitals made it eminently clear during the course of our hearings that it was their view that the involvement of the Commission began when, and only when, the parties had agreed between themselves on a contract and submitted it to the Rate Setting Commission for approval. For this reason, there is not a great deal of information concerning the substance of the negotiations that are in the hands of the State agencies at this point. [537]

If the Massachusetts experience illustrates the difficulty of effective public or regulatory involvement in the negotiation process, recent Pennsylvania experience illustrates the importance of such involvement. In 1971 Philadelphia Blue Cross requested rate increases of $37 million in emergency funds and another $37 million in annual rate adjustments. State Insurance Commissioner Herbert Denenberg refused to approve the increase and instead ordered all Blue Cross hospital contracts to be negotiated in accordance with specific guidelines developed by his office. [538] The guidelines urged that the contract incorporate provisions to: phase out or control construction of duplicative and underutilized facilities; eliminate unsafe and otherwise substandard beds; limit the number of employees; reallocate responsibility for the financing of residents and interns; limit financing for depreciation; institute prospective reimbursement; require prior submission and review of hospital budgets; adopt known cost-saving devices, such as preadmissions testing and graded care; require disclosure of information and control of payments to hospital-based physicians; deny reimbursement for dues paid to trade associations; assure adequate consumer representation on hospital boards; eliminate the system of staff privileges and allow all qualified physicians to admit patients to any hospital; allow pharmacists to substitute less expensive drugs where they are chemically identical to prescribed brand-name drugs; allow reimbursement for general management surveys; provide incentives for cost-saving programs; develop accounting procedures to eliminate reimbursement for research costs; provide for public disclosure of information on hospital and Blue Cross operations; protect the patient from charges for medically unnecessary services; strengthen utilization review procedures; institute safety measures to minimize hospital accidents; transfer the risk of bad debts from Blue Cross to the hospitals; subscribe to services providing comparative data on utilization; accept tests and examinations done outside hospitals by licensed laboratories; move toward uniform accounting systems; and establish procedures to assure that hospitals are not purchasing merchandise at inflated prices.

After five days of public hearings and six months of negotiations among Blue Cross, the Hospital Association and the insurance commissioner, a new agreement was reached.[539] On many issues, the negotiations were between the insurance commissioner on one side, with Blue Cross and the hospitals united in their opposition to the proposed reforms. The final agreement follows some, but not all, of the commissioner's guidelines. Among the most significant changes adopted were protection of the subscriber from charges for unnecessary medical services,[540] elimination of accelerated depreciation,[541] a requirement that hospitals submit an annual budget to Blue Cross at least 45 days prior to the beginning of the fiscal year,[542] and reimbursement for generic drugs when they are equivalent to brand-name drugs. The contract also includes vague requirements on public disclosure of information and consumer participation in hospital governance.[543] Hospitals and Blue Cross resisted the effort to prohibit reimbursement for trade association dues and to require that interns and residents be paid by the physicians whom they assist.

These cost-saving provisions were incorporated into the Philadelphia Blue Cross Hospital Contract because of the aggressive intervention of the insurance commissioner. The reforms proposed and adopted were not particularly original or innovative. Rather, their significance lies in the fact that official pressure was the impetus for the institution of cost controls that Blue Cross had previously neglected to adopt. The fact that the commissioner sought particularistic, concrete additions to the contract—reflecting a sophisticated understanding of hospital financing and reimbursement—was also important. The new contract provisions have produced substantial savings for Blue Cross subscribers and assure them that they will not be faced with unexpected bills for hospital services prescribed by their physician.[544]

Both private Blue Cross subscribers and the beneficiaries of public health insurance need some means of participating in the negotiation process by which ''reasonable costs'' are defined and applied. All of the reforms urged in the Denenberg guidelines are needed to control Medicare costs and could be required by HEW regulation. The guidelines themselves, though, are of little use unless an informed, aggressive, consumer-oriented advocate has power and authority to participate in the negotiation process. Under the existing Medicare and Medicaid legislation, it would be difficult for HEW to justify direct intervention in the cost negotiations between fiscal intermediaries and providers. Although insurance officials in nearly every state now have authority to participate in this process, few use it.[545] Insurance commissioners are not accountable to subscribers and beneficiaries any more than hospitals or Blue Cross are. Commissioner Denenberg has chosen to act as the subscriber's advocate, but subscribers would have been powerless to force him to take that role.

Another major problem in the administration of hospital payments under Medicare lies in the dual role of the intermediary as private insurer and government agent. As has been shown, the allocation formulas lend themselves to the overloading of costs onto the Medicare program. Deficiencies in the formulas are exacerbated by administrative practices. In 1970, the Senate Finance Committee staff noted:

> A serious conflict of interest situation is also created where Blue Cross plans, acting as subcontractors under the program, have a "carve-out" reimbursement arrangement with hospitals. Under this arrangement the Blue Cross subcontractor first determines the amount the hospital should be paid by Medicare and then, based upon remaining costs, pays the hospital on behalf of its regular Blue Cross subscribers.[546]

Despite strong indications that Medicare and Medicaid are bearing a disproportionately large share of hospital costs, a belief exists among many hospital personnel that the hospital receives less payment for Medicaid and Medicare patients than for patients with private Blue Cross coverage.[547] Prior to 1966 it was true that hospitals were not fully reimbursed for care rendered the poor and the aged. These patients were cared for as charity patients, and as such they received care that was, at least with respect to amenities and accommodations, substantially inferior to that provided private paying patients. In teaching hospitals the quid pro quo demanded of charity patients was that they be available as teaching material. With the enactment of the federal health programs there have been some superficial changes in this pattern. For example, since Medicare and Medicaid require semi-private accommodations, some hospitals have eliminated ward accommodations.[548] However, a Health Law Project study of one teaching hospital, with a reputation for excellence, shows that even though ward accommodations have been eliminated, a sharp distinction persists between ward and private "service." Patients on ward "service" continue to receive inferior accommodations and amenities, are cared for by teams of staff physicians and physicians-in-training rather than by individual doctors, and are discriminated against in the provision of radiology and other ancillary services.[549]

The belief that you get what you pay for is fundamental in our society. So long as hospital personnel believe that the hospital is not receiving full payment for Medicare and Medicaid patients, there will probably be a tendency—in both institutional and individual actions—to provide inferior care to such patients. Particularly with respect to the nontechnical aspects of hospital care, such as condition and age of the hospital room and surrounding areas, presence of telephone or functioning nurse call systems, waiting time for X rays or other tests, and so forth, the tradition of providing inferior services to "charity" patients will persist.

Hospital personnel familiar with the specifics of the Medicaid reimbursement formula frequently argue that, even if the public programs ultimately pay as much, hospitals suffer inordinate delays in receiving payment.[550] However, Medicare payments have been made in advance. There is a need for further research on the disparities in the administration of private Blue Cross and Medicare and Medicaid. To the extent that there are longer delays in the auditing and final settlement of Medicare and Medicaid costs, it is because Blue Cross and its auditors decide to give them a lower priority. [551] In giving priority to its role as a private insurer, Blue Cross defaults on its obligations as administrator of public funds, and the poor and the aged suffer.

When the federal health insurance programs were initiated, Blue Cross was familiar with the differential patterns of care arising from the former charitable status of the poor and the aged. It was obvious that integration of these groups into the mainstream of hospital care would require a large job of education to overcome traditional attitudes and treatment patterns based on financial differences that no longer existed.

The fiscal intermediary role was created at the behest of Blue Cross because of its sophisticated knowledge of hospital operations and close working relationships with hospital personnel. Blue Cross was in fact uniquely qualified to help the hospitals translate the new financial equality into equality of treatment. Instead, Blue Cross has paid hospitals more for Medicare and Medicaid services but paid more slowly and inefficiently, so that the myth of charity service persists. The failure of administration could hardly have been greater.

REASONABLE COSTS UNDER MEDICAID

States participating in Medicaid must provide inpatient hospital services to needy individuals eligible for Aid to the Aged, Blind, Permanently and Totally Disabled and Families with Dependent Children.[552] The federal statute required that the states pay the "reasonable cost" of inpatient hospital services provided under the state plan.[553] The HEW regulations specified that the Medicare reasonable costs principles also governed reimbursement for hospital services for Medicaid eligibles. Hospitals that participated in both Medicare and Medicaid were to receive payments under "the same standards, cost reporting period, cost reimbursement principles, and method of cost apportionment" for both programs.[554] Hospitals not participating in Medicare were to be reimbursed by the same standards, except that the institution could utilize an additional method of apportioning costs.[555] There was no explicit statutory floor on the amount that states should pay for outpatient services provided under Medicaid, and the result with respect to outpatient services has been that Medicaid has often paid "less than adequate prices for frequently less than adequate services." [556]

The United States Supreme Court has held that states participating in Medicaid must pay hospitals the full, actual, and current costs of inpatient services furnished to eligible individuals, including retroactive payments or an allowance in lieu of retroactive payments.[557] This litigation, brought by New York hospitals in response to an attempt by the state legislature to impose a ceiling on Medicaid hospital payments, also established that hospitals may utilize the federal courts to collect the full reasonable costs due them for services rendered Medicaid recipients.

Despite the plain, judicially enforceable, statutory obligation to pay full reasonable costs for inpatient hospital services, there is, as we have noted, a widespread belief among hospital administrators that they are not fully reimbursed for services provided to poor people eligible for Medicaid.[558] This is puzzling. It may be that state agencies and Blue Cross plans administering Medicaid in fact pay less than full reasonable costs, despite the statutory mandate. Or it may be that, even though payments are adequate, there has not been sufficient educational effort to overcome historical belief that the poor do not pay their own way.

The states objected strenuously to the requirement that they pay the full reasonable costs of hospital services for poor people. Many of the objections were well-founded criticisms of the excesses inherent in the reasonable costs concept [559] and applied equally to Medicare and Medicaid. Other critics recommended that reasonable costs standards for services to the poor should not be tied to the Medicare reimbursement principles.[560] The argument was that the states should not be restricted to the Medicare formula "in view of the difference between Medicaid and Medicare in terms of the ages of the populations assisted, sources of financing, and primary administrative responsibility." [561] These differences, if taken into account, would almost surely mean that hospitals would receive less for services rendered the poor. The poor are politically vulnerable. States struggling to meet rising Medicaid costs are subject to greater pressure to save money than is the federally financed Medicare program. However, the evidence is that the poor tend to be more acutely ill as hospital patients than their middle-class counterparts.[562] If Medicaid reimbursement standards are not tied to Medicare standards, disparity in payment is likely to mean that it will be increasingly difficult for the poor to obtain hospital services and that the services they receive will be inferior. Rather than piecemeal cost control reform for the most vulnerable segment of the population, reimbursement methods must be changed across the board.

In response to criticism from the states, the secretary of HEW amended the Medicaid regulations in 1971 to allow states to pay less than full reasonable costs for hospital services to the poor with his prior approval.[563] In 1972 Congress authorized states to develop alternative methods and standards of reimbursement under Medicaid, subject to the secretary's approval.[564] The proposed HEW regulations implementing this provision allow the states to limit Medicaid payments to the lesser of reasonable costs, as determined by Medicare principles, or the customary charges to the general public.[565] To the extent that these changes allow states to pay less than reasonable costs for hospital services to the poor, they are likely to perpetuate differential, inferior hospital care for Medicaid recipients.

ALTERNATIVES FOR HOSPITAL FINANCING

In recent years there has been widespread, high-level criticism of the use of the reasonable cost concept in reimbursement for hospital care.[566] Attempted reforms have been limited. On the federal level, a 1968 amendment to the Social Security Act gave HEW authority to institute experimental projects to test new methods of reimbursement for hospital costs under Medicare—but only with the agreement of the hospitals involved.[567] Not surprisingly, there were few experiments.[568] The Social Security Act amendments of 1972 allow the secretary to conduct experiments in cost control without the permission of the hospitals affected.[569]

Major cost control reforms now in effect or under serious consideration are of three types. First, incentive programs, such as that adopted under New York's Hospital Cost Control Act, provide that hospitals will receive a fixed rate based on their previous expenditure levels. If costs go up more than the fixed rate, the hospital loses. If the hospital can effectuate savings through more efficient management, the excess is a reward to be used as the hospital sees fit. A second type of cost control program would use health maintenance organizations and a variety of other devices to create a more competitive market for hospital services, relying on market influences to encourage higher quality patient services and lower costs. The third type of cost control uses public authority to institute particular reforms in reimbursement and hospital management. Each of these alternative means of cost control will be considered and analyzed.

Several states have enacted hospital costs control legislation,[570] and some Blue Cross plans have initiated experimental cost control programs.[571] New York's Cost Control Act was among the first adopted.[572] It applies to all state purchases of hospital care, as well as Blue Cross reimbursement for private services, and provides that rates for hospital services paid by the state must be approved by the state budget director, and rates of payments by Blue Cross must be approved by the state superintendent of insurance.[573] Rates cannot be approved until the commissioner of health has certified that they are "reasonably related to the costs of efficient production of such services." [574] In making this certification the commissioner of health must take into consideration

> elements of cost, geographical differentials in the elements of cost, economic factors in the area in which the hospital is located, rate of increase or decrease of the economy in the area in which the hospital is located, costs of hospitals of comparable size, and the need for incentives to improve services and institute economies.[575]

Under this mandate the commissioner of health has promulgated regulations providing that all payments to hospitals are to be on a prospective basis of rates fixed at the beginning of each year, and no retroactive rate adjustments are to be made in the absence of a determination of error.[576] For the purpose of making cost comparisons, hospitals are divided into groups on the basis of type of hospital, geographic area, size of facility, and sponsor.[577] A rate is established for each hospital for routine services on the basis of the hospital's recent cost experience. The basic rate for a particular hospital cannot exceed by more than 10 per cent the weighted average of the group into which it falls.[578] This basic rate is then weighted for expected cost increases in the coming year by means of various general price indexes.[579]

The theory of the New York cost control plan is that, in the absence of competitive market influence, an incentive-penalty mechanism is needed to keep hospital prices down. The incentive is the amount of money the hospital can plan on and retain if its annual costs total less than its budget projection. Similarly, the amount by which a hospital's costs exceed its projected budget becomes a financial penalty which the hospital must absorb.

There are several major weaknesses in the New York program. First, it does not apply to many of the most costly elements of hospital care. Specifically exempted from the average basic rate are "capital costs, costs of schools of nursing, costs of interns and residents, and costs of ancillary services." [580] This means that as much as one half of a hospital's operating budget is excluded from controls. A hospital could shift routine costs to ancillary services and be assured of full reimbursement, plus the incentive guaranteed by the base rate.

A second major problem with this program is that it freezes current hospital institutional relationships. The pivotal mechanism in the New York cost control law is the prospective basic rate for routine services as determined by use of hospital comparison groups and previous hospital experience. Under the comparison group guidelines, it is possible to establish some thirty comparison groups. The plan prepared by New York Blue Cross establishes fourteen comparison groups.[581] The law limits cost increases only in terms of a particular hospital's own group, and, with the multiplication of groups, the effect may be to limit costs within a group that as a whole is substantially inefficient or extravagant and can remain inefficient and extravagant or become more so at the rate of 10 per cent per year. Like the reasonable cost reimbursement methods now utilized, New York's program assures that hospitals that spend most, and have spent most in the past, will receive most. In 1971 the state-approved Blue Cross per diem rates for teaching hospitals ranged up to $155, while the per diem rate to municipal hospitals was $103.[582] Conditions in New York's municipal hospitals are deplorable.[583] Despite a need for additional personnel, a hiring freeze was in effect from December 1971 to September 1972 because of lack of funds.[584] The cost control legislation perpetuates a vicious circle in which the hospitals that legitimately need funds to provide adequate services cannot get them, while the better financed institutions continue to receive funds at a higher rate.

The most serious objection to the New York model is that the incentive provided is indiscriminate. If the problem of rising hospital costs were primarily one of inefficiency or incompetence, cost incentives and penalties would be a helpful reform. However, hospitals, and particularly the most expensive teaching hospitals, are often highly structured, well organized, and staffed with efficient, highly motivated, and intelligent people. High costs and inadequate services exist, because the hospital is organized to meet the needs of physicians, research, medical education, and a hospital board and administration oriented toward parochial professional prestige. The basic issues in cost control are questions of priorities, allocation of resources, and allocation of the power to make these judgments.[585] New York's Cost Control Act does nothing to affect these issues.[586] Hospitals retain unfettered freedom to effect savings or to limit the increase in costs in any way they see fit.

The New York legislation now serves as a model for federal reform.[587] Prospective reimbursement is allowed under the 1972 amendments. It is not universally required, however, because Congress was not convinced that it would effectively control costs [588] and was concerned that cost control would be accomplished by reductions in the quality of care rendered.[589]

Health Maintenance Organizations (HMOs) are a second major cost control device. HMOs are a particular form of incentive reimbursement system characterized by the combination of medical services into a single organization capable of providing comprehensive care for a fixed, actuarially determined amount.[590] Theoretically, there are three ways in which HMOs will control costs. First, because the organization receives a fixed amount not based on the kind or amount of service provided to a particular individual, the financial incentive is to provide care in the most economical way possible. Whereas in the fee-for-service system a doctor is encouraged to provide the most expensive treatment available, because the more care he provides the more he will profit, in an HMO the financial incentive is just the opposite. If more expensive treatment can be avoided by the provision of less expensive preventive services, the organization will have an incentive to provide the latter and a disincentive to provide the former.

Second, by combining a comprehensive range of health services, the HMO will have the inducement and opportunity to choose the most efficient form of treatment for its patients. The historic pattern of Blue Cross and Blue Shield coverage adopted by the Medicare and Medicaid programs has encouraged excessive reliance on inpatient hospital services.[591] Since inpatient services are insured, while outpatient services must be paid for by the individual, both physicians and patients tend to utilize hospitals in borderline cases. Where individuals are enrolled in a group prepaid practice plan for outpatient services and are independently insured for hospital care through Blue Cross or private insurance, whatever savings result from the availability of outpatient services and the reduced need for hospitalization accrue not to the individual or the group plan but rather to Blue Cross or the insurance company providing hospital coverage.[592] To the extent that HMOs end this bifurcation of inpatient and outpatient services they may overcome some of the problems outlined above.

The third way in which HMOs may control costs is by introducing competition and informed consumer choice into health services delivery.[593] Reversing the financial incentives in the provision of health care could be dangerous to patients, however. There is little evidence that preventive medical services can prevent most major illnesses requiring hospitalization, for example cancer, stroke, heart disease.[594] Changes in personal habits, for example diet, smoking, exercise, may have a significant preventive effect, but medical services do not have a good record of helping people with these problems. There is no economic incentive for an HMO to provide a prolonged and intensive course of life-saving treatment. Incentives for economy can also be incentives for no care or inferior care. For example, if a hearing defect can be ignored, compensated for with a hearing aid, or permanently corrected with expensive surgery, an HMO will have an economic motive to do nothing or to prescribe a hearing aid.[595] The danger that HMOs will provide inferior care is particularly acute when the organization is a profit-making one, when the physician's compensation is based on a percentage of profit rather than a fixed salary, when physicians work only part-time for the HMO and also have a private fee-for-service practice, when HMO enrollees have no alternative means of obtaining medical care, and when the HMO population is exclusively poor or aged.

The dangers inherent in HMO development could be alleviated by extensive government regulation of the quality of care provided, by a requirement of direct and effective consumer control of the HMO, or by the effective introduction of competition and informed consumer choice into the health care market. None of the current proposals for HMO development include provisions for extensive government regulation. This is understandable, since quality standards are not well defined, there is no government experience in monitoring quality of health care, and the hospital and insurance industries and medical profession vigorously resist government regulation of the quality of medical care. Existing HMOs do not allow for consumer control,[596] and existing federal legislation regarding HMO development does not encourage such control.[597] The 1972 Social Security Act amendments allow Medicare beneficiaries to purchase services through HMOs.[598] Although Congress recognized that HMOs have an economic incentive to provide inadequate care so as to reduce costs and maximize financial gain,[599] the act contains no effective provisions to prevent this unhappy result.[600]

HMO proponents see competition as the primary means of controlling the quality of services they render and also as an additional means of reducing health costs.[601] If an HMO serves a captive population, there is no incentive to provide care of decent quality. Competition among HMOs and between HMOs and the private fee-for-service sector are essential if the danger of inferior and inadequate care is to be avoided. One leading HMO theorist argues that HMOs should be required to enroll one self-paying member for each member enrolled under Medicaid or Medicare and that a variety of legal sanctions should be used to assure and promote the existence of competitive HMOs.[602] On a theoretical level, the notion of competing HMOs offering different combinations of services, quality, amenities and price, which consumers could evaluate and select, is attractive. Increased competition is proposed as a means to make the health services industry more responsive to public and consumer preferences. The call for competition recognizes that the delivery of health services involves social choices that are appropriately made by the public, rather than technical medical issues to be resolved by doctors, administrators, or other experts. It also recognizes a tendency toward excess and waste inherent in an unregulated, noncompetitive industry. However, given the current dominance of health care by a few powerful and, in some cases, monopolistic organizations, it seems naïve to suppose that health services will reorganize themselves along competitive lines.[603] Medical societies, professional specialist organizations such as pathologists and radiologists, hospital associations, and Blue Cross/Blue Shield each have the power to make or break any developing HMO.[604]

A theoretical answer to the problem of maintaining competition in the health care market is to bar Blue Cross and Blue Shield from participation in HMO development. Clark Havighurst, a leading proponent of the competitive HMO model of health care delivery states:

Of course, health insurers might move directly into HMO formation and might profit handsomely in so doing. I see substantial merit, however, in prohibiting health insurers from entering the HMO sector. The obvious reason is to avoid domination of the market by Blue Cross/Blue Shield, which might in some communities come to sell the bulk of the health insurance while also controlling the major HMO and reinsuring the competing HMOs against excessive risks. Since Blue Cross is widely accused of being operated in the interest of the medical establishment, the arguments against Blue Cross's extension into the HMO sector parallel the arguments against medical society sponsorship of prepayment plans: there is good reason to suspect that Blue Cross HMOs would hang back rather than develop the full potential of the HMO concept and that avoidance of the establishment's discomfiture would be their primary raison d'etre.[605]

The reality of HMO development bears little relationship to the theoretical competitive model. Blue Cross and other insurers [606] have in fact moved to control and profit from HMO development. In 1969, when Kaiser-Permanente first held training sessions on HMO management and development, the sessions were sold out to Blue Cross personnel.[607] Since then Blue Cross has begun fourteen HMOs and has over forty more in planning stages.[608] On the national level, the BCA has encouraged the promotion of HMOs and made efforts to dispel criticism of Blue Cross dominance of HMOs.[609]

An examination of the influence of Blue Cross on HMO development in Philadelphia illustrates the power that Blue Cross wields in shaping this new form of health care delivery. In 1970 the president of the BCA acted as a catalyst in the formation of Group Health Planning of Greater Philadelphia (GHP), an umbrella organization for HMO planning and promotion. GHP is engaged in HMO development that would provide services through existing facilities, with Blue Cross/Blue Shield and other insurance companies marketing and underwriting. The organization is committed in a vague way to consumer control, but so far active members consist of 23 hospitals and 9 insurance companies.[610] GHP remains primarily in the planning stage. If its program were to be fully realized, the present dominance of hospitals and insurance companies in the Philadelphia health delivery industry would be consolidated.

Blue Cross has played an important role in relation to each of the developing HMOs in Philadelphia. The one HMO currently functioning is operated by Temple University and serves a Medicaid-eligible population in the neighborhood surrounding the university. Blue Cross serves as the underwriter and fiscal intermediary.[611] Health Service Plan of Pennsylvania (HSP) is a nonprofit corporation attempting to develop HMOs in Philadelphia: its first full-scale HMO would serve 10,000 Medicaid recipients in West Philadelphia.[612] Dr. Newton Spencer, chairman of the board, describes obstruction on the part of Philadelphia Blue Cross ranging from attempts to discourage people from dealing with HSP to an insistence that Blue Cross reinsurance based on an excessive rate of hospital utilization be included in the HMO package.[613] HSP has not gotten off the ground, at least in part because of the lack of Blue Cross cooperation. South Philadelphia Health Action (SPHA) is a consortium of providers and consumers funded by the Office of Economic Opportunity to develop a network of HMOs to serve South Philadelphia. It has close working relationships with both Blue Cross and Group Health Planning of Greater Philadelphia. Its executive director considers cooperation with Blue Cross essential because of Blue Cross control of private health capital and the desire of individuals to have the Blue Cross insignia on their health plan cards.[614]

HMOs are a positive development inasmuch as they encourage the provision of outpatient services and a possible end to the economic bifurcation of inpatient and outpatient care. While the HMO form of organization discourages unnecessary hospitalization, it does nothing to control the unit cost of hospital services. Like prospective reimbursement generally, prepaid group practice requires that costs be limited to a fixed amount, without specifying how such savings shall be effected. It does not alter the present location of the power to decide the form that cost control should take. An HMO can stay within its budget by instituting cost-saving efficiencies and driving hard bargains with the professionals who provide services and the companies that provide drugs and supplies, or it can save money by simply providing less service. Long waits for appointments or nonemergency treatment and the prescription of less expensive and less effective means of treatment are simple means of limiting services. As we will show in chapter 5, the determination of what services are medically necessary is often a difficult job, and no effective means has yet been devised for the review of such judgments. The fact that financial incentives in the fee-for-service system press toward the provision of excessive services creates serious cost problems, but it also affords individuals some assurance that they will not be denied services they really need. Unless the individual can be provided some means of assuring that he or she will obtain necessary services, reversing the fee-for-service economic incentive could be dangerous for all patients and particularly so when the HMO serves an exclusively poor or aged population.[615]

The third model of hospital cost control is that of a public regulatory agency that scrutinizes hospital expenditures or reimbursement formulas and requires particular cost-saving reforms and reallocation of resources. Particularistic public regulation of hospital costs and services could provide a means for public decision making in the allocation of health resources. It could give the public the information and education needed for intelligent participation in making these political and social judgments. If instituted on the federal level, it would allow the possibility of area and national planning and allocation of resources.

One of the most successful regulatory efforts to control hospital and Blue Cross costs is that of the Pennsylvania Department of Insurance under Commissioner Herbert Denenberg.[616] Denenberg came to office in the beginning of 1971 from a professorship in insurance at the University of Pennsylvania's Wharton School of Finance and Commerce. He had an impressive background in law and insurance.[617] In February, the department issued a report to the people of Pennsylvania outlining its philosophy. Noting that insurance regulatory agencies generally have close contact with industry representatives, the report states that the department "intends to avoid that pitfall . . . [and] not only to act in the consumer's interest but to keep the consumer informed of its activities at all times, and to be fully accountable to the public." [618] In March, as we have seen, in response to a requested Blue Cross rate increase, Denenberg ordered Blue Cross to cancel contracts with hospitals, issued guidelines for Blue Cross/hospital relationships, and conducted five days of public hearings on the issues involved.[619] From March until October, Blue Cross, the insurance commissioner, and the hospitals negotiated, with frequent reports from the commissioner to the public,[620] and finally agreed in principle on the content of a new contract.[621] In March 1972, a new contract was finally approved.[622]

The Insurance Department's efforts were most successful in obtaining concrete changes in hospital management and reimbursement formulas (for example, the provisions referred to above encouraging the use of generic drugs and protecting subscribers from retroactive denial of claims). The reforms were highly successful in stemming the rate of increase of hospital and Blue Cross costs.[623] However, hospitals and Blue Cross resisted proposed changes in governance. The guidelines on consumer participation in hospital and Blue Cross governance were reduced to meaningless exhortations that have had no effect. The public information provisions are vague.[624] These reforms, had they been made, could have had effects lasting beyond Denenberg's tenure as insurance commissioner.

The American Hospital Association favors regulation of hospital costs on a public utilities model at the state level. Is it overly cynical to surmise that the AHA favors this alternative because it is predictably ineffective and would allow hospitals to retain the spending autonomy they now enjoy? The AHA plan provides for the appointment of a state commission that would set rates for all health care institutions on a prospective basis. Rates would be based on comparisons with past costs and among institutions. In order to ''avoid conflicts of interest'' the rate commission ''must not purchase or administer institutional health services programs for the state or federal government.'' Current rates ''should be deemed reasonable, adequate and proper, in the absence of evidence to the contrary.'' Rates would need to be sufficient to cover costs of ''patient care, approved educational programs, patient care-related research, the costs of patients who become credit losses or are unable to pay, the costs of preservation, improvement and expansion of plant and equipment and debt service on capital indebtedness, working capital, and return on investment for profit making institutions.'' [625] Public utilities regulation on the AHA model would protect the financial health of the hospital industry but would not control costs or make care more responsive to patients' needs.

Despite the successes of the Pennsylvania Insurance Department, it cannot serve as a model for reform for two reasons. First, given the political and financial strength of the insurance and hospital industries and medical profession, an administrative agency that undertakes regulation on behalf of consumers is politically vulnerable without a strong broad base of public support. Pennsylvania physicians have demanded Denenberg's ouster [626] and have been unsuccessful only because he has actively sought to build public support and sympathy and because he is an extraordinarily charismatic public figure.[627] Second, and more fundamentally, the Pennsylvania department depends almost entirely on the personality and consumer orientation of a particular individual.

The Pennsylvania experience would indicate that in order for a public agency to be effective in controlling hospital costs it must have: strong technical expertise and familiarity with hospital operations; legal authority to insist that the hospitals and Blue Cross institute reforms in management and reimbursement; and the motivation and political power to work on behalf of consumer and public interests. Although the legal authority of the Pennsylvania Insurance Department is not comprehensive or specific, it is at least as great as that available to most other state insurance departments. In at least some states, such as New York, the insurance department also has the requisite expertise. Motivation is lacking. The question then is: How do we create a public agency responsible for the regulation of hospital costs that is motivated to act in the interests of the public and consumers? The even more difficult question is: What kinds of programs and mechanisms will make it possible for the consumer—the public—to know the alternatives possible, voice their concerns, and participate in the governing process? As has been shown, the health care financing area is littered with regulatory agencies that have had little impact upon hospital management or financing—the Social Security Administration, the Medical Services Administration, the Civil Service Commission on the federal level and departments of health, welfare, and insurance on the state level. Traditional public utilities regulation provides few examples of effective regulation responsive to public interests.[628] There are no good models. The question how to create a consumer-oriented regulatory agency will be considered in the last chapter.

5. BLUE CROSS CLAIMS AND UTILIZATION REVIEW

For the individual subscriber or beneficiary, the greatest problem with Blue Cross is that it sometimes, unexpectedly, refuses to pay the bill. The individual goes to the hospital because the physician says it is necessary. Blue Cross coverage is discussed, or the patient simply assumes that Blue Cross will pay. At the hospital, Blue Cross or Medicare numbers are taken, reinforcing the assumption that Blue Cross will pay. The costs of services are not discussed with the patient or family. The physician and hospital personnel assume responsibility for telling the patient when he or she is "ready" to leave. At discharge, an unitemized bill is presented for coinsurance costs or telephone and other personal services not covered by Blue Cross. The hospital submits a claim for payment directly to Blue Cross. Then, months later, the individual is told that Blue Cross has refused to pay, and the hospital collection process begins.[629] The reasons for denial of payment and the process by which the decision was reached are unexplained and murky.[630]

The high cost of hospitalization is a grave problem at the social level; at the individual level it is a disaster. Even with careful planning and saving, the cost of a modest hospitalization is beyond the means of most people.[631] The expectation that Blue Cross will pay, reinforced by doctor and hospital, means that even the most frugal individuals will not have made plans or accumulated savings to meet this expense. The hospital often transfers the bill to a collection agency. The individual's credit rating is destroyed. People with lifelong habits of paying bills on time and buying only what they can afford are suddenly "bad debts." The individual's sense of anger and injustice is often strong, because the debt was not knowingly assumed and the reasons for Blue Cross nonpayment are mysterious or patently unfair.

Retroactive denial of coverage in individual cases is a relatively new Blue Cross policy, at least on the massive scale that it is now practiced. For the private subscriber the most common grounds for denial of coverage are that the care given was diagnostic or for a pre-existing condition.[632] Figures are not available on the extent of denial of private claims. Under Medicare the most common grounds for denying coverage are that the care provided was merely "custodial" or was not "medically necessary." The Social Security Administration estimates that in 1969 261 million dollars was saved in the Medicare program as a result of "tightened administrative procedures that caused closer scrutiny of bills." [633] Program savings were effectuated by passing the costs on to the aged patients.[634]

The reasons for the policy of large-scale denial of coverage and payment are unfortunate and clear. As we have seen, there are great incentives for excessive hospitalization, incentives created at least in part by Blue Cross. Both Medicare beneficiaries and younger people with private health insurance typically have insurance covering inpatient medical care and excluding outpatient care.[635] Especially if a course of treatment is likely to be expensive, it is in the financial interests of both the hospital and the doctor to have the patient in the hospital. In areas where unplanned and unregulated growth have produced an excess of hospital beds, the tendency toward overutilization of hospital beds is exacerbated, since it is about two-thirds as expensive to maintain an empty bed as to maintain a full one,[636] and the income to the hospital is obviously greater when the beds are occupied. As the unit costs of hospitalization have increased, and Blue Cross and federal and state agencies have been unable or unwilling to effectively control overall or unit costs, the problem of "excessive" utilization has become more acute. There is no evidence that there is more "unnecessary" utilization today than there was, say, ten years ago. Both hospital admissions rates and length of stays have remained relatively stable in the past ten years.[637] However, a single "unnecessary" day of hospitalization is a greater problem today, simply because the average per diem rate has gone from $32.23 in 1960 to $81.03 in 1970.[638] Some solution was called for, and Blue Cross found that it was simpler to control total program costs and subscriber rates by denying claims and passing costs back to the subscribers and beneficiaries, than by undertaking the more difficult job of controlling hospital unit costs.

The practice of controlling utilization of services through ex post facto denial of claims has been an administrative and human disaster. Individuals have not been afforded timely notice of termination of coverage or an effective opportunity to contest the administrative decision overruling the physician's judgment that care prescribed was medically necessary. The decision-making process has not been designed to produce uniform or medically sound decisions. Retroactive review of bills has severely discriminated against the poor, who do not have the independent means to assure a hospital or nursing home that the bill will be paid even if Blue Cross denies the claim. Because of the prohospital bias of Blue Cross administrators, claims review has been applied more harshly to nursing home services, and hence claims review has often discouraged provision of care in the most economical setting commensurate with the medical needs of the patient. Penalties and incentives have fallen upon the patient rather than upon the hospitals and doctors, who have the power to change behavior patterns and correct improper utilization of medical facilities and services. These are serious charges, and they will be discussed more fully after a description of the statutory structure and the present Blue Cross claims review practices.

Claims Review under the Medicare Statute

Before examining the claims review provisions of the 1965 Medicare Act, it should be noted that the statute described here is not the statute as interpreted by HEW or administered by Blue Cross. While the act is ambiguous on some of the details of administration, the overall administrative framework for determining when care provided should be paid for under Medicare is quite clear. As will be demonstrated, however, the congressionally mandated structure was never implemented by Blue Cross or HEW. Rather, the administrators abandoned the statutory structure and, through administrative practice and internal memoranda, created an alternative system. Congress is aware at least to some degree that the Medicare program has not been operated in accordance with the original statutory provisions. The 1972 amendments to the Social Security Act, discussed below, create new administrative mechanisms that will supplant both the 1965 statutory structure and the present administrative practice.

The 1965 Medicare Act relied primarily on professional and institutional integrity and self-policing to assure that payment would be made only for medically necessary care. The preamble laid down a sweeping prohibition against federal "supervision or control over the practice of medicine or the manner in which medical services are provided . . . or the administration of any . . . institution, agency, or person [providing health services]." [639] While the concrete legal effect of this preamble may be doubted, particularly where specific statutory provisions ineluctably require federal "interference" with existing delivery mechanisms,[640] it does illustrate the general congressional deference to institutional and professional service patterns.

The statute provided a variety of mechanisms for guarding against unwarranted utilization of hospital and extended care services. The benefit structure itself placed fixed limitations on the number of days of care for which payment would be made in a hospital or extended care facility or from a home health agency. The "spell of illness" concept limited Medicare services to those needed in an acute illness that initially requires hospitalization; home health care and extended care services are available only immediately following hospitalization and only for the conditions or illness for which the individual was hospitalized.[641] This is a significant limitation, since older people often need skilled nursing care or home health services for conditions that do not ever require hospitalization.

In addition to these mechanical limitations, the act provided that no payments should be made for certain types of services. The thirteen statutory exclusions are a mixed bag, including five based on nonmedical factors,[642] six prohibiting payment for easily identifiable types of services,[643] and two based on the medical necessity of care provided. The last two exclusions prohibited payment for services "which are not reasonable and necessary for the diagnosis or treatment of illness or injury or to improve the functioning of a malformed body member" [644] and "where such expenses are for custodial care." [645] Application of the last two exclusions requires medical assessment of the individual's total condition.

Application of the first two types of exclusions is a relatively simple matter, which neither the act nor the legislative history expressly considered. The fair inference is that Congress intended that the fiscal intermediary or HEW would make judgments whether, for example, some other individual has a legal obligation to pay for the services or whether the services are for, say, orthopedic shoes.

The application of the third class of exclusion presents a knottier problem to which Congress and the statute addressed themselves in considerable detail. Three statutory devices were used to assure that Medicare payments would be made only for medically necessary services: (1) the conditions of participation for providers; (2) the physician certification of medical necessity; and (3) the utilization review process which participating institutions had to establish.

Since patients enter hospitals only on the recommendation of physicians, and all Part A benefits are contingent upon hospitalization, the role of the physician is key. The act provided that payment for inpatient hospital service could be made only where

> a physician certifies that such services are required to be given on an inpatient basis for such individual's medical treatment, or that inpatient diagnostic study is medically required and such services are necessary for such purpose.[646]

The certification had to be given by the responsible physician within twelve days after admission. There were parallel physician certification requirements for all Part A services. In the case of skilled nursing home care the physician had to certify that the individual needed "skilled nursing care on a continuing basis." [647] Thus, under the statutory certification requirements, the prime responsibility for determining whether institutional care was medically necessary rested with the attending physician.[648]

The physician's certification was not to be the final determinant of medical necessity, however. Congress also required that, as a condition of participation in Medicare, institutional providers establish "utilization review committees" to check on the medical need of the care provided and to assure that it was of high quality.[649] The committee had to review admission, duration of stay, and professional services furnished in short-term stay cases on a sample or other basis; it also had to review each case of continuous extended duration periodically during the patient's confinement.[650]

When the attending physician decided that the patient no longer needed institutional care, it could fairly be assumed that he would inform the patient, so that the patient and family would know that Medicare payments were ending and make plans in light of that knowledge. However, when a hospital utilization review committee made that decision, there was no presumption that the patient would learn of it in the natural course of things. Congress anticipated this problem and required that patients be given timely notice of utilization review committee judgments that terminated Medicare entitlement. Utilization review committees could overrule the attending physician's judgment on the medical necessity for continued services only after consultation with him. When an adverse judgment was made, the utilization review committee had to promptly notify the institution, the attending physician, *and the individual;* [651] Medicare payments could be made for four days after such notice was given.[652] This permitted the individual and his family time to make alternative plans.

If the hospital or nursing home utilization review committee was not functioning properly, the statute provided two sanctions. First, the provider could be excluded from the Medicare program upon notice to the public.[653] The exclusion was not effective with respect to patients admitted to the hospital or extended care facility prior to the effective date of the exclusion.[654] Since the effective functioning of utilization review was so important to the statutory scheme, and since total exclusion of a provider from participation in Medicare was the sort of drastic penalty which an administrator might be reluctant to invoke, Congress provided a second, more moderate enforcement technique. The secretary could allow a hospital or nursing home to remain a Medicare provider but refuse payment for services rendered after the twentieth consecutive day of the patient's stay where the institution had failed to comply with utilization review requirements.[655] Again, if this sanction was invoked notice had to be given to the public as well as to the institutions involved,[656] and the prohibition of payment for services rendered after the twentieth day did not apply to patients admitted before the effective date of the prohibition.[657]

This complex of provisions assured that the individual would always have timely notice before Medicare payments were terminated on the ground that services were not medically necessary. If the provider was an approved participating institution, the individual could safely assume that it had an adequate utilization review committee and that that committee would give him timely notice if it made an adverse determination on the medical necessity of continued treatment. If the provider was under a twenty-day order, the individual would know, before he or she entered the institution, that care beyond the twentieth day might not be paid for and could make plans depending upon the anticipated length of stay and the availability of alternative institutions.

The institutional utilization review committee was to make the *final* judgment on the medical necessity of care provided to Medicare beneficiaries. The legislative history indicates that Congress was fully aware that, whatever dangers might be involved in placing the final determination of medical necessity in the hands of the professional committee within the provider institution, that was the way it was to be.[658] Wilbur Cohen, then under secretary of HEW, explained to the House Ways and Means Committee that a utilization review committee determination was comparable to a "supreme court decision." "If the [utilization] review board makes a mistake, there is nothing we can do about it, because that is the professional decision of the doctors." [659]

The role of Blue Cross in this statutory scheme was limited. The fiscal intermediary had to be "willing and able to assist the providers to which payments are made through it . . . in the application of safeguards against unnecessary utilization of services furnished by them to individuals." [660] The function of Blue Cross was to provide services to aid providers in establishing utilization review committees, to prepare utilization data, and to monitor the committees to make sure they were functioning effectively.[661] The legislative history shows that Congress understood that Blue Cross would evaluate the operation of utilization review committees but would not make determinations of medical necessity on a case-by-case basis.[662]

THE ADMINISTRATIVE POLICY FOR MEDICARE CLAIMS REVIEW

In the early years of the Medicare program there was no effort to overrule the determinations of physicians and utilization review committees that care was medically necessary.[663] However, the actuarial forecasts had grossly underestimated the cost of Medicare.[664] There was not a substantial increase in demand for services, as some had feared,[665] but rather an enormous increase in the unit costs of services.

Utilization review committees have not functioned effectively, and sometimes have not functioned at all.[666] Committees have not made the reviews required by their own plans, have not consulted with attending physicians on a timely basis, and have not informed patients or institutions of their decisions. The Social Security Administration and Blue Cross failed to educate utilization review committees on the importance of their role or to police their operations.[667] After five years, neither the intermediaries nor the Social Security Administration had developed statistical profiles on length of stay for various diagnoses or guidelines for determining when review should take place.[668] Neither told hospitals and nursing homes that effective utilization review was a condition of participation in Medicare. Since 1966, only one provider agreement has been terminated for failure to comply with utilization review requirements, and no institutions have ever been placed under a twenty-day order.[669]

Physician certification requirements have also been disregarded by Blue Cross. Despite the specific statutory mandate, it has not required physician certifications. The reasons offered have been that withholding payments would penalize the institution for noncompliance on the part of the attending physicians, and "lack of compliance was not considered sufficiently important to warrant measures as drastic as withholding payments." [670]

Thus, the statutory program was casually abandoned by HEW and Blue Cross. Rather than undertaking the difficult task of monitoring hospitals and physicians with respect to utilization review and physician certification requirements, in 1967 HEW authorized Blue Cross to institute retroactive review of the medical necessity of care provided in specific cases and to deny payment where care was judged unnecessary.[671] The new policy, announced in a letter, instructed Blue Cross to review claims to determine whether care rendered was "custodial" and to deny payment when it judged that care was not medically necessary. The letter, which was not published in the *Federal Register* until 1971,[672] justified this departure from the statutory framework and from previous policy, but the attempted justification is confusing. Custodial care and skilled nursing care are defined as mutually exclusive. "A decision that an individual is not receiving custodial care is also a decision that covered care has been provided." A skilled service is defined as one "which *must* be furnished by or under the supervision of trained medical or paramedical personnel," while an uncovered custodial service is one that "can be safely and adequately performed (or self-administered) by the average, rational, nonmedical person." The letter recognized that the attending physician and utilization review committee might already have made a judgment that the care provided was "skilled nursing care," but explained,

Since under the law custodial care is excluded from coverage without regard to the medical necessity for such services, a determination by a physician or utilization review committee that such care is medically necessary and the intermediary's decision that such care is excluded from coverage under the program do not represent incompatible determinations.

The letter did not explain the "compatibility" that exists when the utilization review committee and physician certify that skilled care is being provided, and Blue Cross determines that no skilled care was provided. An administrative fiat of "compatibility" could not change the fact that Blue Cross began to overrule the judgments of physicians and utilization review committees. Utilization review committee decisions and physician certification were "factors to be considered" by Blue Cross in determining whether or not care was medically necessary.[673] As late as 1970, Blue Cross asked Congress to amend the Medicare statute to give it authority to overrule utilization review committee decisions,[674] but Congress did not do so.

Despite the lack of statutory authority for claims review by Blue Cross,[675] the process has effectively denied payment for services provided Medicare beneficiaries. With respect to nursing home services, between January and June 1968 only 1.5 per cent of bills presented were fully or partially denied because of a noncovered level of care. In fiscal year 1969, the denial rate rose to 2.7 per cent, in fiscal year 1970 to 7.9 per cent, and in the first quarter of 1971 to 12.2 per cent [676].

The increased rate of claims denial represented only the tip of the iceberg. The Blue Cross and HEW review process was triggered by a claim for payment for services already rendered. The beneficiary whose claim for payment was denied had obtained the needed services. However, many other beneficiaries were not able to obtain the services in the first instance. If a hospital or nursing home, fearing a retroactive denial of payment, refused service to the beneficiary, the individual had no means of appeal. "Facilities, after experiencing several denials, probably more carefully screen patient admissions and accept those who require the appropriate level of care for which they will be reimbursed." [677] In 1970 one Blue Cross official estimated that "Over the past two years the Social Security Administration, through its elaboration of what constitutes extended care, apparently has effected a 47.5 per cent reduction in inpatient days paid under its Medicare contract.'' [678] Many nursing homes responded to the increase in retroactive claim denials by withdrawing from the Medicare program. [679] Other facilities responded by requiring substantial preadmission deposits or other proof of independent ability to pay, so that when Blue Cross denied coverage the facility would be assured payment from the beneficiary. [680]

The case of Mr. W. well illustrates the defects in the system. In April 1971, he was admitted to a Philadelphia hospital in critical condition, suffering from congestive heart failure, malnutrition, cirrhosis of the liver, gangrene of four toes, dehydration, and edema. The utilization review committee was functioning effectively, and on the first review of his case on May 1, it recommended continued hospitalization. On the second review on May 18, it recommended transfer to a skilled nursing home for continued treatment. [681] Mr. W. had no resources except for social security. For two weeks, the hospital social worker attempted to find a nursing home that would care for him. Even though there is a surplus of Medicare nursing home beds in the Philadelphia area, no facility would agree to take Mr. W. because, after informal consultation with Blue Cross, the homes believed that the claim for payment would subsequently be denied. Mr. W. was eligible for Medicaid, but because those reimbursement rates are substantially less than the Medicare ''reasonable costs'' [682] there is a shortage of beds available to the poor. Skilled nursing homes are particularly reluctant to admit post-hospital Medicaid patients requiring intensive and expensive care. On May 31, even though both the attending physician and the hospital utilization review committee continued to affirm his need for extended care services, Mr. W. was discharged. [683] After two weeks at his daughter's home, during which he received no skilled nursing services, his condition so deteriorated that he was readmitted to the hospital, again in critical condition. [684]

After Mr. W's May 31 discharge, his physician, the social worker, and attorneys from the Health Law Project attempted to determine the grounds for Blue Cross's informal opinion that Mr. W. was not eligible for exended care services. Blue Cross did not provide reasons to support this informal—but decisive—judgment. Both Blue Cross and the Regional Office of the Social Security Administration refused to provide any means whatsoever by which the decision—effectively terminating eligibility for Medicare benefits—could be contested.

The Medicare Act stated in general terms that any individual dissatisfied with determinations as to entitlement or amount of benefits "shall be entitled to a hearing thereon." [685] However, the regulations of the secretary provided for review only *"after* a request for payment . . . is filed with the intermediary by . . . the individual who *received* inpatient . . . services." [686] (Emphasis supplied.) If Mr. W. had been affluent, he would have been able to assure the nursing home that the bill would be paid even if Medicare denied benefits. He could then have received the prescribed nursing home care, presented a bill to Blue Cross, and if it refused to pay the bill he would have been entitled to an administrative hearing and appeal. [687] Since the hearing process is contingent upon initial receipt of services, the poor who are denied admission to a hospital or extended care facility are excluded from it.

Blue Cross Administration of Claims Review

Because HEW did not issue regulations describing the review process that should be utilized by Blue Cross to determine whether care was covered, the procedures for review have varied from plan to plan. We will examine Blue Cross claims review in New York City and in Philadelphia.

Associated Hospital Services (AHS, Blue Cross of New York City), favored an educational approach, particularly with respect to hospital care, and was initially resistant to the HEW requirement of retroactive denial of payment. AHS has been reviewing claims under its private contracts since 1940. However, plan officials saw a sharp line between claims review to determine whether a particular service is excluded by a specific contract provision and review of the physician's judgment as to the level of care required in a given case. [688]

As a Medicare intermediary, AHS felt that the attending physician and hospital utilization review committee had primary responsibility for level of care determinations. The plan attempted to strengthen provider utilization through sample reviews and consultation with hospital personnel. AHS provided the hospital committees with data on length of stay for common diagnoses. Where utilization review was not function-

ing, AHS arranged conferences with physicians and hospital administrators, conducted on-site visits, and attempted to educate the committees on utilization theory.[689]

> During 1969 and the first 2 months of 1970, the Plan conducted a
> postpayment medical review of a sample consisting of 21,454 bills as
> part of its utilization review system. The data obtained is used by the
> Plan's medical staff primarily as material for an ongoing provider in-
> formation and education program. However, this program as a Plan
> policy did not result in the denial or reduction of a single bill.[690]

The AHS attitude toward nursing homes was less respectful, and
since the beginning of the Medicare program it has reviewed all such
claims. Initially, this review did not lead to denial of claims, but at the
insistence of HEW the percentage of claims denied in whole or in part
as medically unnecessary reached about 10 per cent by 1970.[691] This
review was conducted entirely by physicians.[692] HEW urged the plan to
prepare medical screening parameters, so that review could be conducted by nonprofessional personnel.[693] The plan argued that the use of
statistical data was complicated in the case of patients over 65 by
frequent multiple diagnoses, and hence review should be done by a
physician studying the entire record.[694]

In March 1970, HEW conducted a Contract Performance Review of
the plan and recommended that "the Plan should now consider information and education aspects of its utilization review program as secondary and proceed to use the program to deny and reduce bills." [695] In
response, AHS instituted prepayment claims review of all hospital stays
over 60 days. The review was conducted by a medical clerk, who "receives a three-day company orientation session when she [sic] comes on
duty," and was reviewed by physicians.[696] This process resulted in
rejection in whole or in part of about 2 per cent of the hospital claims for
stays in excess of 60 days. The plan was not enthusiastic about allowing
clerks to review the professional decisions of doctors but felt that hiring
nurses or additional physicians to do this work would be too expensive.
(New York Blue Cross has the highest administrative costs of any plan
in the nation.) [697]

Philadelphia Blue Cross operated on different assumptions, dictating
a divergent approach to claims review. Plan officials, skeptical of the
value of provider utilization review, did not expect that it could be made

effective and directed very little energy toward helping provider committees to function well.[698] The Philadelphia plan was a pioneer in
reviewing claims for the purpose of denying payment because of inappropriate utilization.[699] Nurses reviewed all bills submitted against data
for diagnosis, age, and type of hospital (teaching/nonteaching).[700] If
there was any question, the nurse went to the hospital and examined the
medical records or asked the hospital to submit copies of the progress
notes. If the nurse believed a claim should be disallowed, it was
reviewed by a physician on the Blue Cross staff or a consulting physician.[701] When an adverse determination was made on a Medicare
claim, notice was given to the provider utilization review committee,
and the committee was given fifteen days to submit additional information. (For private claims, notice is given to the attending physician, and
he has thirty days to contest the decision. For Medicaid claims, notice is
given to the provider utilization review committee. After Blue Cross has
made its final determination, all Medicaid claims are again reviewed by
the state agency, which sometimes disallows claims Blue Cross would
have paid.)

No comprehensive information is available on the rate of claims denial over the years, for hospitals or for extended care facilities. In 1970
the denial rate for extended care facility claims was just under 8 per
cent.[702] With respect to the review of hospital claims, there appear to be
glaring differences in the denial rates for different institutions. For example, at the Hospital of the University of Pennsylvania, although
many claims were questioned, since 1966 only ten Medicare claims
have been denied in whole or in part, and in two cases the disallowance
was reversed on appeal by the patient.[703] By contrast, Philadelphia
General Hospital submitted 2,000 Medicaid claims in 1969, of which
1,200 were disallowed by Blue Cross.[704]

Often, Blue Cross did not review claims for payment until months
after the service was rendered.[705] This long delay meant that when
review was finally made the facts were stale, the attending physician
and others involved in determining whether continued care was needed
were perhaps unavailable, and certainly their memories had faded.

This delay also distorted the substantive determinations made. The
physician and institutional utilization review committees had to make
judgments on the basis of a projection of the course the patient's illness
might take. In the ex post facto review of claims for payment, the

decision maker knew the course the illness in fact took. The question on review was, ''Who should pay the bill, the patient or the Medicare program?'' If the review had been made in a timely fashion, the issue would have been, at least in the case of the poor, ''Does this individual in fact need the hospital or skilled nursing services prescribed by his or her physician?'' Where individual health, and indeed life, is at stake there is, of course, a tendency to prescribe potentially critical services that may turn out not to have been needed. A timely review to determine whether or not services should be provided, based on a projection of the course the patient's illness may take, is bound to produce fundamentally different decisions from an ex post facto review to determine who is to pay the bill.

Delay in the review process and the lack of reasoned decisions made it difficult to know the standards and principles for determining whether or not care was covered in a particular situation. The people who in practice made these judgments—hospital social workers, doctors, nursing home administrators—did not learn what constituted a covered service.[706] Claims review could have been an important educational tool to explain the scope of coverage of the Medicare program and to encourage health personnel to provide care in the most economical setting possible. Such a process is possible only if there is a decision-making process that develops coherent standards and applies them in a timely fashion.

Ex post facto Blue Cross claims review also resulted in serious misallocation of medical resources. Because Blue Cross established more rigorous procedures for the review of the medical necessity of care provided in nursing homes than in hospitals,[707] patients were sometimes kept in hospitals to avoid denial of Medicare benefits.[708] Data on the extent to which this was true are incomplete and inconclusive.[709] The historic and present relationship between Blue Cross and hospitals created incentives for Blue Cross to be more generous in paying claims for hospital services than for care provided in nursing homes, with which Blue Cross does not have a similar historic alliance.[710] The ex post facto denial of nursing home claims caused many nursing homes to withdraw from the Medicare program, despite a general need for long-term care facilities.[711]

A final and fundamental defect in claims review as a means of assuring that payment is made only for medically justified care was that the penalties fell upon the individual, who was powerless to determine whether he or she would receive care in a hospital, nursing home, or at all, rather than upon the physicians and institutions that made these judgments. A related problem was that Blue Cross claims review of institutional bills and Blue Shield review of bills for physicians services were often not coordinated.[712] This meant that, for the same services, the doctor would collect insurance payments, while the hospital or nursing home would have to try to collect from the individual.

In Pennsylvania, the insurance commissioner has required Blue Cross to shift the penalty of nonpayment for services subsequently found to be medically unnecessary from the individual to the hospital.[713] Hospitals have been prohibited from collecting payments from individuals for services that Blue Cross determined were unnecessary. Another alternative is to place the burden of payment on the physician who ordered the service.[714] Placing the risk of loss on hospitals and nursing homes certainly creates incentives for those in control of the situation to determine that the services provided are in fact medically warranted.[715] It assures that the subscriber or beneficiary will not be subsequently surprised with a bill for services that he believed would be paid by Blue Cross. It requires hospitals to begin to scrutinize the admitting practices of staff physicians and is likely to fundamentally change the relationship between the hospital and physicians who use it.

A danger in shifting the burden of nonpayment from the individual to the institution, however, is that, if it works, it will create pressures on institutions to refuse care whenever there is any question as to medical necessity. In effect, it formalizes the situation that now exists with respect to the poor. Particularly in areas in which hospitals and nursing home beds are in short supply, whole classes of patients may be excluded if the institution determines that there is an inordinately high risk of nonpayment in identifiable types of cases, for example hospitalization for the chronically ill. The individual is powerless to challenge the institution's determination that he is not entitled to payment for services under his policy. It is not difficult to imagine a situation arising in which the attending physician prescribes inpatient hospital treatment, and the hospital, while perhaps concurring with the physician's judgment of medical need, refuses to admit the patient because it fears that Blue Cross will later deny payment. This determination of entitlement to services and payment for services should not be left to the uncontrolled discretion of the hospital, which may, especially when beds are in short supply, act conservatively to admit only those patients whose eligibility for payment is clear.

THE 1972 AMENDMENTS TO THE SOCIAL SECURITY ACT

The 1972 amendments to the Social Security Act contain a variety of provisions in response to the problems of ex post facto Blue Cross claims review. They are not wholly satisfactory solutions, however. One major reform is the creation of a new agency called a Professional Standards Review Organization (PSRO), which, beginning in 1974, has the responsibility to determine whether institutional and physician services provided to Medicare and Medicaid beneficiaries were medically necessary and provided in accordance with professional standards.[716] The only statutory function for Blue Cross in determinations of medical necessity is to provide utilization data and other information.[717] A PSRO is an organization of a substantial number of physicians serving a particular area.[718] Medical societies and foundations are asked to submit plans to establish local PSROs. Blue Cross will be used only as a last resort.[719] Similar statewide and national bodies will also be formed.[720] The PSRO has authority to determine, in advance, whether "any elective admission to a hospital, or other health care facility, or . . . any other health care service which will consist of extended or costly courses of treatment" is medically necessary and provided in the most economical setting appropriate.[721] A National PSRO Council is authorized to establish "norms of care, diagnosis and treatment based upon typical patterns of practice . . . as principal points of evaluation and review." [722] These norms are also to be used to "specify the appropriate points in time after the admission of a patient for inpatient care . . . at which the physician shall execute a certification stating that further inpatient care in such institution will be medically necessary effectively to meet the health care needs of such patient." [723] Where the PSRO finds that the utilization review committee of a particular institution is functioning well, it may delegate responsibility to that committee.[724] If the program is implemented, the organization of PSROs and the development of norms for care can be expected to have a substantial impact on medical practice.[725]

A second major provision of the 1972 amendments makes absolutely clear that Blue Cross is not supposed to deny payment for prescribed services on grounds that the care provided was not medically necessary or was custodial, at least where the beneficiary and the provider acted in good faith.[726] Blue Cross may review claims to determine whether the care was medically necessary or custodial, but unless the provider and the beneficiary knew, or should have known, that the care was not covered by Medicare, payment must be made and notice given, so that in similar future cases the provider will be on notice as to the level of care requirements. The provision could have an important effect in encouraging extended care facilities to remain in the Medicare program and to accept chronically ill patients with the assurance that, if they operate in good faith, the bill will be paid. Congress intends that the government's liability for payment for noncovered care will thus be progressively limited.[727] Where the provider knew, or should have known, that the care being provided was not medically necessary, but there was good faith on the part of the beneficiary, liability will shift to the provider. If the provider attempts to collect payment from the individual, Medicare will indemnify the beneficiary, the indemnification will be treated as an overpayment to the provider, and recovery will be effected through a setoff against any future amount otherwise payable.[728]

On August 15, 1973, the HEW Bureau of Health Insurance telegraphed instructions to intermediaries on the implementation of the statutory limitation on liability that was supposed to have gone into effect on January 1, 1973.[729] The instructions stated:

> Whether a beneficiary or the provider had or could have had reasonable knowledge of noncoverage is often a judgmental issue which would be very difficult and costly to decide without the use of administrative presumptions. For this reason, decisions as to waiver of liability on cases normally will not be developed on a case-by-case basis but, instead, decisions will be made on the basis of presumptions . . .
>
> The provider would be entitled to the waiver of liability when: (1) it did not have actual knowledge of the noncoverage of services in a particular case and (2) it has made all reasonable efforts to obtain knowledge of Medicare coverage criteria and has correctly demonstrated that knowledge in its general handling of Medicare cases.[730]

The criteria for determining that a provider has made all reasonable efforts to obtain knowledge of Medicare coverage criteria include: all admissions notices, bills, and medical information must be submitted in a rigorously timely fashion; [731] the state agency must find that the provider complies with all standards for utilization review and that the intermediary does not have information to contradict that finding; [732] and the current average rate of intermediary denial of claims submitted by the provider must be below a specified amount (5 per cent in the case of hospitals and home health care agencies and 10 per cent in the case of extended care facilities).[733]

These provisions effectively nullify the limitation on liability that Congress sought to create. In the first quarter of 1971, the most recent date for which figures are available, an average of 12.2 per cent of the extended care facility bills submitted to Blue Cross were denied in whole or in part on the ground that the care provided was not medically necessary.[734] HEW has, in effect, instructed Blue Cross to presume that most of the facilities throughout the country are not entitled to the limitation of liability that Congress tried to create. By establishing a flat percentage denial rate for determining the applicability of the statutory limitation, the instructions fall most harshly on those institutions that provide care to the chronically ill. For example, a teaching hospital that limits admissions to cases requiring surgery or complex medical treatment will probably have a claims denial rate below 5 per cent, while a general hospital that tries to provide ordinary care to the chronically ill will almost certainly have a denial rate above 5 per cent.[735] Under these instructions, it is doubtful whether any public general hospital in the nation will be able to qualify for the limitation on claims denial ordered by Congress in 1972.

As of this writing, a year after the effective date of the statutory limitation, nothing on this provision has been published in the *Federal Register,* and there has been no opportunity for public comment. Even if the HEW telegraphic instructions are subsequently published and public comment solicited, the administrative changes mandated are so far-reaching that there will undoubtedly be a tendency, as there was in 1965,[736] to reject any suggestion, however well conceived, on the grounds that the procedure has already been established and it is too late for change.

In 1972 Congress evidenced concern that a more generous, pragmatic, nontechnical approach be taken in determining whether hospital care should be paid for by Medicare. The availability of skilled nursing home services has been introduced as a factor in determining whether a hospital and physician acted reasonably in keeping an individual in the hospital.[737] When there is no nursing home available for transfer, it seems reasonable to keep an individual who needs some institutional care in the hospital; in the past, however, it has been the Blue Cross/HEW policy to deny coverage.[738] The Senate Finance Committee recognized that

> Under certain circumstances, it may be reasonable to keep a medicare patient in the hospital even though he required only an extended care facility level of care. Sometimes there may be no extended care facility bed available. Or, there may be a period of a few days at the conclusion of a hospital confinement when a convalescing patient requires only an extended care level of services but where, as a practical matter, it would be unreasonable to transfer the patient to an extended care facility for such a short period of time. Similarly, there are situations where a terminal hospital patient could be discharged to another institution or his home a few days before his death but where it would not be economical or humane to do so. In these cases, it would continue to be appropriate to approve the few additional days of the hospital stay that are involved.[739]

Several provisions of the 1972 amendments attempt to reverse the restriction of skilled nursing home services created by the policies of Blue Cross and HEW.[740] First, the definition of what constitutes skilled nursing home care is expanded to include non-nursing rehabilitative services, which "as a practical matter can only be provided in a skilled nursing facility on an inpatient basis." [741] The legislative history indicates that nonmedical factors, such as the cost and inconvenience of transporting a patient to an outpatient rehabilitation center or bringing the services to the patient's home, should be considered in determining whether skilled nursing home care is warranted.[742]

Second, the statute makes an explicit presumption that skilled nursing home care is covered when the attending physician certifies that such care is needed and provides a plan for treatment.[743] The secretary of HEW (in cooperation with the PSROs when they become functional) is to establish norms for presumed coverage and for review of the need for continued care that take into account the diagnosis, the medical severity of the individual's condition, the degree of incapacity, and other similar factors. As has been noted,[744] it is very difficult to develop uniform standards for the care of aged patients, who often present multiple diagnoses and varying degrees of overall physical strength. Although Congress has mandated that the secretary develop standards for determining the appropriate length or stay in extended care cases, the legislative history also shows recognition that whether or not care is needed often depends on the gestalt of factors presented in the individual case. The Senate Finance Committee report says:

> If a patient needed a variety of unskilled services on a regular daily basis, that patient could, nonetheless, be considered a skilled care patient if the planning and overseeing of the aggregate of the unskilled services required regular daily involvement of skilled personnel . . . The controlling factor in determining whether a person is receiving covered care is the skill and frequency involved and the supervision that the patient requires, rather than considerations such as diagnosis, type of condition, or degree of functional impairment.[745]

This conflict between the desire for generally applicable norms and standards and the recognition that each case must be determined on its particular complex of facts is not peculiar to Congress but rather seems to arise in any serious consideration of the problem of determining the medical necessity of institutional services for the aged.[746] It underscores the need for a fair, timely, and reasoned decision-making process.

The 1972 Social Security amendments remove the penalty of retroactive denial of claims and substitute a variety of penalties that may be imposed upon physicians and institutions for irresponsibly prescribing services that are not medically justified. Providers are required to assure that care given Medicare beneficiaries is only provided to the extent medically necessary, is of professional quality, and is supported by such evidence of quality and necessity as the PSRO may require.[747] If, after notice and opportunity for hearing, the PSRO finds that a provider failed to comply with these obligations in a substantial number of cases or grossly violated such obligations in one or more instances, the provider may be fined or may be excluded from eligibility to provide Medicare services on a reimbursable basis either permanently or for a specified period of time.[748] The public must be given adequate notice when a provider is excluded from Medicare, and the exclusion is effective only with respect to services provided after such notice.[749]

In addition to this general obligation and penalty structure, the section affirming the presumption that nursing home care certified as necessary by a physician is in fact necessary provides that the presumption of coverage may be removed with respect to physicians who frequently submit erroneous certifications or inappropriate plans for care.[750] Unfortunately, there is no statutory requirement that beneficiaries be provided notice when this penalty is imposed upon physicians. In view of the general statutory pattern requiring notice to the public whenever a penalty is imposed upon a provider of services, the secretary could and should correct this omission by regulation.[751] Beneficiaries need to know when a physician has been found to be unreliable or incompetent in the services he prescribes. Criminal penalties are imposed on beneficiaries and providers for willful misrepresentation, concealment of information with fraudulent intent, and offering or accepting bribes, kickbacks, or rebates for referring individuals for services.[752]

THE NEED FOR DUE PROCESS FOR AGGRIEVED INDIVIDUALS

One of the major problems in the current operation of Medicare is that beneficiaries do not receive timely notice of decisions terminating entitlement and have no effective means of contesting those determinations. Under the 1972 amendments the points at which determinations may be made that effectively deny or terminate services to beneficiaries are:

—when the PSRO denies authorization for services recommended by the attending physician,[753]

—when the secretary, PSRO, or intermediary determines that services are no longer necessary.[754]

The appeals section of the PSRO amendment says:

Any beneficiary or recipient who is entitled to benefits under this Act (other than Title V) or a provider or practitioner who is dissatisfied with a determination with respect to a claim made by a Professional

Standards Review Organization in carrying out its responsibilities for the review of professional activities in accordance with paragraphs (1) and (2) of section 1155(a) [which provide for prior authorization and retrospective review of medical necessity, quality of care, and level of care], shall, after being notified of such determination, be entitled to a reconsideration thereof by the Professional Standards Review Organization.[755]

The section goes on to provide for a further reconsideration, if the matter in controversy is $100 or more, by the statewide PSR council, and where adverse to the recipient he or she is "entitled to a hearing thereon by the Secretary to the same extent as is provided in Section 205(b)," of the Social Security Act and thereafter to judicial review if the amount in controversy is $1,000 or more.[756]

The review process outlined is fundamentally defective, at least in the context of the history of HEW's restrictive attitude toward appeals under the Medicare statute and the experience of the states with prior authorization requirements under Medicaid. In order to be effective and fair, a prior authorization procedure must require prompt initial determinations, an expedited appeal and decision where the initial determination is adverse, and the administrative mechanisms and incentives necessary to assure that needed services are not delayed or denied because of bureaucratic lethargy or red tape. The need for prompt, simple, and fair review procedures is particularly acute, since what is at stake is prescribed health services for the aged and infirm.[757]

The statute leaves these matters for HEW regulation. Regulations should establish a mechanism by which patient and physician can obtain a determination from the PSRO, set time limits for such determinations, and outline the form and content that the notification of determination must take. Regulations will also be needed to prescribe the form of review on a reconsideration determination, to assure that beneficiaries and physicians will have a statement of the reasons for the initial decision and access to information needed to present their case for reconsideration. An impartial decision maker is essential, and the decision maker must state the reasons for the determination and the standards and evidence relied upon. These elements of fundamental fairness are essential to a just and effective program and are constitutionally required.[758] Most critically, the regulations must develop imaginative incentives and sanctions to assure that initial determinations are made promptly.[759]

Prior authorization requirements have been used increasingly in Medicaid,[760] applying standards essentially similar to those which are to be applied by the PSROs.[761] Even though Medicaid beneficiaries are legally guaranteed the right to a prompt determination and a fair hearing with respect to any claim denied or "not acted upon with reasonable promptness," [762] in practice the prior authorization requirements often serve as a means to deny or delay the receipt of needed services. Prior authorization may be an effective cost-saving device,[763] but it is possible that savings result because eligible patients "are denied outpatient and inpatient care by arbitrary, nonclinical regulations." [764] There have been no studies exploring what happens to Medicaid patients when their claims for prescribed services are denied. One state hospital association claims that prior authorization is ineffective even as a cost-saving device, since program administration costs four times as much as the savings it effects.[765] Not only are patients denied services, but physicians, burdened by paperwork and frustrated by arbitrary determinations and delays, have withdrawn from the California Medicaid program as a result of prior authorization requirements.[766]

Apart from the PSRO provisions, the 1972 amendments are deficient in failing to make clear the notice and appeals provisions to be applied in reviewing the need for institutional services beyond the presumptive periods outlined by the regulations or in cases in which specific presumed periods cannot be established. (Indeed, the determination whether a particular case is governed by a specific presumption will often need to be made on an individual basis.) The Senate Finance Committee report says:

> Where a request for coverage beyond the initial presumed period, accompanied by appropriate supporting evidence, is submitted for timely advance consideration, it is expected that a decision to terminate extended care or home health coverage would ordinarily be effected on a prospective basis. For those conditions for which specific presumed periods cannot be established, current procedures for determining coverage would continue to apply. However, the PSRO . . . (or the fiscal intermediary . . .) should be able to make appropriate reviews on a timely basis for such admissions.[767]

This congressional expectation of timely prospective decision making is not mandated by specific statutory provisions. Responsibility for establishing appropriate mechanisms for decision and review is left to HEW.

Blue Cross and HEW have limited experience with contemporaneous review of the need for institutional services. In 1968 HEW instituted an Assurance of Payment procedure, under which a skilled nursing home that has doubts whether the care provided in a given case will be deemed Medicare-covered may submit medical information to the intermediary and obtain a coverage determination.[768] Only those homes with functioning utilization review systems are allowed to participate in this program.[769] The appropriate medical information may be submitted within forty-eight hours of the admission, and if the intermediary finds that care is not covered the home will be paid so long as it has complied with the procedure.[770] Beneficiaries are not given notice of the grounds for termination of Medicare entitlement, and there is no administrative review of the decision. Even under the Assurance of Payment procedure, nursing homes are reluctant to accept a poor person when there is any danger that the intermediary will deny assurance and force the home into the dilemma of continuing service to a nonpaying patient or evicting an often very sick person who does not fall within the intermediary's definition of medical necessity. It is more comfortable to simply deny admission to the poor in questionable cases.

Given the vagueness of the statutory provisions on notice and review and the demonstrated lack of interest of HEW in assuring beneficiaries a means by which to obtain a timely determination of coverage and an opportunity to contest adverse determinations, it is useful to consider the extent to which notice and opportunity for hearing on the denial or termination of Medicare benefits is constitutionally required. The answer to this question requires examination of three issues: Is entitlement to Medicare an interest of sufficient magnitude to warrant due process protection? If due process protections apply to Medicare rights, what sort of notice and hearing must be given to meet the constitutional requirements of fundamental fairness? Finally, in what circumstances do the actions of HEW, Blue Cross, and PSROs, or the providers participating in Medicare constitute government action denying entitlement to statutory benefits?

While there was once doubt whether the individual interests and benefits conferred by federal social legislation fell within the ambit of "life, liberty and property" protected by the Fifth and Fourteenth Amendments,[771] the Supreme Court's landmark decision in *Goldberg v. Kelly,* 397 U.S. 254 (1970), settled that, where an individual claims government largess as a matter of statutory entitlement, the interest is one to which due process protection attaches. The right to Medicare, like the right to public assistance at issue in *Goldberg,* is a statutory entitlement, afforded as a legal right to all persons who meet the statutory criteria. The Medicare statute specifically states that "the benefits provided to an individual under this part *shall consist of entitlement* to have payment made on his behalf." [772] (Emphasis added.) In the case of Medicare benefits, as in *Goldberg,* the crucial fact "is that termination of aid pending resolution of a controversy over eligibility may deprive an eligible recipient of the very means by which to live while he waits. Since he lacks independent resources, his situation becomes immediately desperate." [773] While of course not all those eligible for Medicare are poor, an enormous and disproportionately large number are,[774] and the institutional services needed to enable an individual to survive a spell of illness are costly beyond his or her means. To the extent that access to the hearing and appeals process is made contingent upon independent ability to guarantee payment for services, the process raises issues of substantive as well as procedural due process.[775]

Each of the factors traditionally requiring full notice and an opportunity for full adversary administrative hearing prior to the termination of entitlement applies when entitlement to Medicare services is denied or terminated on grounds that services prescribed are not medically necessary. Administrative action denying or terminating coverage is plainly adjudicatory, entailing both particularistic findings about an individual and the binding application of coverage rules to such findings.[776] When the decision maker misunderstands the medical facts or misapplies the law, the resulting harms are wholesale and immediate: extended debilitation and even death.[777] The complexity of the factual and evaluative issues involved supports the need for adequate notice and hearing. Judgments of medical necessity are not per se immune from due process scrutiny, and courts have increasingly recognized the need for due process protections in situations involving medical expertise.[778] The coun-

tervailing interests of the state are administrative convenience and protection of public funds—interests that are not sufficient to override the
need for a fair procedure.[779]

Assuming that this analysis is correct and that the entitlement to
Medicare payments may not constitutionally be denied or terminated
without affording the elements of fundamental fairness required by the
Constitution, what sort of process is necessary?

Minimal due process fairness requires the opportunity to be heard "at
a meaningful time and in a meaningful manner." [780] *Goldberg* reaf-
firmed the established principle that the issue of *when* a hearing must be
afforded is usually synonymous with the question *whether* due process
requires an opportunity to be heard.[781] Once it is determined that a hearing is constitutionally required, it must be provided at a time and in a
manner that permit effective protection of the right at issue. Where entitlement is terminated during a spell of illness, notice and hearing must
be given prior to termination. Where entitlement is denied at the beginning of an elective course of treatment, as in the case of PSRO prior authorization, due process requires prompt decision and review.

Goldberg also affirms the individual's right to "timely and adequate
notice detailing the reasons for a proposed termination [or denial] and
an effective opportunity to defend by confronting any adverse witnesses
and by presenting his own arguments and evidence"; [782] the right to
an impartial decision maker; and the right to a decision based "solely
on the legal rules and evidence adduced at the hearing." [783] These elements are required in a pretermination hearing or an expedited hearing
on the denial of benefits where there is a subsequent opportunity for a
full adjudicatory hearing with "complete record and comprehensive
opinion, which would serve primarily to facilitate judicial review." [784]

Since constitutional requirements of due process apply only to the
government, the final issue is, in what circumstances are Medicare
benefits terminated as a result of governmental action? Under the program as presently administered, the individual often finds that entitlement has terminated because of the combined actions and inactions
of the federal agency, the quasi-public intermediary, and the private
provider. Is that governmental action? In form the decision often appears to be a private determination of a private nursing home denying
admission to the facility. In substance, the decision is one made by the
federal administrator and its agent intermediary and is a termination of

the entitlement established at the beginning of the spell of illness. A few principles provide guidance on the question of governmental action. "Consideration of what procedures due process may require under any given set of circumstances must begin with a determination of the precise nature of the government function involved as well as the private interest that has been affected by governmental action." [785] The parameters of procedural due process are traditionally defined through particularistic analysis of the nature of the decision makers, the decision-making process, and individual and governmental interests.

Three questions are key in determining whether a particular instance is governmental action that must meet due process requirements. First, is the decision one that determines entitlement for Medicare benefits? When a nursing home turns an individual away, because it has no empty bed or because of religious or racial discrimination, or when a physician refuses to prescribe treatment, because he does not believe it is necessary, the judgment is not one that determines statutory entitlement. But when a nursing home turns away a patient, whom it would otherwise serve, solely because Medicare coverage may not be available, the action is one terminating entitlement. A second factor is, does the decision turn upon the application of legal standards of Medicare entitlement? As has been shown, the question whether a particular service is medically necessary in the professional judgment of a physician or institution is not the same as whether the service meets the Medicare requirements of medical necessity. Where the decision-making process involves the application of *legal standards* to the facts of a particular case, due process requires procedures to assure that the standard is correctly understood and applied. [786] A third factor to consider is, does the decision maker operate as an agent of the government? For example, when Blue Cross terminates home health care benefits to individuals, a prior notice and hearing should be provided. [787] Blue Cross, acting as an agent of the government, [788] applies legal standards to terminate established statutory entitlement. [789] Or, for a second example, when the intermediary or HEW terminates or denies entitlement under the Assurance of Payment procedure or the presumptive eligibility standards to be developed under the 1972 amendments, the decision involves governmental action terminating statutory entitlement. The PSROs, although composed of private physicians, should be considered governmental agents, since they will be a creation of federal statute and will determine entitlement to federal statutory benefits through the application of standards having the force of law.

A more difficult situation is that in which a hospital or nursing home, not operating under Assurance of Payment, denies the patient admission because of fear that the care will not be covered by Medicare. Here the individual suffers not because of the positive action of the government terminating entitlement but rather because of the failure of the system to make any determination. The institution second guesses the intermediary and gives practical—and final—effect to the decision to terminate even before it is formally rendered. The right to adequate and timely notice should include the right to have a determination made in the first instance.

To suggest that the Constitution requires timely notice and opportunity to be heard on issues of entitlement to federal health benefits is not to imply that these problems should be left to the courts. The Constitution defines only minimum standards and principles, and far more is needed to effectuate the practical application and implementation of a system to assure that individuals who are aged, infirm, and often alone are given effective opportunity to contest termination decisions that involve complex judgments of fact, medicine, and law. The challenge for humane and creative administration is enormous. The past few years have seen a rapid transformation in attitudes toward patterns of treatment and toward the physician-patient relationship. In the traditional one-to-one relationship between private patient and physician, the doctor's discretion is unfettered and unsupervised. The patient's power is the power to change doctors. The ability to find another doctor is dependent on ability to pay his fee, so service of this kind has never been widely available to the poor. With the beginning of federal payments under Medicare and Medicaid, the idea of peer review has gained general acceptance—in theory if not in practice. Despite strong opposition from the medical profession, Congress adopted the PSRO amendments and has made the development of standards for quality of care and evaluation of medical care a matter of federal policy. At least where the state is paying, decisions of medical necessity are no longer to be determined in the sole discretion of the individual physician.

The patient may, however, have been lost in the shuffle. This is unfortunate but not surprising. The role of the patient in determining the course of his care and treatment was not large in the traditional patient-physician relationship. The disregard of Blue Cross and HEW for the individual in the institution of retroactive denial of claims for payment was astounding. It was accomplished without even the formal nod to public opinion and participation that publication of regulations in the *Federal Register* affords.[790] Utilization review committees, where they functioned, rarely complied with the statutory requirement of notice to patients, and neither HEW nor Blue Cross ever sought such compliance.

The apparent lack of interest in the patient's role in evaluating care received and determining course of treatment reflects a basic attitude toward patients as people. What could the individual possibly contribute to an evaluation of the quality of care he or she is receiving or the medical necessity of a particular course of treatment? The physician can describe the patient's situation and advocate his or her cause. This view of the individual as a "case" to be dealt with by professional application of technical knowledge is fundamentally wrong. It is also, to an unfortunate degree, self-fulfilling.

There are many reasons why an individual should be provided an effective means of participating in the process of determining medical care. Most basic is that patients are people, and people should, to the greatest extent possible, control their own lives. As a practical matter, the patient (or his family or someone else he has chosen to act in his behalf) has the greatest possible interest in making the process work. The individual whose health or even life is at stake has the strongest incentive to move the process along and to help the doctor or other professional to be honest and accurate in describing the problem. The individual is an independent source of information. People normally have a legitimate curiosity in their own fate. The physician should not have the whole burden and responsibility of dealing with the PSRO or intermediary. At least as presently defined and educated, the physician has no particular competence to assist the individual in learning the possible alternatives for care or in obtaining the care he or she desires. Performing these important tasks may be a waste of the skills the physician does possess. In a fee-for-service system the physician has a financial incentive to serve as the patient's advocate in obtaining the care prescribed. If, as in a health maintenance organization, the financial incentive is reversed, the physician may be less likely to go through the processes needed to obtain authorization for care that produces no financial benefit.

Providing for effective individual participation in the evaluation of medical care and determination of course of treatment is an enormously difficult task. Legal requirements can assure that individuals have access to information about their own case, about the standards and norms applied to determine medical necessity and to evaluate quality, and about the decisions applying such standards to the facts of other cases.[791] The law can also require reasoned decisions and uniformity of treatment. However, if this information is to be useful to people, a whole new class of health service worker is needed to work in close conjunction with physicians and individuals to make information accessible to patients, to know and explain alternatives, and to represent individuals in the decision-making process.

The idea of patient advocates is not a new one.[792] However, virtually no public funds have ever been appropriated for the training and support of such workers.[793] The PSRO amendments place great emphasis on the need to have only physicians involved in the evaluation of other physicians' work and the determination of medical necessity. To the extent that judgments are made on the basis of purely medical considerations, this emphasis is an important antidote to Blue Cross's practice of allowing workers with minimal training to play a large role in overruling professional medical judgments. However, the evaluation of quality of medical services and the determination of the course of appropriate and necessary treatment are generally not simply a technical medical process. There is a great need to involve personnel with other skills in this process. A recent General Accounting Office report notes:

> Frequently, the hospital's social work department can assist the physician, the patient, and the patient's family to plan for and obtain appropriate care for the patient before discharge. It has been shown that the length of stay in acute hospitals can be significantly reduced, by nearly 40 per cent in some cases, through discharge planning to insure the timely transfer of patients to facilities that are less costly and better suited to their needs. However, at present only about one of four community general hospitals has a social service department.[794]

6. BLUE CROSS AND NATIONAL HEALTH INSURANCE

This final chapter considers the question, what role, if any, should Blue Cross have in future national health insurance? It is a big question. Congressional debate has avoided this fundamental issue, though it has relied heavily on Blue Cross and hospital spokesmen for ideas about structuring the administration of federal health programs.

Some form of national health insurance will probably be adopted in the next decade.[795] There are two reasons why it has become inevitable. First, people are simply not able to get, or afford, the care and services they need. There is a growing sense that health services, like schools, police and fire protection, should be available to everyone and that the availability and quality of services should not depend upon ability to pay.[796] Health services are considered a right. To the extent that resources are limited, they should be distributed on the basis of medical necessity rather than on the basis of wealth, and services should be equally available to all. If enough people believe that equal access to health services is a right, it becomes possible for rhetoric to be translated into concrete programs. This sensibility is important, but it is not a full explanation of why national health insurance is now likely to be enacted. Popular opinion and public need do not necessarily determine national policy.

The second reason is that government programs for the poor and the aged and private health insurance no longer provide a stable source of income to support the increasing costs of health care institutions, particularly research-oriented hospitals.[797] The creation of Blue Cross and Blue Shield, controlled by hospitals and doctors, has, for a time, assured a stable source of financial support.

Like all social and institutional relations in capitalist societies, these institutions [medical schools and teaching hospitals] operate in a competitive atmosphere, and compete, in part, like universities for prestigious faculty and medical staffs. The norms, again like the universities in general, are quality and quantity of research output, where the standards are determined by the profession itself . . . As medical care tended more and more toward the dictates of research-oriented providers, the allocation of medical resources became less and less relevant to consumer needs.[798]

This dynamic is

simply pricing the middle-income consumer out of the market. Blue Cross and private carrier premiums roughly reflect hospital per diem charges, which in turn reflect the rising (research-oriented) overhead expenditures . . . There is no way strictly within the private sector for third parties to roll back these costs, since they reflect the prevailing professional dynamics of the delivery system.[799]

Industries and corporations that find themselves in this dilemma have historically sought help from the public sector.[800] Medicare and Medicaid, far from being the beginning of an austere "socialized medicine," have been a bonanza to Blue Cross and the hospitals. As a matter of rhetoric, probably everyone would agree that the ultimate purpose of a national health insurance program is to make quality health services available to all of the people at reasonable costs. In translating rhetoric into legislation, it is essential to recognize that the interests of the health industry, the medical profession, and the health consumer are not identical and that the industry and medical profession are well organized and articulate in asserting their respective interests, while the health consumer is not.

There are three types of proposals for the reform of the health delivery system.[801] The most conservative proposals would provide government subsidies to individuals, particularly the poor, to enable the purchase of health services through existing delivery mechanisms.[802] Individual consumer choice would be the means by which the health delivery system was made responsive to consumer need. These proposals are supported by the medical profession but almost no one else. They represent a defense of the status quo and deny the existence of a crisis of costs, accessibility, and quality in health services delivery. In its most sophisticated form this system would encourage competition, particularly through the development of health maintenance organizations. For reasons that have been discussed, it is extremely unlikely that the oligopolistic health industry would ever reorganize itself along competitive lines, and to the extent that the free enterprise model is realized there would be serious dangers that care would be inaccessible and of poor quality.

The second type of proposal would preserve present structures, recognize the hospital as the key location and organizer of health services, and increase government power in coordination, planning, and financing. Actually there are a variety of proposals of this type concerning health manpower, area planning, institutional licensing, and so forth.[803] Proposals for increased regulation through existing agencies or new agencies created along traditional lines are supported by Blue Cross, the hospitals, most academics, state and federal officials, and government commissions created to study the health delivery crisis. Study commissions are overwhelmingly dominated by individuals affiliated with the hospital/health insurance industries, with little participation by either private practitioners or health consumer advocates.[804]

The most serious criticism of these proposals is that the agencies, both state and federal, tend to be primarily responsive to the industry regulated rather than to the general public good. The process by which regulatory agencies are captured is well enough understood.

Most regulatory issues are of deep interest to regulated industries, with a very substantial amount of income for these industries riding on the decision. The stake of the general public may in the aggregate be even higher, but it is diffused among a large number of unorganized individuals.[805]

In the hospital/health insurance industry, interests are defined in terms of professional prestige, interesting cases, research grants, and innovative equipment, as well as income. Other debilitating characteristics of regulatory agencies flow from the disparity between the organized intensity of the industry's interest and the disorganized diffusion of the public interest. (For example, the tendency to depend upon the industry for information and data, the practice of appointing regulators who have the approval of the regulated, and agency secrecy, which protects the industry at the expense of the public's interest in knowing.) [806] The most immediate concrete indicator of the success of a regulatory agency is the satisfaction of the industry regulated. This examination of the role that

Blue Cross has played in the administration of federal health programs illustrates again and again the predictable failure of regulation in the traditional model. Blue Cross fails as a regulator of hospitals. HEW and state insurance departments fail as regulators of Blue Cross.

The third force pressing for national health insurance consists of the " 'equal health advocates,' who seek free, accessible, high-quality health care which equalizes the treatment available to the well-to-do and to the poor. They stress the importance of community control over the supply and deployment of health facilities." [807] Equal health advocates do not have well-formulated proposals for national health insurance. "Nationalization" of health resources is favored by some,[808] but it is not clear what that would mean in concrete terms. Further, "nationalization is an emotional issue in the United States," both when advocated and when condemned.[809] Other equal health advocates favor regulation of health services but regulation responsive to consumer concerns in a way radically different from the existing practice of regulatory agencies.

How do we begin to create a consumer-responsive regulatory agency? On a theoretical level it is essential first to recognize the phenomena and fact of institutional self-interest. Quite simply this means that the interests of even benevolent institutions and the "public interest" [810] do not necessarily coincide, and institutional assertions of public interest must be taken with a large measure of skepticism. Second, it is essential to recognize that the allocation of resources involves social policy judgments about which reasonable people can disagree. It seems plain that this is the case with respect to health services. However, because good health and life itself are at stake, there may be a reluctance to recognize the social nature of the judgments being made. Traditional regulatory theory assumes that Americans are relatively homogeneous and in general agreement about social policy and that consequently a "best" public policy exists and is both recognizable and feasible.[811] The social nature of regulatory judgments must be dealt with more openly. Third, traditional regulatory theory assumes that government interference in private decision making should be minimized.[812] This assumption was a major factor in the structuring of the Medicare program, particularly its reliance upon Blue Cross. It seems to be most clearly an issue of fundamental political philosophy. However, in recent years government has become increasingly involved in the regulation of health services on an ad hoc basis and to an even larger degree in the financing of health services. No one today argues for less government financing of health services. The issue is no longer whether government should interfere with private decision making but how government should interfere. Even if competition is to provide the solution to the nation's health crisis, massive government interference would be required to structure and encourage a competitive situation. A consumer-responsive regulatory agency is possible only when we stop assuming that noninterference is a primary goal and begin addressing the issue of how government interference is best structured.

Finally, the development of a consumer-responsive regulatory agency requires recognition that democracy is a value in its own right. A structure that gives people, individually and collectively, an opportunity to participate in making decisions about the health services they receive is better structure even if the same substantive result can be achieved more cheaply and efficiently through professional, technical, or bureaucratic decision making. In fact, of course, a system in which decisions about the allocation and manner of delivery of health services was democratized would not produce the same substantive results as professional, technical, or bureaucratic decision making. The results of the decisions now being made by professional and bureaucratic processes are, by any standard, unsatisfactory. A consumer-responsive administrative agency would involve greater administrative costs than professional or bureaucratic decision making. But the costs would be purchasing not simply more responsive health services but also the democratization of decision making. If democracy is a value in its own right, it must be paid for, certainly in lost "efficiency" but also in more direct administrative costs.

Moving from the theoretical to the concrete, we find that conscientious regulators are beginning to develop proposals for making regulatory agencies more responsive to the public interest. For example, Nicholas Johnson, former commissioner of the Federal Communications Commission, suggests that failure of the regulatory system results from the cumulative effect of inadequate representation of the public interest:

First, due to insufficient citizen participation and inadequate investigative facilities, the agencies lack the necessary facts for adequate decision making. Second, regulatory decision making is dominated by the so-called "subgovernment phenomenon" [i.e. agency staffing and policy making is dominated by industry lobbyists, experts, lawyers]. Third, decisions tend to be made ad hoc rather than as the implementation of a conscious, well developed policy. Finally, reform movements which do arise tend to suffocate under the weight of regulatory delay.[813]

Philip Ellman, former commissioner of the Federal Trade Commission, also emphasizes the need for greater public participation in agency decision making. Particularly where an agency has broad discretion, it should "lay open its proceedings to public view, permit advocates for the public interest an opportunity to comment on proposed actions, and endeavor to state publicly the reasons and grounds for whatever actions it adopted." [814] Both Ellman and Johnson suggest specific reforms that would make agencies more open to public interest influence: relaxation of the requirement that an individual demonstrate an injury peculiar to himself (standing to sue); requirement of more effective public notice of proposed decisions; limitation of *ex parte* communications between the regulators and the regulated; an end to unpublished rules and guidelines having the effect of law. These changes would help, but there remains a need to "institutionalize the means whereby the public may be aware of, and participate in, political and governmental processes that affect the quality of our lives." [815]

If the regulation of health services is to allow for public participation in policy making, citizens need forums for participation, experts who are primarily accountable to the public interest, and real power. While opening existing institutions and structures to public scrutiny would certainly be a step in the right direction, it is not sufficient. The health industry has large resources devoted to gathering information, developing policy alternatives, and influencing decision making. Consumers must have similar resources for knowing alternatives and influencing policy if public participation in the administration of health services is to be effective. To date citizen advocates in the regulatory process have come from two main sources: the private public interest bar, as exemplified by Ralph Nader, and publicly funded OEO Legal Services and state and local consumer advocate offices. These resources are wholly inadequate. In the entire nation there are very few lawyers, public or private, who have an understanding of the basic legal structure of the health delivery system and commitment to work in the public interest, however defined.[816] There are even fewer public accountants, economists, sociologists, or experts in other fields who are available as a resource to citizens concerned about participating in the formulation of health services policy.

Furthermore, existing public interest advocates are often not accountable to the public they purport to serve. Tragically, this fact is being used as an excuse for cutting federal funds for law reform lawyers who have attempted to represent the interests of the poor in public regulatory agencies and the courts.[817] Because federally funded public interest advocates are politically vulnerable, Nicholas Johnson concludes that "true citizen advocacy is at its best when it is truly independent of the political process, both in spirit and in funding. This to a large extent explains the effectiveness of Ralph Nader who accounts to no one, inside or outside government, save himself." [818] Public interest advocates must be sufficiently independent of the traditional political process to survive when they challenge powerful established interests, but it should be possible to structure such independence and at the same time promote accountability to the consuming public. The notion of independent "experts" operating on behalf of the people in an area in which social policy judgments play such an important role as they do in health services is disturbing. No cost-benefit analysis is going to tell an expert whether resources that are, at least immediately, limited should be invested in efforts that save a few from premature death or make life richer in some significant respect for a larger number of people. Certainly experts accountable to no one but themselves and struggling to serve the public interest as best they see it are sorely needed and much to be admired. Development of such self-directed "public interest" expertise may be an essential first step, particularly if the self-directed experts also strive to provide people with the information, knowledge of alternatives, and means of expression that will enable them to control their own experts. Experts accountable to no one but themselves are a vast improvement over experts and agencies accountable to special interests, but our goal should be experts accountable to the people.

The traditional political process often does not provide ordinary people with an opportunity to determine public policy in a technological society. There are too many issues, and issues such as health services delivery are simply too complex to be decided in general elections.

Rather what is needed is a structure that will enable those citizens who have a particular interest in health services to participate in the formulation of local health delivery policy, within the framework of a national health system that makes basic allocations of available resources in response to local expressions of need.

There are major objections to the idea that health services delivery can be reformed through radical restructuring to assure greater consumer control of health policy. For example, there is little evidence that ordinary people have any interest in doing the hard work necessary to understand the alternatives, to reach decisions, and to monitor the actual delivery of services on a day-to-day basis. Individuals are often uninterested in health services when they are well and incapable of doing any more than coping with the immediate personal problem when they are ill. Further, unless there is a broad base of community understanding and participation there is a danger that consumer representatives will be co-opted or will become isolated and lose motivation.[819] Token representation without accountability to any larger community, such as labor representation on Blue Cross boards, gives an aura of social responsibility that does not exist in fact.

Perhaps the largest objection to a proposal for a regulatory structure that includes a massive, broad-based community organization component is that it is impractical to assume that Congress would ever create such an agency. Radical critiques of health care delivery are generally disappointing in their pessimism and lack of positive program.[820] Ultimately it is Congress that must formulate a national health insurance policy. The national health delivery crisis must be solved on the national level. Problems are national. Blue Cross, medical schools, the organized medical profession, and the drug industry do not confine their efforts to a community or a state. They have self-defined, organized, national interests and power, which must be met with national power on behalf of the public interest. Further, given the present and foreseeably regressive nature of state and local taxation, solutions must be federally funded.

Unfortunately Congress is ill equipped to do this job. Congressional action in the area of health services delivery tends toward ad hoc responses to particular crisis situations and the creation of categorical, uncoordinated programs. The lack of independent expert staff is crippling and makes Congress heavily dependent upon the executive branch for information and the formulation of alternatives, particularly in areas such as this in which the technological and mystical professional knowledge is so substantial.[821] The executive is similarly ill equipped and in turn depends upon the industry for information and policy. Certainly both Congress and HEW are more sophisticated in their knowledge of health services delivery than they were in 1965, but the experience gained under Medicare is experience under a mandate of deference to the medical profession and the hospital/Blue Cross industry. For all these reasons, Congress is probably incapable of formulating a sane national health policy at this time. But ameliorative steps can and are being taken by Congress, some state officials, academics, and interested consumers.[822] To say that ultimately Congress must determine the structure of a national health program is not to derogate the importance of immediate local reforms. For example, the efforts of Commissioner Denenberg in Pennsylvania illuminate what reforms are useful and possible. Citizen participation in Regional Comprehensive Health Planning provides an invaluable pool of people with knowledge of health care alternatives and decision-making processes.

The national health insurance proposals before Congress bear out this analysis. Despite the failings of the private health insurance industry, which have been examined here with respect to Blue Cross, all of the 1972 proposals for national health insurance with the exception of the Kennedy-Griffiths bill provided in a variety of ways for government purchase of health insurance through the private insurance industry.[823] Indeed, the failures of the private sector to control costs, monitor quality, provide comprehensive benefits for preventive rather than acute care are cited as reasons why national health insurance is needed.[824] While Congress, in enacting a national health insurance program, can correct some of the specific defects of the present health delivery system (for example, by providing more comprehensive benefit coverage), to the extent that problems result because administrative structures are responsive to the needs of the medical profession and hospital industry rather than to the needs of the consumers of health care, a national health system built on the private insurance industry assures that there will be no fundamental change in the present system. Blue Cross is certainly the most closely regulated segment of the health insurance industry and is probably the most consumer-responsive. It is, at least as a matter of rhetoric, committed to community service and nonprofit operation. But as this examination has shown, Blue Cross as presently structured is responsive and accountable first to the hospitals and only second to subscribers and beneficiaries. In health, as in society generally, wealth and control of resources is increasingly concentrated in the hands of a few powerful interests—particularly the banking and insurance industries.[825] A national health insurance program that relied upon Blue Cross, Blue Shield, and the commercial insurance companies would increase concentration of power and money in the private insurance industry.

Obviously many people believe that there are virtues in using private health insurance in the administration of a national health program. Dr. Herman Somers cites the following as reasons why the government needs the private sector in the administration of national health:

> It needs the managerial expertise and experience of the private sector, if only for purposes of effective decentralization and exposure to varieties of administrative alternatives.

> It needs the diversity and competitiveness that capacity for risk-taking, innovation, and experimentation make possible.

> It needs the political protection of a spread of responsibility and blame for mishaps.

> It needs the involvement of large portions of the private sector to make possible broader understanding and tolerance of the immense difficulties of running such a system.

> It needs the support of the private sector as a counterforce to the tendency of governmental budgets to be unduly restrictive.[826]

The purported virtues of the use of Blue Cross do not withstand scrutiny. Where managerial or other expertise is needed, it can be purchased by the government, as indeed Blue Cross purchases the accounting services needed to audit hospital books. In most aspects of health services administration, management consists of an intricate mix of social policy determination and application of technical knowledge. Managerial expertise is not a neutral skill but an efficient means of achieving particular ends. The history and organizational structure of Blue Cross assure that managerial expertise will be directed toward preservation of the financial stability and autonomy of the insurance organization itself and of the hospitals it serves.

The claim that private administration provides ''diversity and competitiveness that capacity for risk-taking, innovation and experimentation make possible'' is frankly unintelligible. Blue Cross does not take risks under either Medicare or the FEBP. If the thought is that the agency administering national health insurance should have some leeway in instituting new methods of administration and some funds without strings attached, this can be accomplished with either a publicly or privately administered program.[827]

The use of private insurance in the administration of health benefits can spread responsibility and blame and increase tolerance for the difficulties and defects of the system. This is not necessarily a virtue. Diffusion of responsibility can mean simply that no one is responsible. Fixing of blame is generally a useful part of analyzing problems and formulating solutions. When responsibility is diffuse, delegated, and subdelegated, tolerance may increase among the various sectors of the administrative apparatus. For example, Blue Cross and HEW are tolerant of each others' failings. As responsibility is delegated to the private sector, it becomes more difficult for the public to understand the reasons for systematic failures or to seek reform or redress. This is not tolerance but powerlessness.

The argument that involvement of the private insurance industry provides protection against underfinancing raises a serious issue. The possibility that health services would be constrained by the sort of chronic underfinancing that exists with respect to the public school system, municipal hospitals, police, and fire services is certainly a legitimate concern. Blue Cross has a proven ability to influence legislative policy to assure generous and stable funding for itself and the hospitals. However, the apparent unwillingness of taxpayers to tax themselves for the adequate provision of municipal services, schools, etc. may result largely from the regressive nature of state and local tax structures, imposed on top of a large federal tax.[828] Federal funding is, in general, more stable and less subject to underfinancing based on taxpayer desire to avoid tax burdens without regard to popular judgment on the value of the services in question. Adequate and stable financing could be further assured by the use of the trust fund device. (Trust funds, such as those established under social security or Medicare, are traditionally associated with a regressive tax on payroll. This association is merely traditional and not necessary. Financial stability could be assured through a trust fund created from general revenues raised on a more progressive basis.) [829] Of course, to the extent that concern for under-financing of health services represents a desire to preserve the excesses and inefficiencies of the present system or to perpetuate the present practice of financing medical research and education through revenues allocated for patient care, more effective public control of costs will represent a loss to hospitals. However, these are losses a national health insurance system should seek rather than avoid.

Perhaps the strongest argument for preserving a role for private insurance in the administration of national health insurance is that a system operated by the federal government could be similarly inaccessible and unresponsive to consumer and public interests. Prior to the enactment of Medicare in 1965, the Social Security Administration of HEW enjoyed a reputation as a fair and efficient administrator of the Old Age, Survivors and Disability Insurance Program (OASDI). Administration of OASDI requires a balancing of the claims of individuals against the statutory limitations of the Social Security Trust Fund. This experience, in a program in which there are no powerful, organized interest groups, did not prepare the SSA to deal effectively with institutional providers and intermediaries under Medicare. SSA manifests the general bureaucratic tendency to pursue the course of action that produces fewest headaches and complaints. Beneficiaries and taxpayers have no effective means by which to influence SSA policies, whereas the hospitals and Blue Cross are capable of mounting strong and effective opposition to policies inimical to their interests. Periodic congressional scrutiny is not effective to make an administrative agency responsive to consumer and public interests on a day-to-day basis.

Would federal administration of national health services under the Kennedy-Griffiths Health Security Act be any more effective? Of all the programs proposed to date, this one comes closest to meeting the problems raised in this book. It would provide fairly comprehensive benefits [830] to all citizens and permanent residents,[831] financed by a combination of payroll taxes and general revenues.[832] It proposes "a working partnership between the public and private sectors . . .[with] Government financing and administrative management, accompanied by private provision of personal health services through private practitioners, institutions, and other providers of health care.'' [833] It would be administered by a five-person, full-time National Health Security Board appointed by the president with the advice and consent of the Senate and under the authority of the secretary of Health, Education and Welfare. [834] A National Advisory Council, composed of representatives of both consumers [835] and providers of health services would advise the board on general policy and regulations and prepare an annual report for Congress. [836] Actual administration would be carried out by 10 existing HEW regions and approximately 100 health subareas to be designated by the council. Advisory councils would also be established at the regional and subarea level. [837] A national Health Resources Development Fund would be used to support innovative health programs in manpower, education, and group practice development. [838] The national board would conduct continuous planning in coordination with the existing comprehensive health planning agency. [839] Planning would be coordinated with the administration of payments to providers. [840] The board could, after public notice and opportunity for hearing, order providers to discontinue or initiate particular services. [841]

This bill would solve some of the administrative problems of the present system. Since the basic benefits would be available to all citizens regardless of income or age, there would be no need to allocate costs among different groups. Fairly comprehensive benefits, with financial incentive for health maintenance arrangements, [842] would reduce the presently excessive reliance on hospital services. However, the new administrative structure would have to deal with the same major problems that now vex Blue Cross. Payments would be made only for medically necessary services, and the mechanisms for making judgments would be essentially the same as those provided in the present act. [843] Hospitals would be paid their ''approved operating costs,'' determined on the basis of a prospective budget submitted annually by the hospital to the board. [844] The bill provides little substantive definition of ''approved operating costs.'' [845] The primary cost control mechanism is to fix the amount of money available. Revenues appropriated to the Health Security Trust Fund would be allocated, under statutory formula, to a health services account, health resources development account, and an administrative account. [846] The health services account would be allocated by regions. [847] Finally, the regional health services account would be allocated by types of services, including institutional services.[848] Since total program funds would be fixed, unless unit costs were subject to effective control the program would be "underfinanced." Of course, only a completely open-ended financing system is capable of paying everything that providers of services might conceivably define as "necessary" at salary levels that scarce workers might define as reasonable. Research, education, and patient care are each infinitely expandable. Unless unit costs are controlled, any program with limited funds will be "underfinanced."

The provisions for consumer and public participation could be a good deal stronger. At the national level, providers may be appointed to the Health Security Board, and there is no requirement that consumers of health services be represented. At the regional and local levels, there are no policy boards at all but only administrative offices and advisory boards. The local and branch offices must receive and investigate complaints by eligible individuals and providers and take or recommend appropriate corrective action.[849] Technical support is provided for the national consumer advisory council but is not assured for the local or regional councils.[850] The members of the local advisory councils are to be appointed by the national Health Security Board, with no provision for local participation in this selection process. There is no guarantee of public access to the budgets submitted by hospitals and no provision for public participation in the approval process.[851] Thus, the program does not provide sufficient opportunity for public initiative or power at the local level.[852] In introducing the act, Senator Kennedy quoted Thomas Paine, "Give us a lever and we shall move the world." If hospital costs are to be controlled and spent in a fashion responsive to consumer and public interests, consumers need more levers than this act presently provides.[853]

A major strength of Blue Cross in the administration of a national health system is that it exists and has an identity, organizational structure, buildings, and staff in most areas of the country. It seems clear that decentralized, local control and administration of some aspects of health services delivery are necessary and important.[854] Creating local structures and institutions on a national scale is an enormous task, and the advantages of building upon an existing institution are obvious. It is possible that the present Blue Cross organization could be transformed, so that the resource it represents could be used to administer a national health program primarily responsive to the needs of consumers of health services rather than to the research and professional needs of providers. Federal legislation could provide for contracting only with fiscal intermediaries that met specific requirements. For example, Congress could require that, in order to participate in the administration of national health insurance, a fiscal intermediary must be governed by a board that does not include providers of services but is composed of individuals who represent the population served with respect to income, age, ethnic background, and sex and who are selected and removed in some democratic fashion.[855] Constitutional requirements of due process, normally applicable only to public agencies, could by statute be made explicitly applicable to the fiscal intermediary. Consolidation of Blue Cross and Blue Shield could be required so as to end the present destructive bifurcation of inpatient and outpatient services. The new Blue Cross could be prohibited from lobbying and allowed to develop and supply information for use in the legislative process only at the request or with the consent of Congress or HEW. Full public disclosure of information on operations could be required. With the enactment of national health insurance, the private business of Blue Cross would naturally diminish, but because of dangers inherent in a single organization administering both private and public programs, fiscal intermediaries participating in the administration of national health insurance could be prohibited from conducting private insurance business.[856]

Of course, a Blue Cross that met these requirements would no longer be Blue Cross. There is no reason to believe that Blue Cross will move toward greater consumer control and accountability in the absence of hard and specific requirements to do so. Despite growing consumer discontent and criticism [857] and a rhetorical public commitment to community service, the evidence is that Blue Cross actively seeks both a major role in national health insurance and the preservation of its present orientation and autonomy. There is no evidence that Blue Cross is interested in reforming itself in response to consumer discontent. For example, the Blue Cross lobbying strategy in opposition to the Kennedy-Griffiths bill is based entirely on the skillful use of personal influence at high levels with no attention to substantive issues.[858] No doubt there are individuals within Blue Cross who would welcome federal pressure to orient the organization toward consumer and public control. But if, as is likely, those in control of this powerful organization are determined to resist fundamental change, then the effort to enact and enforce requirements to reform Blue Cross might be more difficult than the effort required to create a new public administrative agency. The hospitals and insurance companies now have control of health services resources, money, and expertise. The public has no counterbalancing power to make an administrative agency responsive to consumer needs. Making health services delivery publicly responsive is certainly an important value in itself. But the underlying value, one that transcends health services, is the need to develop means by which people can control their own lives and the institutions and programs upon which they depend in an increasingly technological society. From an individual perspective, things seem to be out of control, chaotic, random, and at the mercy of some autonomous technology or system. To some extent this perception is accurate, but to an important degree power, money, and knowledge have become more concentrated in the hands of the institutions and professionals who have always had them. Examination of Blue Cross reveals not so much a system out of control as a system that is quite effectively designed to meet needs and interests that are not the needs and interest of those who use and pay for health services. There are enormous obstacles involved in creating a means whereby people can participate in the determination of social policy in this highly technological society, in which resources and power have become concentrated in the hands of the wealthy, the professionals, and the technicians. The analysis and approach presented here is not offered as a "cost efficient" or easy solution or with any näive sense of optimism. Rather, the consequences of our present course seem so grave, and the stakes so high, that it seems important to articulate democratic alternatives and to struggle to make them happen.

NOTES

1. See, e.g., "The Role of Prepaid Group Practice in Relieving the Medical Care Crisis," 84 *Harv. L. Rev.* 887, 892 (1971); D. Schorr, *Don't Get Sick in America* (Nashville, Tenn.: Aurora, 1970), p. 18; Ed Cray, *In Failing Health* (Indianapolis, Ind.: Bobbs-Merrill, 1970), pp. 12–13.

2. *Basic Facts on the Health Industry,* Report by the Staff of the House Committee on Ways and Means, 92nd Cong., 1st Sess., pp. 8–9 (1971). The 1971 *Survey of Current Business,* U.S. Dept. of Commerce, shows that in 1971 the health industry was second only to contract construction in average number of full and part-time employees. From 1966 to 1971 the number of people working in the health industry rose 38.9%, from 2,257,000 to 3,135,000. This survey also shows that the health industry's national income, or "aggregate earnings of labor and property which arise in the current production of goods and services," rose 87.2% from 1966 to 1971. Health income rose from $17.9 billion to $33.5 billion in five years to overtake agriculture and machinery as producer of national income. See "Health is No. 2," 8 *Perspective, The Blue Cross Magazine,* No. 3, p. 12 (2nd Quarter 1973).

3. *Basic Facts on the Health Industry,* id. at pp. 2 and 10.

4. The American Hospital Association's figures on average hospital expenses per patient day show increases of 15% in 1968, 13.6% in 1969, and 15.1% in 1970. *Basic Facts on the Health Industry,* id. at pp. 50–51.

5. M. S. Mueller, "Enrollment, Coverage and Financial Experience of Blue Cross and Blue Shield Plans, 1969," *Research and Statistics Note,* No. 4 (Washington, D.C.: HEW, SSA, April 21, 1971). For analysis of this data, see Robert J. Weiss, William H. Wiese, and Joel C. Kleinman, "Trends in Health-Insurance Operating Expenses," 287 *New Eng. J. of Medicine* 638, 639 (Sept. 28, 1972).

6. See HEW Public Health Service, National Center for Health Statistics, *Vital and Health Statistics, Data from the National Health Survey;* United Nations Statistical Papers, *Population and Vital Statistics Report,* Ser. A., Vol. 14, No. 1, and Vol. 22, No. 2.

7. Report of the National Advisory Commission on Health Manpower, p. 2 (1967). "The United States has failed to provide adequate health services to the vast majority of its citizens . . . Without a drastic alteration of the present delivery system, the adoption of a [national health financing] program or any other massive infusion of new federal monies will simply compound the failure of the present system." *Heal Yourself,* Report of the Citizens Board of Inquiry Into Health Services for Americans, p. 71 (1970).

8. See Herman M. and Anne R. Somers, "Private Health Insurance: Problems, Pressures and Prospects," 46 *Calif. L. Rev.* 508, 555–57 (1958). See also L. Barrett, "Retreat From Idealism: Blue Cross," *The Nation,* Jan. 9, 1960, pp. 26–32; E. T. Chase, "Can Blue Cross Survive Its Own Success?" 21 *The Reporter* 18–19 (Oct. 29, 1959).

9. *Basic Facts on the Health Industry,* supra n. 2, at pp. 8 and 42.

10. Figures for Medicare and other federal programs are from SSA, BHI, *Quarterly Report to Providers* (1970). Medicaid figures are from internal data, Research and Development Dept., Blue Cross Association.

11. The nurse call system consists of a buzzer system that lights at the nurses' station and over the patient's door. It also lights when the bathroom is in use. The system has an intercom so a nurse can speak to a patient from her station and a device to indicate when the buzzer is malfunctioning should the plug be pulled loose. The call system greatly facilitates rapid communication between the patient and nursing staff, thus enabling the staff to maintain a more constant monitor over the patient's condition. The system costs approximately $7500–8500 for a 25–30 bed unit. Interview, Albert Sutter, Director of Buildings and Grounds, Hospital of the University of Pennsylvania.

Hyperbaric chambers are used in treatment where a high pressure, oxygen-rich atmosphere facilitates recovery. Common usages for the chamber are for the treatment of gas gangrene and other anaerobic infections, air embolism and the bends, carbon monoxide poisoning, and congenital conditions in which oxygen transport of tissue oxygenation is affected. National Academy of Sciences, Committee on Hyperbaric Research, *Fundamentals of Hyperbaric Oxygenation,* p. 1 (1966). Hyperbaric chambers range in cost from $250,000 to $1,000,000. From 4 to 6 people are required to keep the system operating. The University of Pennsylvania chamber serves an area encompassing Pittsburgh, Baltimore, mid-New Jersey, and Delaware, and is eventually expected to serve one patient a week. At present it serves about one patient a month. Interview, Mr. Paddock, School of Environmental Medicine, University of Pennsylvania.

12. See Eliot Freidson, *Professional Dominance* (N.Y.: Atherton, 1970), and sources cited therein.

13. James S. Turner, *The Chemical Feast,* The Ralph Nader Study Group Report on Food Protection and the Food and Drug Administration (N.Y.: Grossman, 1970), pp. vi–vii, 3–4, 248–249; Robert C. Fellmeth, *The Interstate Commerce Omission: The Public Interest and the ICC,* The Ralph Nader Study Group Report on the Interstate Commerce Commission and Transportation (N.Y.: Grossman, 1970), pp. 78, 311–312, 317; Theodore J. Lowi, *The End of Liberalism: Ideology, Policy* (N.Y.: Norton, 1969), pp. 85–97; Nicholas Johnson, "A New Fidelity to the Regulatory Ideal," 59 *Georgetown Law Journal* 869, 874 (1971); Richard A. Posner, "Regulatory Aspects of National Health Insurance Plans," 39(1) *U. Chi. L. Rev.* 9 (1971).

14. In 1970 Blue Cross made payments to 6,574 contracting hospitals under private insurance plans. Internal data, Research and Development Dept., Blue Cross Association, Chicago. As fiscal intermediary, Blue Cross made payments to 10,300 hospitals in 1970. SSA, BHI, *Quarterly Report to Providers* (1970). In 1970 Blue Shield made payments to over 195,000 physicians. *Health Care Crisis in America,* Hearings before the Subcommittee on Health of the Senate Committee on Labor and Public Welfare, 92nd Cong., Pt. 5, p. 931 (March 23, 24, 31, and April 6, 1971).

15. Robert Eilers, *Regulation of Blue Cross and Blue Shield Plans,* Huebner Foundation Studies (Homewood, Ill.: Irwin, 1963), pp. 97–129. Hereinafter cited as Eilers.

16. Social Security Act, §1816 (Blue Cross), §1842 (Blue Shield). 42 U.S.C. §§1395h and 1395u (1971).

17. Eilers, supra n. 15, at pp. 128–29.

18. Dr. Odin W. Anderson, quoted in F. R. Hedinger, *The Social Role of Blue Cross as a Device for Financing the Costs of Hospital Care,* Health Care Research Series, No. 2, Iowa, p. 3 (1966). Hereinafter cited as Hedinger.

19. For a description of pre-Blue Cross hospital insurance, see T. J. Richardson, *"The Origin and Development of Group Hospitalization in the United States, 1890–1940,"* 20 *University of Missouri Studies,* No. 3, pp. 15–18 (1945). See also Hedinger, supra n. 18, at pp. 6–9; Eilers, supra n. 15, at pp. 8–9.

20. R. G. Brodrick, M.D., Presidential Address, *Bulletin of the American Hospital Association,* October, 1927, pp. 25–27.

21. "Economic preparedness of the individual in connection with the use of the modern hospital is largely a matter of public education and training . . . Practicable and easy plans might well be formulated to encourage use of the item 'sickness' in the family budget as actively as the items 'Insurance' and even 'Clothes' are budgeted." Asa S. Bacon, "Hospital Budget-Savings Plan for Prospective Mothers," *Bulletin of the American Hospital Association,* January 1928, p. 68.

22. "A Statistical Analysis of 2,717 Hospitals," *Bulletin of the American Hospital Association,* July 1931, p. 68.

23. Louis S. Reed, *Health Insurance: the Next Step in Social Security* (N.Y.: Harper, 1937), p. 189.

24. See Hedinger, supra n. 18, at pp. 4–13.

25. Justin Ford Kimball, "Prepayment and Hospital," *Bulletin of the American Hospital Association,* July 1934, p. 44. On the early history of Blue Cross, see also Duncan M. MacIntyre, *Voluntary Health Insurance and Rate Making* (Ithaca, N.Y.: Cornell University Press, 1962), pp. 166 et seq.; HEW, SSA, *Private Health Insurance and Medical Care* (1968); O. W. Anderson, *State Enabling Legislation for Non-Profit Hospital and Medical Plans,* Public Health Economics, Research Series, No. 1 (Ann Arbor, Mich.: University of Michigan, 1944).

26. Harry Becker, ed., *Financing Hospital Care in the United States* (N.Y.: McGraw-Hill, 1955), p. 7.

27. R. Rorem, *Non-Profit Hospital Service Plans* (Chicago: Commission on Hospital Service, 1940), p. 29.

28. Reported in Hedinger, supra n. 18, at p. 11.

29. *Hospitals, Journal of The American Hospital Association,* February 1938, p. 77. Item 14 stated: "A hospital care insurance plan should meet with the general approval of the Committee on Hospital Service of the American Hospital Association."

30. Hedinger, supra n. 18, at p. 52, says: "This social characteristic anticipated the enrollment of low income members of the community and their being provided with protection equal to that received by the more affluent community members at a lower cost. The implication, if not the stated goal, of this element as recognized by various state lawmakers was that Blue Cross would serve as an income redistribution device, a role, customarily reserved for governmental action, and more particularly, governmentally owned or controlled social insurance and public assistance schemes."

31. Rorem, supra n. 27, at pp. 92–93.

32. Dr. Odin W. Anderson, an early historian of the health insurance industry, states that the Blue Cross plans adopted the following characteristics "to differentiate themselves from the private insurance companies," and to justify the competitive advantage granted to them under the special enabling legislation:

1. They were incorporated as nonprofit organizations, and, therefore, had no stockholders or profits for individuals.
2. Their boards of directors represented hospitals, physicians, and the general public.
3. They were supervised by state insurance departments.
4. As nonprofit corporations they held low cash reserves since hospitals were assumed to provide a reserve of service instead of cash.
5. They placed emphasis on hospital benefits in the form of service rather than a cash indemnity.
6. They placed all employees on salaries and offered no commissions to salesmen.

Odin W. Anderson, "The Development of Health Services and Public Policy in the United States, 1875–1965" (unpublished manuscript), chap. XV, quoted in Hedinger, supra n. 18, at p. 17.

33. N.Y. Laws 1934, c. 595, adding Art. 14, §§452–461, to the New York Insurance Law. Amended, June 15, 1939, and recodified, Art. IX-C, §§250–259.

34. Hedinger, supra n. 18, at p. 51.

35. Nathan Sinai, Odin W. Anderson, and Melvin L. Dollar, *Health Insurance in the United States,* (N.Y.: Commonwealth Fund, 1946), p. 46. In 1939 the Blue Cross Commission of the American Hospital Association developed a Model Law to Enable the Formation of Non-Profit Hospital and/or Medical Service Plan. Eilers, supra n. 15, at p. 101.

36. *Ala. Code* tit. 28, §§304-316 (Supp. 1969); *Alaska Stat.* §§21.20.140-.20.200; *Ariz. Rev. Stat. Ann.* §20-821 to -840 (Supp. 1973); *Ark. Stat. Ann.* §§66-4901 to -4920 (Supp. 1971); *Cal. Ins. Code* §§11491-11517 (West 1972); *Colo. Rev. Stat. Ann.* §72-24-1 to -24-25 (Supp. 1967); *Conn. Gen. Stat. Rev.* §§33-157 to -167 (Supp. 1973); *Del. Code Ann.* tit. 18, §§6301-6309 (Insurance Pamphlet 1971); *Fla. Stat.* §§641.01-641.38; *Ga. Code* §56-1701 to -1721 (Supp. 1972); *Hawaii Rev. Stat.* §433-1 to -19 (Supp. 1972); *Idaho Code* §41-3401 to -3436 (Supp. 1972); *Ill. Rev. Stat.* ch. 32, §§551-562 (Supp. 1973); *Iowa Code* §§514.1-.18 (Supp. 1973); *Kan. Stat. Ann.* §§40-1800 to -1816 (Supp. 1972); *Ky. Rev. Stat. Ann.* §§304.32-010 to .32-270 (Supp. 1972); *La. Rev. Stat.* §§22.1661-.1663 (Supp. 1973); *Me. Rev. Stat. Ann.* tit. 24, §§2301-2315 (Supp. 1973); *Md. Ann. Code* art. 48A, §§354-361A (Supp. 1973); *Mass. Gen. Laws* ch. 176A, §§1-30 (Supp. 1973); *Mich. Comp. Laws Ann.* §§550.501-.517 (Supp. 1973); *Minn. Stat. Ann.* §§62C.01-.23 (Supp. 1973); *Miss. Code Ann.* §§83-41-1 to -41-19 (Supp. 1973); *Mont. Rev. Codes Ann.* §§15-2301 to -2397 (Supp. 1973); *Neb. Rev. Stat.* §§21-1509 to -1521 (1970); *Nev. Rev. Stat.* §§696.010-.300; *N.H. Rev. Stat. Ann.* §§419:1-:12 (Supp. 1972); *N.J. Stat. Ann.* §§17:48-1 to 48-18 (Supp. 1973); *N.M. Stat. Ann.* §§58-25-1 to -25-49 (Supp. 1973); *N.Y. Ins. Law* §§250-260 (McKinney Supp. 1973); *N.C. Gen. Stat.* §57-1 to -20 (Supp. 1971); *N.D. Cent. Code* §§26-26-01 to -26-14 (Supp. 1973); *Ohio Rev. Code Ann.* §§1739.01-.15 (Supp. 1972); *Okla. Stat. Ann.* tit. 36, §§2601-2621; *Ore. Rev. Stat.* §§750.005-.065 (Supp. 1972); *Pa. Stat. Ann.* tit. 40, §§6101-6127 (Supp. 1973); *R.I. Gen. Laws Ann.* §§27-19-1 to -19-16 (Supp. 1972); *S.C. Code Ann.* §§37-441 to -445 (Supp. 1971); *S.D. Compiled Laws Ann.* §§58-40-1 to -40-19 (Supp. 1973); *Tenn. Code Ann.* §§56-3001 to -3018 (Supp. 1972); *Tex. Rev. Civ. Stat.* art. 20.01-.21 (Supp. 1972-1973); *Utah Code Ann.* §§31-37-1 to -37-26 (Supp. 1973); *Vt. Stat. Ann.* tit. 8, §§4511-4522 (Supp. 1973); *Va. Code Ann.* §§32-195.1 to -195.20:1 (1973); *Wash. Rev. Code Ann.* §§48.44.010-.44.220 (Supp. 1972); *W. Va. Code Ann.* §§33-24-1 to -24-11 (Supp. 1973); *Wisc. Stat. Ann.* §182.032 (Supp. 1973).

37. *Ariz. Rev. Stat. Ann.* §20-837 (Supp. 1973); *Ark. Stat. Ann.* §§66-4917, -4918 (special 1% tax); *Cal. Ins. Code* §11493.5 (West 1972); *Conn. Gen. Stat. Rev.* §33-165 (Supp. 1973); *Ga. Code* §56-1718 (Supp. 1972); *Idaho Code* §41-3427; *Ill. Rev. Stat.* ch. 32, §562; *Ky. Rev. Stat. Ann.* §136.395 (Supp. 1972); *La. Rev. Stat.* §22:1661 (Supp. 1973); *Me. Rev. Stat. Ann.* tit. 24, §2311 (Supp. 1973); *Mass. Gen. Laws* ch. 176A, §19; *Mich. Comp. Laws Ann.* §550.515; *N.J. Stat. Ann.* §17:48-18; *N.Y. Ins. Law* §251 (McKinney Supp. 1973); *N.C. Gen. Stat.* §57-14 (Supp. 1971); *Ohio Rev. Code Ann.* §1739.07; *Okla. Stat. Ann.,* tit. 36 §2617; *Vt. Stat. Ann.* tit. 8, §4518; *W. Va. Stat. Ann.,* §33-24-4; *Wisc. Stat. Ann.* §182.032(8).

38. The federal tax exemption is provided under §501(c)(4), Int. Rev. Code of 1954, for "civic leagues or organizations not organized for profit but operated exclusively for the promotion of social welfare."

39. Cases denying tax exemption include: *United Hospital Service Assn. v. Fulton County,* 216 Ga. 30, 114 S.E.2d 524 (1960); *Hospital Service Assn. of Toledo v. Evatt,* 144 Ohio St. 179, 57 N.E.2d 928 (1944); *Oregon Physicians' Service v. Horn,* 220 Ore. 487, 349 P.2d 831 (1960), (Blue Shield); *Hassett v. Associated Hospital Service Corp.,* 125 F.2d 611 (1st Cir., 1942). *Associated Hospital Service, Inc. v. City of Milwaukee,* 13

Wis.2d 447, 109 N.W.2d 271 (1961), upholds Blue Cross tax exemption. See also *Cleveland Hospital Service Assn. v. Ebright,* 142 Ohio St. 51, 49 N.E.2d 929 (1943). See generally 37 ALR 3rd 1232, 88 ALR 2d 1414.

40. In *United Hospital Service Assn. v. Fulton Co.,* supra n. 39, the exemption was struck down because under the Georgia constitution only institutions of "purely public charity" may be exempt from taxation. In *Hospital Service Assn. of Toledo v. Evatt,* supra n. 39, a property tax exemption was struck down under a similar provision of the Ohio constitution. In *Oregon Physicians' Service v. Horn,* supra n. 39, the Blue Shield organization was denied exemption under a statute applicable to "civic leagues or organizations not organized for profit but operated exclusively for the promotion of social welfare." In *Hassett v. Associated Hospital Service Corp.,* supra n. 39, a U.S. court of appeals held that Massachusetts Blue Cross was not exempt from the payment of social security taxes on wages because it was not a corporation "organized and operated exclusively for . . . charitable . . . purposes," under Sec. 811(b)(8) of the Social Security Act, even though the Massachusetts statute characterizes the corporation as "charitable."

41. *United Hospital Service Assn. v. Fulton County,* supra n. 39, 216 Ga. at 32, 114 S.E.2d at 527. The court found, "Not the public, not just the poor and the needy, but those and only those whose application is approved by the petitioner are allowed to obtain the benefits covered by the policy . . . Once [a policyholder] has received the amount of services paid for, he must either leave the hospital before he is physically able or look elsewhere for charity to provide such needed services."

42. *Associated Hospital Service Inc. v. City of Milwaukee,* supra n. 39, 13 Wis.2d at 471, 109 N.W.2d at 283.

43. The principle challenge rested upon the constitutional due process and equal protection rights of commercial insurers. Since Blue Cross enabling legislation involves no fundamental human liberties and no inherently suspect classification, the court utilized the narrowest constitutional standard. Id., 13 Wis.2d at 470, 109 N.W.2d at 282. Presumably, under this decision, if Blue Cross were to stop providing subscribers with service benefits, its tax exemption would be jeopardized.

44. The BCA Legal Department states that all of the plans and the national association are exempt from payment of federal taxes under §501(c)(4). Interview by author with an official, BCA Legal Dept. Sept. 12, 1972.

45. "It is my recollection that Blue Cross was ruled to be a Section 501(c)(4) organization sometime during the 1930's or 40's. I suspect that the primary reason for classifying them under that Section is that the service did not at the time know what else to do with them. Section 501(c)(4) has traditionally been the garbage can into which has been dumped organizations that in some way benefit the community, but for one reason or another . . . do not qualify under Section 501(c)(3)." Unofficial comment of a tax attorney and former IRS staff member.

46. Blue Cross is essentially an insurance company in direct competition with commercial insurance companies. Although fraternal insurance organizations are explicitly exempt, Int. Rev. Code, §501(c)(8), the insurance business normally is not. Exemptions under 501(c)(4) are not generally available where membership is restricted on the basis of ability to pay. Further, if membership in the organization is primarily to benefit the individual member and only incidentally to further the public welfare, then the organization is not exempt under §501(c)(4). See Rev. Ruling 62–167 and 69–280, and *Consumer–Farmer Milk Coop Inc. v. Comm.,* 186 F.2d 68, 71 (2nd Cir. 1950). Further, Blue Cross may not involve sufficient civic or citizen participation to qualify for a 501(c)(4) exemption. See *U.S. v. Pickwick Electric Membership Corp.,* 158 F.2d 272, 276 (6th Cir. 1946), *Comm. v. Lake Forest Inc.,* 305 F.2d 814, 818 (4th Cir. 1962), *Erie Endowment v. U.S.,* 316 F.2d 151 (3rd Cir. 1963).

There seems to be no discussion of the Blue Cross tax exemption in academic tax literature. One author, arguing that group prepaid practices actually delivering health services should be exempt, notes: "We must distinguish between organizations which merely provide insurance for hospital and medical care, such as Blue Cross–Blue Shield, and those organizations that themselves provide the medicine and hospital services with the members paying under a prepayment plan." Bromberg, "Charity and Change: Current Problems of Tax Exempt Health and Welfare Organizations in Perspective," in *Tax Problems of Non-Profit Organizations* (N.Y.: Journal of Taxation, Inc., 1970), p. 284.

47. See *Hassett v. Associated Hospital Service Corporation,* supra n. 39, which holds that the Blue Cross plan is conducted "more on a business than a charitable basis. The payment of a fee is prerequisite to the receipt of benefits. . . . The corporate capital is not composed of charitable contributions . . . Membership is not limited to the needy but as a matter of fact is composed largely of the middle class and well-to-do. . . . Here we have what is essentially a business arrangement." Id. at 614. See also *La Societe Francaise Etc. v. United States,* 57 F. Supp. 201 (N.D. Calif. 1944). Plaintiff society sued for a refund of taxes assessed under the Social Security Act, arguing that it was "a corporation organized and operated exclusively for charitable purposes" under Int. Rev. Code, §§1426(b)(8), 26 U.S.C. Int. Rev. Code §1426(b)(8), relating to the old age pension, and 1607(c)(8) relating to unemployment insurance. Plaintiff was an organization of individuals who pay membership fees in return for the benefit of receiving hospital and medical care at hospitals operated by the organization. The federal court found that the organization was "charitable" because the hospital maintained two free beds for nonmembers unable to pay for hospitalization and gave free emergency treatment, and the amount of benefits was not directly related to the amount of payment. The court distinguished *Hassett* on the grounds that Blue Cross did not own or operate a hospital or receive charitable donations. *Contra La Societe Francaise, Etc. v. California Employ. Comm'n,* 56 C.A.2d 534, 133 P.2d 47 (Calif. Sup. Ct. 1943). The same organization was denied exemption from payment of state social security taxes. The court in the state case seemed to be applying the same standards as the federal court but denied exemption on the basis of findings that insurance organizations are not charitable, and the hospital was not open to the poor. "[The] one factor . . . which means almost more than anything else . . . is . . . 'Are the doors of the hospital open to all, poor patients and pay patients alike? ' " Id. at 544 and 552.

Smith v. Reynolds, 43 F. Supp. 510 (D. Minn. 1942), held that the Northern Pacific Beneficial Association was not a "charitable" organization for purposes of exemption from social security taxes. Members paid monthly fees in exchange for hospital service benefits. Id. at 513. "Some charity cases were taken care of, but that fact does not in itself make the Association a charitable organization." Id. at 514.

48. Eilers, supra n. 15, at p. 269.

49. See *Prudential Insurance Co. v. Benjamin,* 328 U.S. 408 (1946), on the power of the states to impose a tax on premiums. See also R. Eilers and R. Crowe, *Group Insurance Handbook* (Homewood, Ill.: Irwin, 1965), pp. 248, 259; O. D. Dickerson, *Health Insurance,* 3d ed., (Homewood, Ill.: Irwin, 1968), pp. 690–92.

50. Mark Greene, *Risk and Insurance* (Cincinnati: South–Western Publishing Co., 1968), p. 739.

51. See *Green v. Kennedy,* 309 F. Supp. 1127 (D.C.D.C. 1970), holding that Negro federal taxpayers have standing to challenge the exempt status of a segregated school established to perpetuate segregated education. See generally *Flast v. Cohn,* 392 U.S. 83 (1968); *Data Processing Service Organizations v. Camp,* 397 U.S. 150 (1970); *Peoples v. U.S. Dept. of Agriculture,* 427 F.2d 561 (D.C. Cir. 1970). See also *Cook v. Ochsner Foundation Hospital,* 319 F. Supp. 603 (E.D.La. 1970); *Euresti v. Stenner,* 458 F.2d.

1115 (9th Cir. 1972); and *Organized Migrants,* in *Community Action v. James Archer Smith Hospital,* 325 F. Supp. 268 (S.D. Fla. 1971), holding that indigent plaintiffs have standing to enforce the promises made by private hospitals as a condition for receiving federal construction grants under the Hill-Burton Act.

52. Approval Program for Blue Cross Plans, AHA, 2M–12/70–1575, 1964, Standard No. 5.

53. There has been some overlap in the territorial jurisdiction of two Illinois Blue Cross plans. The Illinois Supreme Court struck down a provision of the state enabling act requiring hospital service corporations to obtain contracts with at least 30% of the hospitals in the area served.

The court described the situation saying: "[In 1957 the Illinois Hospital Association] formulated a policy to solve a problem which had concerned it for 'several years.' The problem was whether the two Illinois Blue Cross Plans, one known as the 'Chicago' plan and the other, the plaintiff in this case, known as the 'Rockford' plan, should be allowed to operate concurrently in the same areas in the State. 'On this question,' the Association stated, 'it is the opinion of the Board of Trustees that the public is better served and confusion avoided if only one Blue Cross Plan operates in a given area.' Since the plans were unable to 'agree upon territories,' the Association directed the attention of its members to [the state enabling law requirement], and recommended that no member hospital have a contract with more than one Blue Cross Plan. 'If this is done, the Plan not selected would be restricted from operating in that County under the provisions of the State Statutes.' " *Illinois Hospital Service, Inc. v. Gerber,* 18 Ill.2d 531, 165 N.E.2d 279 (1960).

On June 30, 1972, the function of authorizing use of the Blue Cross insignia was transferred from the AHA to the BCA. As of this writing, the BCA is using the same authorization standards as the AHA, although the standards are being reviewed and some revisions will be made. Telephone interview with Robert L. Mickelsen, Senior Director, Approval and Licensure Program, Blue Cross Association, June 28, 1973.

54. Hedinger, supra n. 18, at p. 24; MacIntyre, supra n. 25, at p. 155.

55. Harry Becker, ed., *Financing Hospital Care in the United States* (N.Y.: McGraw-Hill, 1955), pp. 8–11.

56. *Research and Statistic Note,* No. 17 (Washington, D.C.: HEW, SSA, Oct. 13, 1965), p. 6; M. S. Mueller, "Enrollment, Coverage and Financial Experience of Blue Cross and Blue Shield Plans, 1969," *Research and Statistic Note,* No. 4 (Washington, D.C.; HEW, SSA, April 21, 1971), p. 1; *National Health Insurance Proposals,* Hearings before the House Committee on Ways and Means, 92nd Cong., 1st Sess., p. 342 (1971).

57. R. Rorem, *Non-Profit Hospital Service Plans,* supra n. 27, at p. 24.

58. Herman M. and Anne R. Somers, *Doctors, Patients, and Health Insurance* (Washington, D.C.: The Brookings Institution, 1961), p. 304.

59. Eilers, supra n. 15, at p. 89; MacIntyre, supra n. 25, at p. 154. The commitment to provide equal rates to the entire community was expressed in general terms, and the term *community rating* was not coined until the late forties. For example, "Hospital service plans have based their rate structures upon the anticipated utilization of hospital service for the community as a whole . . . The plans have felt that if their project is one community-wide in nature, no special consideration could be given to units making up the community." Norby, "Hospital Service Plans: Their Contract Provisions and Administrative Procedures," 6 *Law and Cont. Prob.* 545, 557 (1939). See also J. Stuart, "Blue Cross and Insurance: The Difference;" 33 *Hospitals* 51 (Feb. 16, 1959).

60. See O. D. Dickerson, *Health Insurance,* 3d ed. (Homewood, Ill.: Irwin, 1968), ch. 18, pp. 568–601; Frank Joseph Angell, *Health Insurance* (N.Y.: Ronald Press, 1963), pp. 363–66 and 478–90; and Edwin J. Faulkner, *Health Insurance* (N.Y.: McGraw-Hill, 1960), ch. 11, pp. 364–405, for an explanation of rate setting by commercial insurers.

Moral, racist, and sexist factors not based on actuarial experience have played a role in selection of risks and determination of rates. See generally Edwin J. Faulkner, *Accident-and-Health Insurance* (N.Y.: McGraw-Hill, 1940), pp. 115–19 and 126–27. The Baylor plan did not purport to serve the whole community. One early report commented, "Employees who are underpaid and overworked are not considered good risks and applications are not solicited from such groups." Further, "although every member insured at this hospital pays a rate of 50¢ per month, all do not receive the same accommodations. Employees of the so-called lower classes, such as laborers, porters, etc. are given hospital treatment in ward beds at the rate of $3 per day. This discrimination has led to some criticism in the community." "Group Hospital Insurance Plan," a paper read Oct. 13, 1932, before the Hospital Conference of the City of New York by Frank Van Dyk, Executive Secretary, Hospital Council of Essex County, Newark, New Jersey, p. 10.

61. The number of persons hospitalized per 1,000 population per year are the following, broken down by family income:

Family Income	Total Persons Hospitalized per 1,000 population
All incomes	96
Under $3,000	123
$3,000–$4,999	107
$5,000–$6,999	97
$7,000–$9,999	94
$10,000 and over	82

The number of persons hospitalized per 1,000 population per year are the following, broken down by age:

Age	Total Persons Hospitalized per 1,000 population
All ages	96
Under 15 years	51
15–44 years	113
45–64 years	102
65 years and over	155

HEW, Public Health Service, Health Services and Mental Health Administration, National Center for Health Statistics, *Persons Hospitalized by Number of Hospital Episodes and Days in a Year, United States—1968*, National Health Survey, Series 10, Number 64, DHEW Publication No. (HSM) 72–1029, p. 4 (1971).

62. On pressure by organized labor for experience rating see MacIntyre, supra n. 25, at pp. 155 et seq.; Hedinger, supra n. 18, at pp. 65 et seq. As late as 1953 a special Blue Cross committee was appointed to consider whether Blue Cross was "a community social agency or an insurance company," whether plans should ban or outlaw experience rating outright, and if no agreement could be reached on an outright ban whether Blue Cross should ban future use of experience rating. The annual national Blue Cross meeting adopted a resolution stating that the "overwhelming majority of Blue Cross Plans have not deviated from presently known Blue Cross practices to the point of offering experience rating" and urging "those Plans not yet engaged in experience rating programs to make an honest effort to withstand the pressures which arise for experience rating." MacIntyre, supra n. 25, at p. 161.

63. Unpublished data provided by the Public Relations Department of the Blue Cross Association, 840 N. Lake Shore Drive, Chicago, Ill. 60611. The Vermont-New Hampshire plan has remained committed to community rating.

64. Dickerson, supra n. 60, at p. 329. See George E. McLean, "An Actuarial Analysis of a Prospective Experience Rating Approach for Group Hospital-Surgical-Medical Coverage," 48 *Proceedings of the Casualty Actuarial Society* 155.

65. A 1964 report by the Subcommittee on Health of the Elderly of the Senate Special Committee on the Aging studied the problem of Blue Cross moves toward experience rating and concluded, "Blue Cross and its older subscribers are in very serious trouble. . . . The route of experience rating and abandonment of service benefits is nothing less than a complete denial of the basic reasons for the existence of Blue Cross. There is, however, an alternative—enactment of a program of hospital insurance benefits for the elderly financed through the social security mechanism." *Blue Cross and Private Health Insurance Coverage of Older Americans,* 88th Cong., 2d Sess. p. 35 (1964).

66. In 41 states, the insurance department has responsibility for supervising Blue Cross. In two other states Blue Cross is regulated by some other state agency. A. L. Mayerson, "State Laws and Health Insurance," *Private Health Insurance and Medical Care,* Conference Papers (Washington, D.C.: HEW, SSA, 1968), p. 21. Cf. O. W. Anderson, *State Enabling Legislation for Non-Profit Hospital and Medical Plans,* Public Health Economics, Research Series, No. 1 (Ann Arbor, Mich.: University of Michigan, 1944). In some states, there is no regulatory agency responsible for the supervision of Blue Cross. For example, Virginia, infra n. 137.

67. In 1868 the Supreme Court ruled that "issuing a policy of insurance is not a transaction of commerce," and hence the power to regulate insurance was reserved to the states. *Paul v. Virginia,* 75 U.S. 168. It was not until 1944, in a case that involved a blatant violation of the Sherman and Clayton antitrust acts, that the court ruled that the commerce clause grants to Congress the power to regulate insurance transactions stretching across state lines. *United States v. South-Eastern Underwriters Assn.* 332 U.S. 533 (1944). After the SEUA decision, state regulation and taxation of insurance were given specific congressional sanction in the Insurance Regulation Act. Public Law 79-15, 59 Stat. 33, March 9, 1945. See A. L. Mayerson, "State Laws and Health Insurance," *Private Health Insurance and Medical Care, Conference Papers* (Washington D.C.: HEW, SSA, 1968), pp. 19 et seq.

68. K. Davis, *Administrative Law,* 3d ed. (1972), §29.02. See also *New Jersey State AFL-CIO v. Bryant,* 55 N.J. 171, 260 A.2d 225 (1969). An unusual exception is *Mass. Hospital Service Inc. v. Comm.* 351 Mass. 248, 218 N.E.2d 383 (1966), in which the court overruled an administrative determination that Blue Cross rates to hospitals were unreasonable. However, the court found that the commissioner had rested his decision "not upon the exercise of a discretionary power to disapprove a rate formula, but rather on his belief that the statute is being violated. The question then, is whether the commissioner's conclusion is required as a matter of law." Id. at 255 and 388.

69. See the Model Law to Enable the Formation of Non-Profit Hospital Services Plans, proposed by the Blue Cross Commission in 1939, set forth in Eilers, supra n. 15, App. A.

70. Proposed changes in subscriber rates must be filed with the insurance departments in Alaska, California, Colorado, Connecticut, Delaware, Florida, Idaho, Kansas, Maryland, Massachusetts, Mississippi, New Hampshire, New York, Oklahoma, Oregon, Pennsylvania, Rhode Island, Texas, Utah, and West Virginia. The insurance department has standing authority to review rates in Alabama, Illinois, Iowa, Michigan, Nebraska, South Dakota, and Tennessee.

71. *Conn, Gen. Stat. Rev.* §33-166; *Idaho Code* §41-3420(1) (Supp. 1972); *Kan. Stat.*

Ann. §40-1806(c) (Supp. 1972); *Mass. Gen. Laws.* ch. 176a §6; *N.H. Rev. Stat. Ann.* §419.6; *N.M. Stat. Ann.* §58-25-17 (Supp. 1973); *W. Va. Stat. Ann.* §33-24-6(c).

72. *Fla. Stat.* §641.04(3)(c); *Ga. Code* §§56-1710, -1711; *Kan. Stat. Ann.* §40-1806(c) (Supp. 1972); *Me. Rev. Stat. Ann.* tit. 24, §2305.3 (Supp. 1973); *Md. Ann. Code* art. 48A, §355(b)(3) (Supp. 1973); *Mich. Comp. Laws Ann.* §550.506(b); *N.J. Stat. Ann.* §17:48-7 (Supp. 1973); *N.Y. Ins. Law* §254 (McKinney Supp. 1973); *Ohio Rev. Code Ann.* §1739.05(F)(2) (Supp. 1972); *Tex. Rev. Civ. Stat.* art. 20.15; *Wash. Rev. Code Ann.* §48.44.020 (Supp. 1972). See also *Minn. Stat. Ann.* §62C.15(1) (Supp. 1973): "reasonable and not unfairly discriminatory."

73. The Colorado statute seems to be uniquely restrictive. It defines the reasonableness of subscriber rates solely in terms of the level of cash reserves of the corporation. *Colo. Rev. Stat. Ann.* §72-24-12(1)(c) (Supp. 1973). It requires prior submission of proposed rate increases and mandates the insurance commissioner to approve rates that will preserve those reserves.

74. *Alaska Stat.* §21.87.180 (1972); *Del. Code Ann.* tit. 18, §§6304(b)(3)-6306 (Insurance Pamphlet 1971); *Fla. Stat.* §641.03; *Ga. Code* §§56-1710,-1711; *Idaho Code* §41-3419 (1961); *Ill. Rev. Stat.* ch. 32, §555; *Iowa Code* §§514.7,.8 (Supp. 1973); *Kan. Stat. Ann.* §§40-1803,-1804; *Md. Ann. Code* art. 48A, §356 (Supp. 1973); *Mich. Comp. Laws Ann.* §550.503 (Supp. 1973); *Minn. Stat. Ann.* §62C.16(3) (Supp. 1973); *Miss. Code Ann.* §83-41-3 (1972); *Mont. Rev. Codes Ann.* §15-2304; *Neb. Rev. Stat.* §21-1513 (1970); *N.D. Cent. Code* §26-26-09; *Okla. Stat. Ann.* tit. 36, §2606; *R.I. Gen. Laws Ann.* §27-19-14 (Supp. 1972); *Tenn. Code Ann.* §56-3014; *Tex. Rev. Civ. Stat.* art. 20,14; *Wash. Rev. Code Ann.* §§48.44.020,.070 (Supp. 1972); *W. Va. Stat. Ann.* §33-24-6.

75. *N.J. Stat. Ann.* §17:48-7 (Supp. 1973).

76. *Mass. Gen. Laws,* ch. 176A, §5, as amended by St. 1969, ch. 874, §1, approved Aug. 29, 1969.

77. The health commissioner must certify that such payments are "reasonably related to the costs of efficient production of such [hospital] service," and then the superintendent of insurance must approve the rates as to "reasonableness." *N.Y. Ins. Law,* §254. *N.Y. Pub. Health Law,* §2807.

78. *Ala. Code* tit. 28, §304-316 (Supp. 1969); *Ariz. Rev. Stat. Ann.* §20-821 et seq. (Supp. 1971); *Ark. Stat. Ann.* §§66-4901 to -4920 (Supp. 1971); *Conn. Gen. Stat. Rev.* §33-157 to -167 (Supp. 1971); *Hawaii Rev. Stat.* §433-1 to -19 (Supp. 1972); *Kan. Stat. Ann.* §§40-1800 to -1816 (Supp. 1972); *La. Rev. Stat.* §§22:661-63 (Supp. 1973); *N.H. Rev. Stat. Ann.* §§419:1-:12 (Supp. 1972); *Okla. Stat. Ann.* tit. 36, §§2601-2621; *Ore. Rev. Stat.* §750.005-.065 (Supp. 1972); *Pa. Stat. Ann.* tit. 40. §§6101-6127 (Supp. 1973); *S.D. Compiled Laws Ann.* §58-40-1 to -40-19 (Supp. 1973); *Utah Code Ann.* §31-37-1 to -37-26 (Supp. 1973); *Vt. Stat. Ann.* tit. 8, §4511-4522 (Supp. 1973); *Va. Code Ann.* §§32-195.1 to 195.20:1 (1973); *Wisc. Stat. Ann.* §182.032 (Supp. 1973).

79. Adjudication of Francis R. Smith, Ins. Commissioner, Commonwealth of Pennsylvania, April 15, 1958, in re Associated Hospital Service of Philadelphia, p. 3, 12. Other states in which the authority to review subscriber rates could be interpreted as encompassing the authority to review rates paid to hospitals include Alabama, California, Connecticut, New Hampshire, South Dakota, and Utah.

80. *N.Y. Ins. Law* §254.

81. *Thaler v. Stern,* 44 Misc.2d 278 (Sup. Ct. 1964).

82. The court criticized the superintendent, noting that "Choosing to do the very least required, he conducts but one audit every three years, regardless of the frequency of rate increase requests." 44 Misc.2d at 284. The court added that "sound judgment would seem to dictate against almost exclusive reliance on facts and figures supplied by those

seeking a rate increase, if for no other reason than the obvious realization that honest advocacy can do strange things to the accuracy of figures." Id. at 285.

83. Id. at 285.

84. Id. at 286.

85. Id. at 288–89.

86. Supra n. 77.

87. *Procaccino v. Stewart,* 25 N.Y.2d 301, 305, 251 N.E.2d, 802, 803, 304 N.Y.S.2d 433, 435 (Court of Appeals, 1969), affirming, 32 App. Div.2d 486, 304 N.Y.S.2d 55, reversing 60 Misc.2d 551 (Sup. Ct.).

88. Id. 25 N.Y.2d at 304, 251 N.E.2d at 804, 304 N.Y.S.2d at 436.

89. Id. at 307, 804, 436.

90. Id. at 306, 804, 436.

91. The rate increase proposed did not take account of a general trend toward decreased utilization of hospital services, the addition of coverage for benefits such as extended care treatment and outpatient diagnostic testing, which should further reduce hospital utilization, the federal wage-price freeze, and the institution of prospective reimbursement, which Blue Cross was to begin in the coming year. The decision required that Blue Cross include investment income in determining the need for a rate increase. Opinions, Findings and Order Relative to the Petitions of New Hampshire-Vermont Blue Cross and New Hampshire-Vermont Blue Shield for Blue Cross Basic Contracts, etc. State of New Hampshire, Insurance Department, John A. Durkin, Commissioner, May 8, 1972.

92. The proposed legislation would require public disclosure of hospital budgets, prior state approval of subscriber elections of Blue Cross board members, and at least 70% of the board to consist of subscribers and other members of the public who have no connection with the profession or hospital industry. House Bill No. 61, introduced by Rep. Coughlin in the N.H. House of Representatives, 1972, and referred to Committee on Banks and Insurance.

93. The decision of the director of the Department of Business Regulation, Oct. 22, 1969, stated, "We believe that Blue Cross was chartered to provide hospital insurance for Rhode Islanders at the most reasonable costs. If that be so, Blue Cross would seem to be obligated at a rate hearing to establish the reasonableness of the hospital charges." Decision at p. 7. See *Hospital Services Corp. of R.I. v. West,* C.A. #72-1486, Sup. Ct., Sept. 27, 1972 (upholding commissioner's partial denial of proposed increases to subscribers over age 65, on the ground that he has a duty to regulate Blue Cross rates in the public interest).

94. The Health Law Project of the University of Pennsylvania submitted a questionnaire to the insurance commissioners of 50 states, inquiring into the regulatory activities of their departments. The questionnaire dealt with the nature of the insurance department in question—its yearly budget, staff size, and staff qualifications. Inquiry was also made into the departments' activities with regard to Blue Cross rate regulation, e.g., whether hearings had been required and held for rate increase requests, whether requests for increases had been denied, and what standards had been used to decide such requests. Questions were asked regarding the departments' control over hospital costs and the role the federal government should play in regulating the health insurance industry.

Of the 19 states answering the question, "Is it the responsibility of your office to control rising hospital costs?" 15 replied negatively. Five of the commissioners answering negatively are explicitly required by statute to review the contracts between Blue Cross and the hospitals; only one such state gave an affirmative answer and one an indecisive answer. Ten of the 19 commissioners felt they had no "authority to participate in reimbursement negotiations between insurers and providers." Seventeen of the 19 responded negatively to the question, "Do you feel you have enough legal authority to control rising hospital costs?" Negative responses were given by the 7 commissioners from states where there is statutory authority to review Blue Cross/hospital contracts. Thus, whether or not the insurance commissioners actually have statutory authority to review such contracts and thereby to regulate hospital costs, their responses indicate that they generally feel that they lack such authority.

Responses are on file at the Health Law Project, 133 So. 36th Street, Philadelphia, Penn. 19104.

95. *National Health Insurance Proposals,* Hearings before the House Committee on Ways and Means, 92nd Cong., 1st Sess., pp. 420–21 (1971).

96. *N.Y. Ins. Law* §255 (Supp. 1973); *R.I. Gen. Laws Ann.* §27-19-6; *Wash. Rev. Code Ann.* §48.04.010 (see also Opinions Att. Gen. 63–64 No. 59); *Mass. Gen. Laws* ch. 176A, §6.

97. Hedinger, supra n. 18, at p. 54.

98. Eilers, supra n. 15, at p. 231.

99. Id. at p. 235. Eilers is opposed to public rate hearings. He urges insurance commissioners to "consider the following potentially adverse features of public hearing. Rate hearings . . . have provided an arena for many witnesses who are not typical subscribers. . . . Another bad feature of rate hearings has been improper press reporting or radical views. [For example, press coverage of criticism of Blue Cross television advertising]."

100. The Health Law Project questionnaire, supra n. 94, showed that, of the 19 states responding, 13 have never conducted a public hearing on Blue Cross subscriber rates. Of the 6 states holding public hearings, 2 were required by statute to do so. North Carolina, New Jersey, and Pennsylvania have voluntarily held public hearings since the 1960s. The New Hampshire insurance department held the first public hearing on a Blue Cross rate increase in 1972.

101. Hedinger, supra n. 18, at p. 56. Eilers found that over half of the insurance commissioners responding to a questionnaire answered affirmatively the query, "Do you feel that Blue Cross and Blue Shield plans are sufficiently similar to health insurance companies for both types of organizations to be treated alike by regulatory agencies?" Supra n. 15, at p. 114.

102. Testimony of National Association of Insurance Commissioners before the House Committee on Ways and Means, supra n. 95, at 421. The NAIC does not have information on the numbers of regulatory personnel with special responsibility for health insurance or on the education, training, and experience of personnel employed. Letter to author from an official, NAIC, June 29, 1972.

103. R. J. Cole, "N.Y. Insurance Regulation Paces the Nation," New York *Times,* Feb. 21, 1971, Sec. F. p. 3, col. 5. This reporter comments, "few, if any, consumers are aware that New York has one of the finest—if not the finest—insurance regulating agencies in the country."

104. An official in the Pennsylvania Insurance Department reports that the department has 246 personnel and that the ratio of nonprofessionals to professionals is about 2:1. An official in the New York Insurance Department estimated that it has 800 employees of which 500 are professional.

105. U.S. Service Mark Registration Number 554,448, registered Feb. 5, 1952; No. 554,817, registered Feb. 12, 1952; and 554,818, registered Feb. 12, 1952.

106. "The name 'Commission on Hospital Service' was subsequently changed to 'Hospital Service Plan Commission' and, finally, to 'Blue Cross Commission' in 1946. Legally, the Blue Cross Commission was a subordinate trust of the American Hospital Association. The Board of Trustees of the AHA could disapprove any course of action of the

commission. Thus, the Blue Cross Commission was in a literal sense an arm or 'commission' of the American Hospital Association." Eilers, supra n. 15, at p. 58.

107. "AHA and Blue Cross Split but Still a Twosome," *Medical World News,* Sept. 10, 1971, p. 20.

108. Telephone interview with Robert L. Mickelsen, Senior Director, Approval and Licensure, Blue Cross Association, June 28, 1973. (Prior to the transfer Mr. Mickelsen was an employee of the AHA, with the title Blue Cross Specialist.)

109. Bylaws, AHA and BCA. The 1971 organizational changes are reported in *AHA Convention Daily,* Aug. 25, 1971; *Modern Hospital,* September 1971, p. 37.

110. *Modern Hospital,* ibid. In June 1972 the AHA committee searching for a new president of that organization recommended Walter J. McNerney, President of BCA. *Washington Report on Medicine and Health,* No. 1305, July 3, 1972. The committee's recommendation was not accepted.

111. Approval Program for Blue Cross Plans, AHA 2M-12/70-1575, AHA, 1964: Approval Standards for Non-Profit Hospital Service Plans Within the United States, Standard No. 2. The interpretation does not define the required community service.

112. Id. Standard No. 1. The interpretation requires that at least one-third of the members of the board be representatives of the participating hospitals and that one-third be representatives of the public. It also requires that "the interests of any officer, director or trustee of a plan shall not be in conflict with the interests of the plan."

113. Id. Standard 3.

114. Id. Standards 4 and 6. The interpretation of standard 4 requires that reserves be sufficient to meet expenses for three months, or that reserves have been increased by at least 3% of gross income during the preceding twelve-month period, or that there is at least an expectation that reserves will be increased or not drastically reduced during the forthcoming year.

115. Id. Standards 7 and 10. The interpretation of standard 10 requires semiannual meetings with the local hospital association and regular exchange of information.

116. Id. Standard 9.

117. Id. Standard 5. Standard 5 requires that the agreement between Blue Cross and the hospital include "a definition of the method of hospital reimbursement based on the AHA's Principles of Payment for Hospital Care."

118. Telephone interview with Robert L. Mickelsen, AHA Blue Cross Specialist, April 28, 1972. For example, with respect to the provision prohibiting persons with conflicts of interest from becoming board members, Mr. Mickelsen explained that compliance was determined on the basis of the plan's response to a questionnaire.

119. From time to time, plans that were seen to be "in trouble" were placed on probationary status by the AHA. The plan then either shaped up or merged with another plan. Ibid. In 1971, 86 Philadelphia area physicians in a petition to the AHA charged the Philadelphia Blue Cross plan with violation of the approval standards. The plan was then $4.5 million in the red and had approved a bylaw change providing for a maximum of 6 provider representatives on the plan's 34-member board of directors. The petition sought to have AHA ensure the plan's compliance with the standards of approval. *American Medical News,* Aug. 16, 1971, p. 9. No action was taken by the AHA.

120. *Guidelines for Using the Blue Cross Service Marks* (AHA, 1968) is a 32-page publication on the proper use of the service marks. It states, at p. 5: "The service marks BLUE CROSS and the BLUE CROSS Symbol are valuable business assets; however, they can easily be destroyed. It is, therefore, important that a constant effort be made to protect them. Inadvertent and careless misuse of a mark can result in the loss of rights; the service mark can then become the descriptive or generic name of the services to which it refers. . . . Protecting the service marks . . . requires constant vigilance. . . . If an

unscrupulous infringer appears, it is necessary to take action, since one means of safeguarding the service marks is an unrelenting fight against encroachment.''

121. Testimony of Walter J. McNerney, *High Cost of Hospitalization*, Hearings before the Subcommittee on Antitrust and Monopoly of the Senate Committee of the Judiciary, 91st Cong., 2nd Sess., Pt. 2, p. 205 (January 1971). Hereinafter cited as Hart Committee Hearings.

122. Id. at p. 206.

123. The "External Relations Division" works to "extend the influence of the Blue Cross system in the opinion-making provider and consumer segments of the environment external to the Blue Cross system, and to relate back to the system the conditions and circumstances of that environment for the purpose of aiding in the determination of the role of Blue Cross." External Relations also maintains intelligence on over 300 provider and consumer organizations. Id. at pp. 197–98.

124. BCA Bylaws, Art. 3, Sec. 4, "Visitation," quoted in id. at p. 184.

125. Hart Committee Hearings, supra n. 121, at p. 176. Walter J. McNerney stated, "The Blue Cross Association conducts intensive reviews of plan performance and makes recommendations for improvement. . . . These reviews all are designed to help plans improve performance on a timely and efficient basis." He described three types of review conducted by BCA: a total plan review, a national account review to assure that particular contract specifications are met, and a review in special circumstances. Id. at p. 185. BCA began doing comprehensive plan reviews in the fall of 1967, and as of January 1971 35 such reviews had been conducted in plans representing 58% of United States subscribers. Id. at p. 186.

126. BCA maintains information on some factors that provide some indication of plan functioning, at least relative to other plans, for example administrative expense per claim, staff ratios, productivity. An internal BCA memo dated May 1971 stated that the figures for the Virginia plan have "been unsatisfactory for some time and each periodic reading shows greater deterioration." Id. at p. 51.

127. Id. at pp. 31, 54.

128. Ibid.

129. Id. at pp. 32–33, 61.

130. Id. at pp. 36–37, 48.

131. Id. at p. 188.

132. Id. at pp. 188–89.

133. Id. at p. 55. Another BCA memo, dated May 11, 1970, stated, "The uncontrolled increase in administrative cost has created an explosive situation regarding Medicare and could generate bad publicity coupled with SSA and Congressional reactions even worse than those encountered by the Washington D.C. plan." Id. at p. 51.

134. Supra n. 109.

135. Hart Committee Hearings, supra n. 121, at p. 192.

136. Asked about the furniture purchases substantially above market prices from a company whose sales manager was chairman of the Blue Cross Building Committee, the Richmond executive director stated, "But he was not involved in the sale of this equipment. It was not in his area. He did not get a commission. . . . We have investigated and find nothing wrong with that relationship." Id. at p. 33. A BCA memo reports that "The Plan's attitude is that they are on top of the situation and can handle the Fountain Committee or any other problems that may arise. I believe much of their confidence stems from a lack of understanding and respect for the talent they may encounter if called before the Fountain Committee." Id. at p. 36.

137. Id. at p. 13. See also *Washington Post*, Jan. 29, 1971, p. B1, col. 7. The plan's executive director outlined why the legislature removed the State Corporation Commission's (SCC) power to approve Blue Cross subscriber rates: "the corporation commission

didn't want to raise the rates that were necessary to keep the plan solvent, and we found that we were actually in the red. . . . And the pressures put on by certain individuals tended the corporation commission not to make timely rate adjustments. Delays were very detrimental in keeping a solvent association." Hart Committee Hearings, supra n. 121, at p. 13.

In the aftermath of the 1971 Hart Committee hearings, a state senator introduced legislation to place Blue Cross rates under the supervision of the SCC. *Washington Post,* Jan. 29, 1971, p. B1, col. 7; Feb. 4, 1971, p. B1, col. 2. The SCC stated that it would be "next to impossible" to regulate Blue Cross without also setting hospital and doctor fees but stopped short of outright opposition. *Washington Post,* Feb. 3, 1971, p. A15, col. 4. Blue Cross opposed regulation and instead urged a state study of Blue Cross operations. *Washington Post,* Feb. 2, 1971, p. C2, col. 1. The governor supported the state study and opposed the bill, since previous SCC regulation had been ineffective. *Washington Post,* Feb. 4, 1971, p. B1, col. 2, and Feb. 5, 1971, p. B2, col. 4. Two weeks later the State Senate Insurance and Banking Committee, in executive session, voted unanimously to kill the bill. *Washington Post,* Feb. 19, 1971, p. C5, col. 6. A majority of the members of that committee had previously cosponsored the bill, but sentiment for controlling Blue Cross apparently cooled. *Washington Post,* Feb. 20, 1971, p. B2, col. 4.

138. Hart Committee Hearings, supra n. 121, at p. 28.

139. *Blue Cross-Blue Shield Fact Book 1972,* (Chicago, BCA), p. 12.

140. Hart Committee Hearings, supra n. 121, at p. 26.

141. For example, the Evaluation of Part A Intermediary Performance, SSA, March 19, 1971, based on the 18 months ending December 1970, indicated that the Richmond plan was one of the three Blue Cross plans in the nation that had an "unsatisfactory" composite of unit cost per bill processed. The other plans with an unsatisfactory rating were New York City and Puerto Rico. In addition, seven plans were evaluated as having "substandard" costs per bill processed: Buffalo, N.Y.; District of Columbia; Maryland; Minnesota; New Mexico; Los Angeles, California; Jamestown, N.Y.

142. The Washington Blue Cross is called Group Health Association Inc. See *Administration of Federal Health Benefit Programs,* Hearings before a Subcommittee of the House Committee on Government Operations, 91st Cong., 2nd Sess., pp. 274–75 (1970).

143. Id. at pp. 274–75. The chairman of the board and president of the National Savings and Trust Co. was also a member of the Blue Cross board, its treasurer for over ten years, and a member of both its Executive and Finance and Investment committees. That bank was the primary one used by Blue Cross and also served as investment custodian for all of the funds of the organization. Id. at pp. 228, 261. Other members of the Blue Cross board were officers of other banks, some of which were beneficiaries of Blue Cross noninterest-bearing accounts. Id. at p. 252.

144. The chairman of the Illinois Blue Cross board was senior vice president of the Continental Illinois National Bank of Chicago until recently. When he joined the board in 1947, Blue Cross had less than $1 million on deposit. By 1963, when he became chairman of the board, the plan's balances at Continental had passed $7 million. On December 31, 1971, the plan had $15.3 million on deposit. In addition, the plan has more than $2 million in noninterest-bearing accounts in the Northern Trust Company, one of whose officers is also on the Blue Cross board. In 1971, perhaps in response to the 1970 congressional investigation of Washington Blue Cross, Continental paid Blue Cross interest amounting to $375,339. A. Bajonski, "The Blue Cross Doubled Cross," 5 *Chi. Journalism Rev.,* No. 2, p. 4 (February 1972), and A. Bajonski, "Further Notes on the Blue Cross Double Cross," 5 *Chi. Journalism Rev.* no. 6, p. 19 (June 1972).

145. Hart Committee Hearings, supra n. 121, at pp. 40–41.

146. The BCA responded that information was not available on the following subjects: amount of Blue Cross payments to hospitals under Medicaid; number of days of work on

hand; percentage of Medicaid claims reviewed for medical necessity; breakdown of the types of personnel involved in claims review work; percentages of claims for payment for hospital and nursing home care that were questioned and/or rejected; whether member hospitals had functioning utilization review committees and whether those committees utilized length of stay data; rate of hospital usage by experience-rated groups; comparative information on rates to community- and experience-rated subscribers; increases in rates to community-rated subscribers; the process by which public and provider members are selected to serve on Blue Cross boards. The questionnaire, BCA response, and related correspondence are available from the Health Law Project, 133 So. 36th Street, Philadelphia, Penn. 19174.

147. For example, Philadelphia Blue Cross takes the position that information concerning per diem costs and charges should be made available only to the professional public, because the general public is not in a position to evaluate such information and public disclosure would be unfair to the physicians and hospitals involved. See Sen. Abraham Ribicoff, *The American Medical Machine* (N.Y.: Saturday Review Press, 1972), p. 98.

148. In 1965, Walter McNerney described the members of Blue Cross boards: "the majority are public representatives, and these reflect labor, management, the church, and various facets in the community, and they all serve without pay." Executive Hearings before the House Committee on Ways and Means, 89th Cong., 1st Sess., Pt. 1., p. 181. Before the Senate Finance Committee, he stated, "Blue Cross plans, like many hospitals, were started by thousands of public servants, many of whom were not professionally involved in health. They were labor leaders, businessmen, educators and legislators who saw a vital need to help their fellow citizens have access to health care. They organized hospitals. They wrote, sponsored, and passed enabling legislation authorizing Blue Cross plans. These laws declared public policy to include the functioning of these plans as a public policy, using some of the principles of insurance, but dedicated to obtaining total community membership." Hearings on H.R. 6675 before the Senate Finance Committee, 89th Cong., 1st Sess., Pt. 1 (1965).

Asked "who is it that sets the salaries and provides the costs that are necessary," McNerney responded, "It is a community board. For example, we might have on the board a group of the top industrialists and labor people in the town, representatives of the churches. We might, for example, have people who are providers of care. These people will establish the basic policy of this operation." Hearings on H.R. 3920 before the House Committee on Ways and Means, 88th Cong., 1st and 2nd Sess., Pt. 3, p. 2072.

149. For example, *N.J. Stat. Ann.* §17:48-5 (Supp. 1973); *Calif. Stat. Ann. Insurance* §11498 (1972); *Wisc. Stat. Ann.* §182.032(3)(a) (1957); *N.Y. Ins. Law* §250.1-a (Supp. 1973).

150. Hart Committee Hearings, supra n. 121, Pt. 2, p. 184. These figures do not include hospital trustees as public representatives. Over the past 25 years there has been a slight decrease in the proportion of provider representatives.

	Hospital	Medical
1945	55%	17%
1959	51%	17%
1965	45%	14%
1967	44%	14%
1968	43%	17%
1969	43%	16%

151. Id. at p. 131.

152. Sen. Thomas Eagleton asked, "Since the record is clear, I take it that interlocking

boards of directors are the rule and not the exception. On boards of Blue Cross and Blue Shield plans you will find individuals from hospitals, and in the same area, on the hospital boards you will find Blue Cross and Blue Shield types, and thus with this interlock, with friendly brothers in law, as it were, supervising each other, cost control is unrealistic.

Sen. Hart: It is, as I see it.

Sen. Eagleton: I like those short answers to my demagogic questions.

Sen. Hart: That was not a demagogic question, I assure you."

Health Care Crisis in America, Hearings before the Subcommittee on Health of the Senate Committee on Labor and Public Welfare, 92nd Cong., 1st Sess., Pt. 5, p. 850 (1971).

153. On the basis of questioning of the provider members of the board and examination of the hospital reimbursement contract, the commissioner found:

> The capacity of the board to "negotiate" as a unit and put forth a unified front is clearly diminished in direct proportion to the number of hospital administrators on the board who recognize the interests of their hospitals to be paramount, yet inimical, at least in the area of hospital reimbursement, to the interests of Blue Cross and its subscribers.

> At a minimum, the Commissioner finds that the terms of the reimbursement contract approved by the Board in 1970, were not arrived at through anything resembling true arms length negotiations, and that the bargaining that took place was impaired by a lack of objectivity and independence on the part of some board members.

Memorandum Opinion, *In re Blue Cross,* Administrative Hearing No. 72-10, West Virginia Commissioner of Insurance, pp. 9–10, Nov. 15, 1972.

154. The Massachusetts rate chairman noted, "without in any sense suggesting wrong doing on the part of these 11 [provider representatives on the Blue Cross board]—many of whom are known to me personally as fine, honorable men who act only according to deeply held convictions—I believe their mere duality of roles weakens the resolve of Blue Cross in its dealings with the hospitals." Hart Committee Hearings, supra n. 121, at p. 131.

155. See Sen. Edward Kennedy, *In Critical Condition* (N.Y.: Simon and Schuster, 1972), pp. 209–10.

156. The chairman of the Massachusetts Rate Setting Commission recommends state legislation excluding hospital representatives from the Blue Cross board and providing for a hospital advisory committee. Hart Committee Hearings, supra n. 121, at p. 131.

157. Infra at n. 224.

158. *Health Care Crisis in America,* supra n. 152, Pt. 5 at p. 915.

159. Id. at p. 864.

160. According to BCA data, the board of directors or corporate membership selects the public board members in 44 plans. Hart Committee Hearings, supra n. 121, at pp. 177–82. Often the only "members" of the Blue Cross corporation are the board of directors. Boards are sometimes casually self-perpetuating. For example, J. N. Stanberry, an Illinois Blue Cross director emeritus and retired vice president of Illinois Bell, says, "when I left the Blue Cross board, I suggested my successor at Bell to take my place, and the other directors said it was all right with them." Andrew Bajonski, "The Blue Cross Double Cross," 5 *Chi. Journalism Rev.,* No. 2, p. 4 (February 1972).

161. Hart Committee Hearings, supra n. 121, at pp. 178 et seq. Plans in which the hospital representatives select the public board members include: Los Angeles; Atlanta; Des Moines; Sioux City; Kentucky; New Orleans; Michigan; Minnesota; Kansas City, Mo.; St. Louis; Montana; North Dakota; Canton, Ohio; Lima, Ohio; Youngstown, Ohio; Allentown, Pa.; Chattanooga; Memphis; Parkersburg, West Va.; and Wheeling, West Va.

162. Ibid. In Maine, Nebraska, and Puerto Rico the public representatives are nominated and elected by the subscribers. In Kansas and Wilkes-Barre, Pa., the public representatives are elected by the corporate members chosen from the Subscriber Advisory Board, which represents subscribers in each county served. In Mississippi and Oklahoma the subscribers select public members from a list nominated by the board.

163. See *Philadelphia Inquirer,* Jan. 30, 1972, p. 26; Feb. 14, 1971, p. F17, col. 1; Feb. 23, 1972, p. 17; *Philadelphia Bulletin,* Jan. 26, 1972, p. 9; Feb. 23; 1972, p. 38, col. 4. After the 1972 election it was revealed that the plan management learned of two additional vacancies just prior to the election. The board appointed a former plan executive and a businessman to fill the positions. Subscribers unsuccessfully urged the seating of those receiving the next highest vote in the election. Minutes, Associated Hospital Service of Philadelphia, Consumer Advisory Committee Meeting, May 1, 1972.

164. On Sept. 28, 1972, the Consumer Advisory Board of Philadelphia Blue Cross recommended that the bylaws be amended to provide that no employee of Blue Cross should be allowed to solicit proxy votes. The proposal was rejected. Minutes, Associated Hospital Service, Nov. 22, 1972. The bylaws were amended to provide for the listing of candidates nominated by petition in newspaper advertisements, but the board refused to accept the consumers' recommendation that proxy forms be provided for insurgent as well as management candidates. The board also rejected a consumer recommendation limiting office to six years.

165. Major affiliations of the public board members include food companies (e.g. Horn & Hardart, Tasty Baking Co., Campbell Soups), insurance companies (e.g. Penn Mutual Life Insurance, Fidelity Mutual Life, Lumberman's Mutual Life Insurance), and other businesses such as Sears, Roebuck and Co., Quaker Chemical, etc. Detailed data on each member of the Philadelphia plan board is compiled in an unpublished paper, "Conflicts of Interest on the 1970 Blue Cross of Greater Philadelphia Board," on file at the Health Law Project, 133 So. 36th Street, Philadelphia, Penn. 19174.

166. The 32-person board had 6 physicians, 1 hospital administrator, 15 hospital trustees, and 3 former hospital trustees. Thomas Jefferson University Hospital had 4 representatives; Albert Einstein Medical Center had 3; Temple University Hospital, Pennsylvania Medical College, and Germantown Hospital and Dispensary each had 2. The Hospital of the University of Pennsylvania had only 1 trustee on the board; however, 3 Blue Cross directors were trustees of the university. Ibid.

167. The information upon which this tabulation is based was presented in *Physician Training Facilities and Health Maintenance Organization,* Hearings before the Subcommittee on Health of the Senate Committee on Labor and Public Welfare, 92nd Cong., 1st Sess., Pt. 3, pp. 1043 ff. (Nov. 2, 1971). The other positions listed included: 1 agricultural agent, 1 farm commissioner, 2 farmers, 1 rancher, 5 executive secretaries, 4 secretaries, 1 research nurse, 1 chemist, 2 manufacturers, 1 trustee, 1 congressman, 2 accountants, 1 civic worker, 1 health officer, 5 superintendents, 2 radio and TV staff, 1 office manager, 1 machinery worker, 1 biologist, 3 editors, 5 publishers, 3 hospital officials, 1 comptroller, 3 CPAs, 1 salvage worker, 1 coal operator, 2 supervisors, an executive and an employee of PRWRA (an unidentified Puerto Rican organization), 1 Blue Cross official, 2 government employees, and 1 police officer.

168. For example, although there were labor representatives on the board of the Washington, D.C., and Illinois plans, and an official of George Washington University on the Finance Committee of the Washington board, there was no evidence that these people raised questions about the plan's deposits in noninterest-bearing accounts. *Administration of Federal Health Benefit Programs,* supra n. 142, at p. 228.

169. Walter J. McNerney states, "If you examine what has animated Blue Cross over

the years, you would find, for example . . . that in Michigan the greatest impact on Michigan Blue Cross is derived from the United Auto Workers . . . and other labor unions in that State who were very explicit about what they wanted and the conditions under which they wanted them. In Western Pennsylvania it was steel, and in Cleveland, similarly, and so on around the country. . . . Eighty per cent of our business is through groups. We have seven out of the ten largest industries enrolled in this country and if there is any dominancy, it certainly comes from that source." Hart Committee Hearings, supra n. 121, at p. 220. Dr. Harry Becker, a health economist long associated with Blue Cross and organized labor, estimates that the single most important objective of Blue Cross plan subscriber relations is to keep the blue chip accounts happy. Interview, May 6, 1971, New York, N.Y.

170. C. Silberstein, "Non-Group and Small Group Coverage: What's Available and How Much Does it Cost?" (Unpublished ms, Nov. 11, 1971). See also *The American Health Empire,* A Report from the Health Policy Advisory Center (N.Y.: Random House, 1970), pp. 151–54.

171. The New York Insurance Department recently proposed regulations that would require insurance companies to maintain experience data for determining rates. Proposed Amendments to 11 N.Y.C.R.R. 52, issued Dec. 20, 1972.

172. Dr. Harry Becker explains that labor representatives impressed by the opportunity to meet, work, and socialize with financial and professional leaders take an accommodating and unquestioning role in exchange for amiable relationships on the board. Supra n. 169.

173. Odin W. Anderson, "Compulsory Medical Care Insurance, 1910–1950," in *Medicare: Policy and Politics,* ed. Eugene Feingold (San Francisco: Chandler Publishing Co., 1966), p. 87. Hereinafter cited as Feingold. In the early 1900s the American Association for Labor Legislation (AALL) was the most prominent group pressing for national health insurance. Organized in 1906, by 1913 the AALL had over 3,300 members, mostly professionals. The American Medical Association established a committee on health insurance in 1915, including three members of the AALL. The AALL prepared a model bill for introduction in state legislatures. Ibid., pp. 86–87.

174. *Journal of the American Medical Association,* May 1, 1920, p. 1319.

175. The Committee on the Costs of Medical Care, which issued 28 reports from 1928 to 1932, recommended in its final report that "medical service, both preventive and therapeutic, should be furnished largely by organized groups of physicians, dentists, nurses, pharmacists and other associated personnel" and that "the costs of medical care be placed on a group payment basis" through insurance, taxation, or both. Feingold, supra n. 173, at pp. 89–90.

In 1934 President Roosevelt's Committee on Economic Security did not make recommendations on health insurance but simply provided one line in the original social security bill instructing the Social Security Board to study the problem and report to Congress. Edwin E. Witte, executive director of the committee, wrote, "That little line was responsible for so many telegrams to the members of Congress that the entire social security program seemed endangered until the Ways and Means Committee unanimously struck it out of the bill." Ibid., pp. 91–92.

176. In 1939 Sen. Robert Wagner introduced a bill (S. 1620). A succession of bills providing for a social security type of national health insurance program was introduced without success through the 1940s. In 1947 Sen. Robert Taft introduced a bill (S. 545) to assist states in providing medical care for the indigent. In 1949, after the election of President Truman, a large number of bills was introduced, the major ones being the administration's social security type of health insurance (S. 1679) and an opposition bill (S.

1970) providing grants to states to assist private prepayment plans in serving the poor. See Agnes W. Brewster, *Health Insurance and Related Proposals for Financing Personal Health Services* (Washington, D.C.: HEW, SSA, 1958).

177. Charles Schottland, *The Social Security Program in the United States* (N.Y.: Meredith Publishing, 1963), p. 151.

178. The Special Subcommittee on Problems of the Aged and Aging of the Senate Committee on Labor and Public Welfare was established early in 1959 to conduct a study of the major problems of the aged.

179. The conference was held under the aegis of the departing Eisenhower administration. Although about half of the delegates to the medical care work group, which considered health insurance proposals, were representatives of the medical profession and insurance industry, two prominent Republicans, Marion B. Folson, former secretary of HEW, and Arthur Larson, then under secretary of labor, supported a social security type of hospital insurance legislation, and the conference ultimately endorsed the idea by a close vote. Feingold, supra n. 173, at p. 114. For a discussion of action by the conference on the financing of medical care for the aged, see "Aging Parley Bows to Social Security," *Washington Post,* Jan. 13, 1961. The conference "Basic Policy Statements and Recommendations" and data demonstrating the need for health insurance for the aged are set forth in The 1961 White House Conference on Aging, *Basic Policy Statements and Recommendations,* prepared for the Special Committee on Aging, U.S. Senate, 87th Cong., 1st Sess. (May 15, 1961).

180. *Blue Cross and Private Health Insurance Coverage of Older Americans,* A Report by the Subcommittee on Health of the Elderly to the Special Committee on Aging, U.S. Senate, 88th Cong., 2nd Sess., p. 36 (July 1964). See also pp. 16, 20, 22.

181. In 1957, 1958, and 1959, Rep. Aime J. Forand (D.-R.I.) introduced bills providing for a social security type of health insurance for people over 65 who were eligible for social security benefits, covering 60 days of hospitalization and 120 days of nursing home care. H.R. 4700, 86th Congress. The House Ways and Means Committee first held hearings on these proposals in 1959. The AFL-CIO strongly supported the bill. HEW Secretary Arthur Flemming, for the administration, opposed the bill and did not offer an alternative. It was not reported out of committee. Hearings on H.R. 4700 before the House Committee on Ways and Means, 86th Cong., 1st Sess. (1959).

182. In March 1960, 6,000 people rallied in New York and 12,000 in Detroit in support of the Forand bill. In May 1960, 12,000 attended another New York rally. Feingold, supra n. 173, at pp. 107, 110. National opinion polls in 1961 showed that a majority of people favored social-security-financed health insurance for the aged. *New York Times,* April 30, 1961, p. 18, col. 4.

183. In 1960 the House Ways and Means Committee was deadlocked between the Forand bill and an administration bill authorizing federal grants to states to subsidize the cost of voluntary health insurance for the aged poor. See 106 *Cong. Rec.* 9948–49 (Remarks of Rep. Byrnes). Committee Chairman Wilbur Mills submitted a compromise providing federal grants to the states to pay part of the costs of medical services to the needy aged. Each state would decide whether to participate and would determine standards of eligibility and services to be provided, within broad limits. 86th Cong., 2nd Sess. H. 12580 passed the House on June 23. The national political conventions intervened and on July 12 Democrats adopted a platform calling for health care for the aged financed through the social security system and without a means test. *New York Times,* July 13, 1960, p. 20. Sen. Robert Kerr (D.-Okla.) introduced a Senate companion to the Mills bill, which was supported by the American Medical Association and the administration. Despite Democratic and labor support for a more liberal alternative, the bill became law. 42 U.S.C. 301–4306.

184. The Kerr-Mills Act was denounced by both presidential candidates in 1960. Feingold, supra n. 173, at p. 113.

185. The King-Anderson bill, 87th Cong., 1st Sess., H. 4222, S. 909, §1610.

186. The AHA testified against the bill, urging a program financed by general revenues and administered by the states, with a large role for Blue Cross. Hearings on H.R. 4222 before the House Committee on Ways and Means, 87th Cong., 1st Sess., Vol. 1, pp. 252 et seq. (July 26, 1961). The AMA organized a public campaign against the bill. *New York Times,* Feb. 15, 1961, p. 18, col. 4.

187. Herman M. Somers and Anne R. Somers, *Medicare and the Hospitals* (Washington, D.C.: Brookings Institution, 1967), p. 5.

188. The resolution recommended "the earliest possible implementation of a national Blue Cross program for a voluntary nonprofit plan available to all persons aged 65 and over." It recognized that "Government assistance is necessary to effectively implement this national Blue Cross proposal in order to enable many retired aged persons to purchase this health protection through the voluntary health insurance system . . . If this proposed plan [is administered] by the voluntary, nonprofit, prepayment system, the tax source of the funds is of secondary importance to us." Resolution of the AHA House of Delegates, Jan. 4, 1962, reported in *Medical Care for the Aged,* Hearings on H.R. 3920 before the House Committee on Ways and Means, 88th Cong., 1st and 2nd Sess., Pt. 1, p. 350 (Nov. 18–22, 1963, and Jan. 20–24, 1964).

189. M. J. Skidmore, *Medicare and the American Rhetoric of Reconciliation* (University, Ala.: University of Alabama Press, 1970), pp. 82–84.

190. HEW Memorandum, May 10, 1962, to Wilbur J. Cohen from Arthur E. Hess, Chairman, Sub-Task Force on Use of Blue Cross and other Insurers.

191. Feingold, supra n. 173, at p. 120.

192. Anderson-Javits Bill, S. 3565, 87th Cong., 2nd Sess.

193. Social Security Act, §1816(a), 42 U.S.C. §1395h(a).

194. Ibid.

195. Social Security Act, §1816(b), 42 U.S.C. §1395h(b).

196. Supra n. 195.

197. Social Security Act, §1816(c), 42 U.S.C. §1395h(c).

198. Social Security Act, §1816(c), 42 U.S.C. §1395h(d).

199. Social Security Act, §§1816(f) and (g), 42 U.S.C. §§1395(f) and (g).

200. In 1963 the administration-supported bill was introduced by Cong. Cecil R. King as H.R. 3920, 88th Cong., 1st Sess. The fiscal intermediary is described in Sec. 1715. In 1964 the same provision was introduced as part of H.R. 11865, 88th Cong., 2nd Sess., Sec. 1815. In 1965 the bills introduced by the administration, H.R. 1 and S. 1, 89th Cong., 1st Sess., contained the same provisions on fiscal intermediaries as in previous years.

The compromise bill introduced by Ways and Means Chairman Wilbur Mills after the 1965 hearings and finally adopted contained some modifications in the fiscal intermediary provisions. H.R. 6675, 89th Cong., 1st Sess. It made plain that the secretary could contract with a national organization (BCA) nominated by an association of providers (AHA). Sec. 1816(u). H.R. 1 had simply provided that the secretary could contract with "any organization designated by providers for the receipt of payments." Sec. 1715(a).

The Mills bill required that before contracting with a fiscal intermediary, the secretary *must* find that the organization is willing and able to assist providers in applying safeguards against unnecessary utilization. Sec. 1816(b)(2). (Under previous bills the secretary had the option of assigning this job to the fiscal intermediary if he found that the organization was able to perform. Sec. 1715(b)(3).)

It added a requirement that the fiscal intermediary furnish to the secretary such information acquired by it in carrying out its agreement. Sec. 1816(b)(3).

Finally H.R. 6675 added a provision authorizing the fiscal intermediary to provide consultative services to enable providers to establish and maintain fiscal records and otherwise to qualify as participating provider institutions. Sec. 1816(a)(1).

201. HEW Memorandum, supra n. 190, at p. 1. This document was never included in the legislative history. Copies may be obtained from Social Security Administration, Division of Health Insurance, Office of Program Education and Planning, Room 432 Admin., Baltimore, Md.

202. Ibid.

203. The functions suggested that might be contracted out under such a program included: acting as a communications link between the providers and the federal government; providing assistance in establishing appropriate fiscal records and in calculating provider operation costs; "under general Federal review and auditing authority, apply-[ing] cost reimbursement policies to individual hospitals and other providers"; performing the daily operations involved in the processing and payment of bills for services rendered; receiving federal funds to pay providers' bills; performing routine, periodic auditing of hospital accounts. Ibid.

204. The reasons cited in favor of this alternative were: (1) sensitive areas of provider relations would be reserved for Blue Cross, which had the experience, relationships with hospitals, and skilled staff necessary to perform these administrative functions; (2) federal responsibilities might spur Blue Cross to effect economies for its private subscribers; (3) professional medical organizations would probably find this approach more acceptable; (4) "Blue Cross is basically a public-service oriented organization and is showing signs of interest in and willingness to assume responsibilities to assure more effective use of community health facilities and services."

205. Statutory criteria suggested by the HEW task force included the representativeness of the organization's governing board (at least one-third public representatives); the organization's efficiency in conducting its own affairs; its experience with reimbursement of providers on a cost basis; and its experience with the development of safeguards against unnecessary utilization of health services.

206. Kenneth Williamson, associate director of the AHA, testified that "As requested by the HEW we brought people in on the drafting of the bill previous to the one introduced this year [i.e., the 1962 bill after the HEW Memorandum]. Some of the suggestions that our group made were taken and some were not. But we did have a thorough discussion across the board of problems involved, and the best way we thought of handling various technical matters in the legislation." *Medical Care for the Aged,* Hearings on H.R. 3920 before the House Committee on Ways and Means, 88th Cong., 1st and 2nd Sess., Pt. 1, p. 362 (Nov. 18–23, 1963, and Jan. 20–24, 1964). Hereinafter cited as 1963 House Hearings, Part 1.

207. *Cong. Rec.* (daily ed.), July 8, 1965, pp. 15970–71.

208. Testimony of Dr. David B. Wilson, Chairman, Council on Government Relations, American Hospital Association, before the 1963 House Hearings, Part 1, supra n. 206, at p. 360.

209. Testimony of Walter J. McNerney, President, BCA. *Medical Care for the Aged,* Hearings before the House Committee on Ways and Means, 88th Cong., 1st and 2nd Sess., Pt. 4, p. 2050 (Nov. 18–22, 1963, and Jan. 20–24, 1964). Hereinafter cited as 1963 House Hearings, Part 4.

210. Id. at p. 2055.

211. 1963 Hearings, Part 1, supra n. 206, at p. 364.

212. Id. at pp. 361, 362.

213. Id. at p. 364.

214. Id. at p. 365.

215. Id. at pp. 352, 360, 363, 396, 406–07, 412.

216. Id. at pp. 407–08.

217. In 1964 the AHA reiterated the proposition that the most serious defect in the administration bill was the failure to provide for administration through federal underwriting without federal control. Hearings before the Senate Finance Committee on H.R. 11865, 88th Cong., 2nd Sess., p. 619 (August 1964).

218. Remarks by Sen. Williams (D.-N.J.) *Cong. Rec.* (daily ed.), Oct. 11, 1962, p. 23174.

219. In 1961 the AHA witness noted, "Blue Cross plans have established firm relationships with hospitals." Hearings on H.R. 4222 before the House Committee on Ways and Means, 87th Cong., 1st Sess., Vol. 1, p. 252 (July 26, 1961). In 1963 Walter McNerney concluded that it would be "a great gain for the Government to put a consciously, socially oriented group between it and the provider of care . . ." 1963 House Hearings, Part 4, supra n. 209, at p. 2061. See also Hearings before the Senate Finance Committee on H.R. 11865, 88th Cong., 2nd Sess., p. 619 (AHA) and p. 337 (BCA) (August 1964). With respect to utilization review, an AHA witness noted that the only way the government could serve as administrator "would be by having some sort of governmental doctors going into hospitals checking on the records, and the difficulties that will arise from having the Government appearing to question or interfere in medical practice will cause considerable furor." *Medical Care for the Aged,* Executive Hearings on H.R. 1 and Other Proposals for the Medical Care of the Aged, before the House Committee on Ways and Means, 89th Cong., 1st Sess., Pt. 1, p. 287 (January and February 1965). See also BCA at p. 179.

220. 1964 Senate Hearings, id. at p. 337. 1965 House Executive Hearings, id. at p. 163.

221. See, e.g., 1963 House Hearings, Part 4, supra n. 209, at pp. 2054, 2072, 2039–77.

222. 1961 House Hearings, supra n. 219, at p. 253.

223. Id. at p. 263.

224. 1963 House Hearings, Part 1, supra n. 206, at pp. 363, 395–96, 408.

225. H.R. 3727 introduced by Rep. Herlong (D.-Fla.) and H.R. 3728 introduced by Rep. Curtis (R.-Mo.), 89th Cong., 1st Sess. These bills were identical.

226. H.R. 4351, 89th Cong., 1st Sess., introduced by Rep. Byrnes (R.-Wisc.).

227. H.R. 1, 89th Cong., 1st Sess.

228. The role of the carriers under Part B is different from that of fiscal intermediaries in several important respects. First, carriers are selected by the secretary, rather than by the providers. The secretary is required, to the extent possible, to contract with carriers to carry out the major administrative functions of the medical insurance plans, including determining rates of payment, holding and disbursing funds for benefit payments, and determining compliance and assisting in utilization review. Social Security Act, §1842(a), 42 U.S.C. §1395u(a). Second, while payments under Part A are made on the basis of reasonable costs, Part B payments for physicians' services are made on the basis of customary and prevailing charges. Hence the statute requires that the contract with the carrier provide that, where payments are made on the basis of charges, the charges must not be higher than those paid for comparable services for the carrier's other policy-holders and subscribers and that the carrier take into consideration the customary and prevailing charges in the area. Social Security Act, §§1842(b)(3) and 1861(v)(3), 42 U.S.C. §§1395u(b)(3) and 1395x(v)(3). Third, carriers under Part B are required to afford a "fair hearing" to any individual enrolled in the program when any request for payment is de-

nied or not acted upon with reasonable promptness or when the amount of such payment is in controversy. There is no comparable role for the intermediary under Part A. Social Security Act, §1842(b)(3)(c), 42 U.S.C. §1395u(b)(3)(c).

229. Social Security Act, §1902(a)(5), 42 U.S.C. §1396a(a)(5).

230. Robert Straus suggests that "the sociology of medicine is concerned with studying such factors as the organizational structure, role relationships, value systems, rituals, and functions of medicine as a system of behavior and that this type of study can best be carried out by persons operating from independent positions outside the formal medical setting. Sociology in medicine consists of collaborative research or teaching, often involving the integration of concepts, techniques, and personnel from many disciplines. . . . Research in which the sociologist is collaborating with the physician in studying a disease process or factors influencing the patient's response to illness are primarily sociology in medicine." Robert Straus, "The Nature and Status of Medical Sociology," 22 *American Sociological Review* 203 (April 1957). Eliot Freidson in *Professional Dominance: The Social Structure of Medical Care* (N.Y.: Atherton Press, 1970), p. 42, makes the point that the sociology of medicine has barely begun. See also H. E. Freeman, S. Levine, and L. J. Reeder, eds. *Handbook of Medical Sociology* (Englewood Cliffs, N.J.: Prentice-Hall, 1963); Steven Polgar, "Health and Human Behavior: Areas of Interest Common to the Social and Medical Sciences," 3 *Current Anthropology* 159–205 (April 1962). In the past several years, organizations have been formed that begin to give an independent focus to legal issues (Health Law Project, University of Pennsylvania Law School; National Health and Environmental Law Program, U.C.L.A. Law School) and consumer-oriented problems (Ralph Nader's Health Research Group).

231. For example, Walter McNerney was questioned on the ability of the BCA to control local plans, particularly with respect to racial discrimination. He replied, "If I could leave the question of the Negro to last," went on to assure the committee of the national capacity to control local plans, and never returned to the question of racial discrimination. 1963 House Hearings, Part 1, supra n. 206, at pp. 2061–62.

232. 1965 Hearings before the House Ways and Means Committee, supra n. 219, at p. 171.

233. Executive Hearings on H.R.1 and Other Proposals for the Medical Care of the Aged, before the House Committee on Ways and Means, 89th Cong., 1st Sess., pp. 160, 187–88, 245, 299 (January and February 1965).

234. Compare H.R.1, §1715(a), 89th Cong., 1st Sess. ("Any organization designated by providers for the receipt of payments"), with H.R. 6675, §1816(a), 89th Cong., 1st Sess. ("If any group or association of providers of services wishes to have payments under this part to such providers made through a national, State, or other public or private agency or organization"), 42 U.S.C. §1395h(a).

235. 39 *Hospitals* 21 (December 1965).

236. *Medicare and Medicaid: Problems, Issues and Alternatives,* Report of the Staff to the Senate Finance Committee, 91st Cong., 1st Sess., p. 113 (1970). In September 1970, BCA was acting as intermediary for about 90% of the hospitals and 60% of the extended care facilities and home health agencies participating in Medicare. The remaining participating institutions deal either directly with SSA or with nine other private organizations. General Accounting Office, *Lengthy Delays in Settling the Costs of Health Services Furnished Under Medicare,* B164031, p. 9 (June 23, 1971).

237. The contract provides for automatic renewal for successive two-year periods, unless either party gives notice of intention to terminate at least six months before the end of the contract period. Hospital Insurance Benefits for the Aged, Agreement with Intermediary Pursuant to 42 U.S.C. §1816, 1970, art. XXII. Hereinafter cited as BCA 1970 Contract.

238. "The structure of regulation is not a promising one. The first layer of regulation, private intermediaries, because of their relationship to health care providers and because of the way in which they are compensated (reimbursed for their out-of-pocket costs with no allowance for profit), have little incentive to exercise stringent cost and utilization control. The second layer of regulation, the Social Security Administration, lacks, and is unlikely ever to acquire, the resources that would be necessary to supervise effectively the millions of claims submitted under the program every year." The author summarizes, "The result has been recurrent waste and extravagance, sometimes bordering on outright fraud." Richard A. Posner, "Regulatory Aspects of National Health Insurance Plans," 39 *Univ. of Chi. L. Rev.* 1, 18 (1971).

239. BCA 1970 Contract, art. II, §L.

240. Id., art. II. §F.

241. Id., art. III, §B.

242. HEW, SSA, Audit Agency, Blue Cross Hospital Service Inc. of St. Louis, No. 10036-07, Nov. 30, 1970.

243. *Administration of Federal Health Benefit Programs,* Hearings before a Subcommittee of the House Committee on Government Operations, 91st Cong., 2nd Sess., Pt. 1 Medicare Program, pp. 95–97 (1970). An example of BCA countermanding SSA directives involved a request for local plans to submit all of their publications to SSA. Another example involved an SSA request for "information related to the problem of determining . . . the appropriate amount of owner's compensation, where the owner of a proprietary institution . . . determines his own salary."

244. BCA 1970 Contract, supra n. 237, art. VII, §B.

245. *Medicare and Medicaid: Problems, Issues and Alternatives,* supra n. 236, at p. 115.

246. BCA 1970 Contract, supra n. 237, art. XX, §A.

247. Id., art. XVIII.

248. *Medicare and Medicaid: Problems, Issues and Alternatives,* supra n. 236, at p. 115.

249. 1970 Subcontract between BCA and Blue Cross Plans, art. XXIII, provides that the secretary may terminate the agreement, if he finds that "(1) The Intermediary failed substantially to carry out this agreement, or (2) the continuation of some or all of the functions provided for in this agreement is disadvantageous or is inconsistent with the efficient administration of Title XVIII."

250. The statute provides that the secretary shall not enter into an agreement with any fiscal intermediary unless he affirmatively finds that "to do so is consistent with the effective and efficient administration" of the Medicare program. Social Security Act, §1816(b)(1)(A), 42 U.S.C. §1395h(b)(1)(A). The secretary can terminate an intermediary agreement if he finds "(A) the agency or organization has failed substantially to carry out the agreement, or (B) the continuation of some or all of the functions provided for in the agreement with the agency or organization is disadvantageous or is inconsistent with the efficient administration [of Medicare]." Social Security Act, §1816(e)(2), 42 U.S.C. §1395h(e)(2) (1969).

251. *Administration of Federal Health Benefit Programs,* supra n. 243, at p. 98.

252. The 1962 Task Force Report on the Use of Blue Cross and Other Insurers in the Health Insurance Program for the Aged stated that the authority of the secretary in making agreements with intermediaries "should be broad enough to negotiate for the selection of some components of a contracting organization but not of others. He must have recourse to direct Federal operation in any particular locality in the event that administration by a contracting private organization proves impractical for any reason." With particular reference to Blue Cross, the task force states, "It is assumed that the secretary would

be authorized to select the components of a contracting organization to participate in the administration of the program; thus for example, if the Blue Cross Association were selected as the contracting organization, the Secretary would not be obligated to accept all Blue Cross plans particularly those of small size or any others which for sound reason would not contribute to economical and efficient administration.''

253. The Senate Finance Committee Report notes, ''The arrangement under present law giving providers of services wide latitude in their choice of intermediaries was appropriate at the outset of the medicare program. As the program has matured, however, such unrestricted choice may be an impediment to efficient and economical administration. . . . Unrestricted choice interferes with the Administration's efforts to improve program administration by increasing the responsibilities of the most efficient intermediaries, while decreasing the roles of relatively inefficient intermediaries.'' Excerpt from S. Rept. 92-1230, Report of the Committee on Finance to Accompany H.R.1, The Social Security Amendments of 1972, IV, Provisions Relating to Medicare-Medicaid and Maternal and Child Health, 92nd Cong., 2nd Sess., p. 313 (1972).

254. Social Security Amendments of 1972, H.R.1, Sec. 286, amending Social Security Act, §1816(d), 42 U.S.C. §1395h(d).

255. Some informed commentators praise HEW administrative performance, and particularly the agency's lack of aggressive intervention in the private sector. For example, Anne Somers says, ''The exceptionally competent administrative leadership provided by the Social Security Administration and the lengths to which SSA went to avoid disturbing preexisting institutional relationships, to involve the maximum feasible number of nongovernmental units in administration, and to permit virtually complete free choice to all beneficiaries, have all contributed to [Medicare's] general popularity.'' Anne Somers, *Health Care in Transition: Directions for the Future* (Chicago: Hospital Research and Educational Trust, 1971), p. 60.

256. As of December 1972, HEW had issued 251 audit reports on the activities of the BCA and 74 of its member plans. Letter to author from an official, HEW Audit Agency, Dec. 20, 1972.

257. From 1967 to 1971, the staff of the Contract Performance Review Branch comprised approximately 35 persons and conducted 122 formal reviews of fiscal intermediaries.

258. In 1971 unofficial sources provided the author with Contract Performance Review Reports on the St. Louis and New York City plans.

259. *Dellums v. Richardson,* Civ. No. 181-72, D.C. Dist. Ct., filed Jan. 28, 1972. Plaintiffs included Congressman Ronald V. Dellums (D.-Calif.), journalist James Ridgeway, and the Health Law Project of the University of Pennsylvania.

260. Proposed regulation: 37 *Fed. Reg.* 17978, Sept. 2, 1972. Social Security Act, §1106(d) and (e), 42 U.S.C. §§1306(d) and (e) (1972). Both the statute and regulations require that intermediaries and providers be given 60 days to comment on reports concerning them before the reports are released.

261. It was expected that reports on all Part A intermediaries, including Blue Cross plans, would be completed by June 1973. Letter to author from an official, Bureau of Health Insurance, Jan. 1, 1973.

262. Excerpts from S. Rept. 92-1230, Report of the Committee on Finance to Accompany H.R.1, The Social Security Amendments of 1972, IV, Provisions Relating to Medicare-Medicaid and Maternal and Child Health, 92nd Cong., 2nd Sess., p. 278.

263. Report of the Conferees [to accompany H.R.1], Social Security Amendments of 1972, Report No. 92-1605, 92nd Cong., 2nd Sess., p. 1 (Oct. 14, 1972).

264. *Dellums v. U.S. Department of Health, Education & Welfare,* 2 CCH Medicare and Medicaid Guide ¶26,694 (D.C.D.C. 1973).

265. Social Security Act, §1902(a)(5), 42 U.S.C. §1396a(a)(5) (1969).

266. Social Security Act, §1902(a)(4), 42 U.S.C. §1396a(a)(4) (1969).

267. See BCA, National Association of Blue Shield Plans, *Special Title XIX Conference Proceedings* (Chicago, Ill., 1968). For example, in Pennsylvania, Blue Cross initially became an intermediary "because it stepped forward first and had close ties with the state." Interview by author with a former official, Pennsylvania Department of Welfare, May 28, 1971.

268. Louis Reed, *Private Health Insurance Organizations as Intermediaries or Fiscal Agents under Government Health Programs,* HEW, Office of Research and Statistics, Staff Paper No. 7, pp. 3 and 10 (1971).

269. Id. at p. 10.

270. "A State plan for medical assistance, which provides part or all of its medical assistance through contracts with fiscal agents, must provide that, as a minimum, the contract will:

1. Include the type of functions to be performed by the contractor, the amount to be paid the contractor by the State agency for performing the functions, the basis for the amount, and provision for renegotiation of the amount.

2. Provide that the contractor will make payment for medical care in accordance with the rules and regulations established by the State agency.

3. Provide for duly authorized representatives of the Federal agency and the State to be allowed free access to the contractor's expenditure records relating to the administration of the medical care program for audit and other purposes.

4. Include the period of time the contract will be in effect, together with provisions for termination."

HEW, *Handbook of Public Assistance Administration,* Supp. D, *Medical Assistance Programs,* §5520(B) (May 17, 1966).

271. 45 C.F.R. §249.82(b)(2), adopted 36 *Fed. Reg.* 3874 (Feb. 27, 1971).

272. HEW, *Report of the Task Force on Medicaid and Related Programs,* p. 70 (1970).

273. HEW, SRS, MSA, *Basis for Payment to Fiscal Agents for Administrative Services,* Tech. Asst. Series, No. 3 (July 1970).

274. Ibid.

275. Indiana Blue Cross processes and pays all claims for inpatient and outpatient hospital services, skilled nursing home services, and rehabilitation centers. Iowa Blue Cross processes and pays all claims for hospital and nursing home services. Capital Blue Cross processes all claims from hospitals and home health agencies in Pennsylvania, except for the southeastern area of the state. Minnesota Blue Cross pays all claims for hospital and nursing home services rendered by providers or to recipients in St. Louis County. HEW, SRS, *Characteristics of State Medical Assistance Programs under Title XIX of the Social Security Act,* MSA-PA49-71, pp. 100, 107, 168, 288 (1971).

276. *Basis for Payment to Fiscal Agents,* supra n. 273.

277. Kansas Blue Cross does only processing and not payment but also performs additional services, including provider audits, analysis of provider utilization review, and production of documents. Alabama Blue Cross processes and pays all claims, except those for Medicare deductibles and coinsurance, inpatient and outpatient hospital care, and skilled nursing home care. Vermont Blue Cross processes and pays all vendor claims, except those from skilled nursing homes and institutions for mental diseases. Massachusetts Blue Cross processes and pays claims for inpatient hospitalization, skilled nursing home care, and services provided by home health agencies (blind program only). *Characteristics of State Medical Assistance Programs,* supra n. 275, at pp. 7, 151, 346.

278. See, e.g., GAO, Report to the Congress, *Improvement Needed in the Administra-*

tion of the Iowa and Kansas Medicaid Programs, by the Fiscal Agents, pp. 56–57 (Oct. 20, 1970); HEW Audit Agency Report (Delaware Blue Cross and Blue Shield), Audit Control No. 10006-02, New York Region, Sept. 25, 1970; 2 CCH Medicare and Medicaid Reporter ¶26,334; HEW, Audit Agency, *Report on Review of Selected Audit Areas Grants to States for Medical Assistance Programs Under Title XIX of the Social Security Act,* Aug. 26, 1969.

279. Each of these problems was found in the Blue Cross administration of Medicaid in Kansas and Iowa. GAO Report, id., at pp. 14–50. Delaware Blue Cross and Blue Shield failed to make effective or timely hospital audits or to develop adequate utilization review prodedures. HEW Audit Agency Report, ibid.

280. See HEW. Audit Agency, *Report on Review of Selected Audit Areas Grants to States for Medical Assistance Programs Under Title XIX of the Social Security Act,* pp. 29–30 (Aug. 26, 1969).

281. HEW Audit Agency Report, Audit Control No. 10006-02, Sept. 25, 1970; 2 CCH Medicare and Medicaid Reporter ¶26,334.

282. California, Department of Health Care Services, *Report on Financial and Operational Audit of Electronic Data Processing Installations of Fiscal Intermediaries,* Joint Legislative Audit Committee, March 5, 1971, pp. 9–15; R. Fitch, "H. Ross Perot: America's First Welfare Billionaire," *Ramparts,* November 1971, pp. 43–51.

283. HEW Audit Agency Report (Nevada Medical Assistance Program), Audit Control No. 00127-09, San Francisco Regional Office, May 27, 1970; 2 CCH Medicare and Medicaid Reporter ¶26,338, p. 9895.

284. See HEW Audit Agency Report, supra n. 280; R. Stevens and R. Stevens, "Medicaid: Anatomy of a Dilemma," 35 *Law & Cont. Prob.* 348 (1970); Silver and Edelstein, "Medicaid: Title XIX of the Social Security Act: A Review and Analysis," 4 *Clearinghouse Rev.* 239, 305, 348 (1970; Silver, "Medical Care Delivery Systems and the Poor: New Challenges for Poverty Lawyers," 1970 *Wisc. L. Rev.* 644.

285. HEW monitoring consists primarily of reviewing state plan material and other written information submitted. A GAO study showed that from 1967 to 1970 only five field visits, of one or two days, were made to Kansas and nine to Iowa. The field visits "did not include comprehensive evaluations of the effectiveness of the programs or their administration." GAO, Report to the Congress, *Improvement Needed in the Administration of the Iowa and Kansas Medicaid Programs,* by the Fiscal Agents, pp. 56–57 (Oct. 20, 1970).

286. See, e.g., *King v. Smith,* 392 U.S. 309 (1968), *Rosado v. Wyman,* 397 U.S. 397 (1970), *Townsend v. Swank,* 404 U.S. 282 (1971).

287. See, e.g., *N.W.R.O. v. Finch,* 429 F.2d 725 (D.C. Cir. 1970), holding that welfare recipients have a right to intervene in HEW conformity hearings. See also R. Rabin, "Implementation of the Cost-of-Living Adjustment for AFDC Recipients: A Case Study in Welfare Administration," 118 *U. Pa. L. Rev.* 1143 (1970).

288. See *Bass v. Rockefeller,* 331 F. Supp. 945 (S.D.N.Y. 1971) 464 F.2d 1300 (2nd Cir. 1971).

289. P.L. 92-603, Title II, Sec. 231, Social Security Act, §1902(d); 42 U.S.C. §1396a(d).

290. 5 U.S.C. §8901 et seq. P.L. 86–382, Sept. 28, 1959.

291. 5 U.S.C. §8903.

292. §94X§2; 86th Cong., 1st Sess. (1959). See Hearings before the Subcommittee on Insurance of the Senate Committee on Post Office and Civil Service on S. 94, 86th Cong., 1st Sess. (1959), introductory statement of Sen. Neuberger, p. 2.

293. See Blue Cross comments on S. 94, Hearings before the Subcommittee on Insur-

ance of the Senate Committee on Post Office and Civil Service on S. 94, 86th Cong., 1st Sess., p. 112 (April 1959). See testimony of Douglas Colman, Vice-President of Blue Cross in Hearings before the Subcommittee on Insurance of the House Committee on Post Office and Civil Service on S. 2162, H.R. 8210, 86th Cong., 1st Sess., p. 106 (July-August 1959).

294. Letter of Aug. 5, 1959, to Tom Murrary, Chairman of the House Committee on Post Office and Civil Service, from the Civil Service Commission giving the commission's views of S. 2162 and H.R. 8210. *Cong. and Admin. News,* 86th Cong., 1st Sess., House Report No. 957, p. 2932 (1959). "The Commission assumes, of course, that the national Blue Cross/Blue Shield organization will be the prime carrier for the government-wide service benefit plan."

Andrew E. Ruddock, Director, Civil Service Commission, Bureau of Retirement, Insurance and Occupational Health, notes, "It is significant that the law was so written that Blue Cross/Blue Shield was the only carrier qualified to contract for the service benefit plan." *Administration of Federal Health Benefit Programs,* Hearings before a Subcommittee of the House Committee on Government Operations, 91st Cong., 2nd Sess., Pt. 2, Blue Cross-Blue Shield, p. 278 (1970).

295. 5 U.S.C. §8902(a). The regulations of the CSC provide that, at a minimum, a service benefit carrier "(b) . . . must have, in the judgment of the commission, the financial resources and experience in the field of health benefits to carry out its obligations under the plan." 5 C.F.R. §890.202.

296. The next biggest plan was the Government-wide Indemnity Benefit Plan (Aetna) with 16.3%; fifteen employee organization plans covered 15.6%; fourteen group practice plans had 4.7%; and seven individual practice plans had 1.9%. *The Federal Employees Health Benefits Program, Enrollment and Utilization of Health Services, 1961–68,* prepared by George S. Perrott, HEW, Health Services and Mental Health Administration, p. 4; data calculated from Reports to the Bureau of Retirement and Insurance, U.S. Civil Service Commission.

297. Hearings on Increase in Blue Cross/Blue Shield Health Insurance Premiums before the Subcommittee on Retirement, Insurance and Health Benefits of the House Committee on Post Office and Civil Service, 92nd Cong. 1st Sess., Serial No. 92-28, p. 38 (Dec. 1, 2, 1971). Hereinafter cited as 1971 FEBP Hearings.

298. *Review of Administration of Federal Employees' Health Benefits Program,* Hearings before the Subcommittee on Retirement, Insurance, and Health Benefits of the House Committee on Post Office and Civil Service, 92nd Cong., 2nd Sess., Pt. II, Serial No. 92-43, p. 63 (Feb. 22, April 26, 27, 1972). This means that FEBP subscribers pay proportionately more than other subscribers for Blue Cross coverage. See statement of Fairfax Leary at p. 137.

299. 5 U.S.C. §1803(1).

300. The functions of the CSC include contracting with the carrier, collecting premiums and remitting them to the carrier, promulgating regulations governing the program, which are set forth at 5 C.F.R. §890.00 et seq., developing and distributing educational material about FEBP for federal employees, auditing the financial operation of the program, and compiling financial and statistical reports. *Federal Role in Health,* Report of the Senate Committee on Government Operations, 91st Cong., 2nd Sess., made by its Subcommittee on Executive Reorganization and Government Research, Pursuant to S. Res. 320, 91st Cong., pp. 492–93.

301. The national plans contract with Group Hospitalization, Inc., the Washington, D.C., Blue Cross plan, to handle day-to-day administrative and clerical work.

302. 5 U.S.C. §8902(i).

303. Blue Cross/Blue Shield—high option family plans.

Date Years	Monthly Premium	Government Contribution	Employee Cost	Percentage Increase in Premium
1960–63	$19.37	$ 6.76	$12.61	—
1964–65	23.83	6.76	17.07	23.06/35.4
1967	28.30	8.88	19.42	18.8/13.8
1968	29.46	8.88	20.58	4.1/6.0
1969	35.23	8.88	26.35	19.6/28.0
1970	38.33	8.88	29.45	8.8/10.5
1971	47.91	18.72	29.19	25.0/0.9
1972 * (CSC)	64.59	21.30	43.29	34.8/48.3
1972 * (PC)	58.46	19.42	39.04	22.0/33.8

* 1972 rates reflect rollback of BC/BS premium by the Price Commission. *Review of Administration of Federal Employees' Health Benefits Program,* supra n. 298, at p. 131.

304. Ibid. Increases in the service benefit plan were greater than those in other health insurance programs available to federal employees. From 1960 to 1972, increases, overall and to federal employees, were:

	Overall	Employees' Payments
Blue Cross	202%	210%
Aetna	201%	209%
Letter Carriers (employee organization plan)	122%	80.3%
Group Health Assn. (group practice)	141%	125%

305. 5 U.S.C. §§8906(a) (1973 Supp.) and 8906(c) (1967). The government contribution is fixed at 40% of the average of the premiums charged by the six largest FEBP health benefit plans for their highest level of benefits. 5 U.S.C. §8906(a) (1973 Supp.).

306. 5 U.S.C. §8909(b).

307. 5 U.S.C. §8909(a). Net subscription income received by the Employees Health Benefits Fund is due and payable to BCA/NABSP 30 days after receipt by the fund and in no event later than 45 days following the end of the pay period to which the subscription charges are applicable. Subscription income is sent from the fund to the operations center at Group Hospitalization, Inc. (GHI) in Washington, D.C. A decision is made at GHI as to how much money is needed for daily disbursements. BCA/NABSP contract with Civil Service Commission, as amended, effective Jan. 1, 1971, art. IX(b).

308. 5 U.S.C. §8909(b).

309. 5 C.F.R. §890.503(c)(1).

310. *Administration of Federal Health Benefit Programs,* Hearings before a Subcommittee of the House Committee on Government Operations, 91st Cong., 2nd Sess., Pt. 2, p. 298 (1970).

311. CSC/BCA NABSP, Federal Employee Health Benefits Program, Contract No. CS 1039, as amended, effective Jan. 1, 1971, Service Benefit Contract, Schedule A, art. X, para. (b)(1).

312. Testimony of William E. Ryan, Senior Vice President, National Association of Blue Shield Plans, *Review of Administration of Federal Employees Health Benefits Program,* supra n. 298, Serial No. 92-14, p. 104 (April 21, 22, May 24, July 12, 20, 1971).

313. Testimony of Andrew E. Ruddock, Director, Bureau of Retirement Insurance

and Occupational Health, U.S. Civil Service Commission, 1971 FEBP Hearings, supra n. 297, at p. 32.

314. 5 C.F.R. §890.503(c)(2).

315. Since 1965, payments have been made each year from the contingency reserve to keep the cash and special reserves at required levels. *Administration of Federal Health Benefit Programs,* supra n. 310, at p. 292 (June 30, 1970). Testimony of Andrew Ruddock, Director, Bureau of Retirement Insurance.

316. Testimony of Andrew Ruddock, Director, BRI, *Review of Administration of Federal Employees Health Benefits Program,* Hearings before the Subcommittee on Retirement, Insurance, and Health Benefits of the House Committee on Post Office and Civil Service, 92nd Cong., 2nd Sess., Pt. III, p. 81 (Aug. 10, Sept. 13, 19, 1972). Hereinafter cited as 1972 FEBP Hearings, Pt. III.

317. Id. at p. 81.

318. Id. at p. 83.

319. Id. at p. 85.

320. CSC/BCA NABSP FEBP Contract No. CS 1039, as amended, effective Jan. 1, 1971, art. X, para. f.

321. *Review of Administration of Federal Employees Health Benefits Program,* Hearings before the Subcommittee on Retirement, Insurance, and Health Benefits of the House Committee on Post Office and Civil Service, 92nd Cong., 2nd Sess., Pt. II, Serial No. 92-43, p. 235 (Feb. 22, April 26, 27, 1972). Hereinafter cited as 1972 FEBP Hearings, Pt. II.

322. 1971 FEBP Hearings, supra n. 297, at p. 32.

323. The practice of Group Hospitalization Inc. of investing cash reserves in noninterest-bearing accounts of banks of GHI board members is discussed supra n. 142.

324. *Administration of Federal Health Benefit Programs,* supra n. 310, at pp. 236–83 (May 21, June 30, July 1, 1970).

325. CSC/BCA NABSP FEBP Contract No. CS 1039, as amended, effective Jan. 1, 1971, Schedule A, art. X, para. (a)(3)(A).

326. Id., Schedule A, art. X, para. (e).

327. 1972 FEBP Hearings, Pt. II, supra n. 321, at p. 157.

328. Id. at p. 158.

329. Id. at p. 62.

330. Id. at p. 158.

331. Id. at p. 159.

332. 1972 FEBP Hearings, Pt. III, supra n. 316, at pp. 29–30. Blue Cross administrative expenses under the Medicare programs, while lower than the FEBP costs, are not strictly controlled. See n. 444 infra.

333. Id. at pp. 89–90. The CSC pays a profit on all FEBP contracts with insurance companies, both profit and nonprofit, but not on the four self-insured union contracts. Id. at p. 100.

334. 41 U.S.C. §254(b) prohibits use of cost plus percentage of cost contracts by federal agencies. See *Washington Post,* Jan. 28, 1972, p. A1, col. 6. A spokesman for the Civil Service Commission said CSC attorneys had never considered the possibility that the contract was illegal.

335. 1972 FEBP Hearings, Pt. III, supra n. 316, at p. 98.

336. 1972 FEBP Hearings, Pt. II, supra n. 321, at pp. 113–14.

337. Andrew Ruddock, Director of BRI, said, ''We agreed to pay it to them because when the Congress in 1960 said in effect to the Civil Service Commission, you will contract for a service benefit plan and with specifications under which Blue Cross/Blue Shield was the only carrier that could possibly meet the intent of Congress and when we found that Blue Cross/Blue Shield applied by whatever term, something over and above expenses

with everybody it does business with—and this is true today in every one of its national insurance contracts—we agreed that we would do as any other large employer contracting with the Blues. We would not say, well, so far as we are concerned you will have to get your profit, risk, public service charge, contribution to capital, whatever you want to call it—you will have to get that from somebody else.'' 1972 FEBP Hearings, Pt. III, supra n. 316, at p. 91.

338. 1971 FEBP Hearings, supra n. 297, at p. 108.

339. Rep. Waldie questioned Andrew Ruddock on this point:

"Mr. Waldie: It is unhappy that you do not have a provision in the contract saying if this is a public service charge as contractor on behalf of the public, I want to guarantee that it is being used for public benefit. You do not believe that is any of your responsibility?

Mr. Ruddock: No, sir.

Mr. Waldie: Do you not believe they are trying to put a big facade upon this money by listing it as public service?

Mr. Ruddock: Yes, sir.

Mr. Waldie: You do? . . . Does that not disturb you?

Mr. Ruddock: Morally: yes, sir. In my responsibility for administering this contract, it does not bother me.''

1972 FEBP Hearings, Pt. III, supra n. 316, at p. 93.

340. *Council for the Advancement of the Psychological Professions and Sciences, Inc. et al. v. Blue Cross Ass'n Inc. et al.,* District Court for the District of Columbia, filed Aug. 16, 1973.

341. The actual deficit for 1971 was only $15.3 million. 15 *American Medical News,* No. 33, p. 8 (Aug. 21, 1972).

342. Letter, June 30, 1971, from Joseph E. Harvey, Vice President BCA/NABSP and Director of FEBP, p. 2. The primary factor in the underprojection and rate inadequacies in 1970/71 was an unexpected increase in utilization of outpatient diagnostic X-ray and laboratory procedures. (This letter and others concerning the 1972 rate negotiations are on file at the Health Law Project, 133 So. 36th Street, Philadelphia, Penn. 19174.)

343. Letter, Andrew Ruddock to Joseph Harvey, Aug. 27, 1971.

344. This amendment had initially been suggested by Blue Cross/Blue Shield in their June 30 letter. They offered to reduce their 1972 special reserve objective from one month's to one-half of one month's subscription income in exchange for a pledge of the contingency reserve.

345. See also letters from Ruddock to Harvey, May 26, 1971, p. 2, and from Harvey to Ruddock, June 30, 1971, p. 6.

346. The negotiations were called "cavalier horse trading" by the director of the National Association of Government Employees. 1972 FEBP Hearings, Pt. II, supra n. 321, at p. 49. Witnesses and congressmen expressed disbelief at the CSC's total reliance on Blue Cross data and the contract concessions granted. Id. at pp. 114–15.

347. The FEBP is no longer accurately characterized as an "insurance" program. Rep. Waldie notes, "What we really have here is a self-insured program. You have now guaranteed them recoupment of any losses and you have eliminated the risk. What is the difference? Why is this an insurance program if those two things are eliminated? Why do we pretend it is insurance?" 1972 FEBP Hearings, Pt. II, supra n. 321, at p. 114. See also 1972 FEBP Hearings, Pt. III, supra n. 316, at p. 89. (Waldie: "It seems to me we ended the insurance concept a long time ago.")

348. *Study of Financial Experience of Government-Wide Service Benefit Plan,* prepared by the Wyatt Co., Aug. 20, 1971, cited in 1972 FEBP Hearings, Pt. II, supra n. 321, at p. 263.

349. Telegram from Andrew Ruddock, Oct. 15, 1971, to all carriers in the Federal Employees Health Benefits Program. The guidelines required that new premiums could be increased using the existing formula to reflect experience on actual costs through August 15, 1971, or latest data available from that date. Anticipated cost or price increases beyond August 15, 1971, could not be used in calculating renegotiated premiums. Based on Phase I Economic Stabilization circular 102, Title 32(a) National Defense Appendix, ch. I, §4072.

350. Three factors are presumed to have been involved in the rate adjustment: (1) CSC did not permit recoupment of deficits; (2) CSC has said that companies must reduce their allowance for inflation to 62.5% of present forecasts; (3) insurance companies would not be allowed to pass on in rate increases more than a 2.5% advance in company-controlled expenses, such as administrative costs. *New York Times,* Dec. 23, 1971, p. 13, col. 5.

351. 1972 FEBP Hearings, Pt. II, supra n. 321, at p. 175. The Price Commission actuaries had originally recommended a 16% increase, and Blue Cross testimony was persuasive in obtaining the final 22% increase. Id. at pp. 144, 207. See also *New York Times,* Dec. 23, 1971, p. 13, col. 5.

352. Blue Cross/Blue Shield have a tendency to consistently overestimate projected deficits. Rep. Waldie summarizes:

> In December of 1971, Mr. Harvey wrote a letter to all Members of Congress to the effect that the 1970–71 deficit will be $68 million and that refusal of the [34%] increase in premium rates . . . would put your deficit at $146 million at the end of 1972.

> In a February 22, 1972 hearing of this committee, Mr. Ryan said that he agreed with that deficit amount but that it had now been revised down to a deficit, not of $68 million but of $45 million.

> In March—a month later—the Blues announced the deficit had actually been only $16 million.

> In the April 26 hearing, before this committee, Mr. Ruddock revised that estimate down to a $15 million deficit.

1972 FEBP Hearings, Pt. III, supra n. 316, at p. 24.

353. 1972 FEBP Hearings, Pt. II, supra n. 321, at pp. 76–77. A memo from Greater New York Blue Cross to all member hospitals advised them of the new policy, saying, "We have recently received a directive from the Administrators of the program requesting that we be particularly strict in enforcing those sections of the FEP contract under which benefits may be limited or denied entirely." Id. at pp. 110–11.

354. The new policy had a substantial effect on the number of claims paid in the latter half of 1971. 1972 FEBP Hearings, Pt. II, supra n. 321, at pp. 110–11.

355. The CSC and the Phase II Price Commission did not know of the new restrictions in benefits until the February 1972 congressional hearings. 1972 FEBP Hearings, Pt. II, supra n. 321, at pp. 74, 206, 209. A Federal Insurance Administration official testified that increases allowed by the Price Commission would have been lower had the existence of this new policy statement been known. Id. at p. 210. Another Federal Insurance Administrator said, "We think it is inexcusable that this 35 page document, which existed since June 1971, and even to the most naive observer would have to have a significant impact on claims, was not presented to every interested party, including the Civil Service Commission, the Price Commission, and us." Id. at p. 211.

356. Id. at pp. 69, 154–55.

357. *National Association of Internal Revenue Employees v. Blue Cross Association,* Civ. No. 909-72, D.C.D.C., filed May 8, 1972.

358. The settlement, reached in August 1972, applies to the 1.6 million federal employees covered by Blue Cross and Blue Shield and requires these two organizations to pay "all costs, including hospitalization, subject to a $100 deductible, for claims filed during 1971 and 1972." 46 *Hospitals,* No. 17, p. 180 (Sept. 1, 1972). *Washington Post,* Aug. 2, 1972, p. B13.

359. 1972 FEBP Hearings, Pt. II, supra n. 321, at p. 248.

360. 5 U.S.C. §8904(1) of the act requires that the service benefit program include six basic services: hospital benefits, surgical benefits, inhospital medical benefits, ambulatory patient benefits, supplemental benefits, and obstetrical benefits.

361. See HEW, Health Services and Mental Health Administration, *Towards a Systematic Analysis of Health Care in the United States; A Report to the Congress,* p. 12 (October 1972).

362. Under the act, federal employees must be offered both a high option and low option service benefit contract. 5 U.S.C. §8903(1). The options differ in the range of covered services, coinsurance, deductibles and dollar maximums, and subscription rate. Eighty-five percent of federal employees electing the service benefit coverage have chosen the high option plan.

For rate-making purposes the experience of both options is combined. The low option plan has had better financial experience than the high option plan. For example, in 1970 the low option plan had an operating gain of $8 million, and the special reserve amounted to $74 million at the end of the year. The high option plan had an operating loss of $59 million in 1970 and finished the year with a deficit of $50 million in the special reserve. Hearings on Increase in Blue Cross/Blue Shield Health Insurance Premiums before the Subcommittee on Retirement, Insurance, and Health Benefits of the House Committee on Post Office and Civil Service, 92nd Cong., 1st Sess., p. 32 (December 1971).

The value of the product being delivered to the low option subscriber, as reflected in the pure premium, has been consistently below the subscription charge. The pure premium value for the high option subscriber has been consistently higher than or comparable to the subscription rate. See *Study of Financial Experience of Government-Wide Service Benefit Plan* prepared by the Wyatt Co., Aug. 20, 1971, for the Civil Service Commission, Bureau of Retirement Insurance, p. 7 (table 1).

363. A similar problem exists under Medicare and is discussed p. 135 infra.

364. After the 1972 contract was negotiated, subscribers were informed that they had a right to an "impartial review by the CSC if dissatisfied with the final determination of the Blues on a denial of benefits." The CSC inserted this provision in the contract in response to congressional criticism. See letter from CSC to all FEB carriers, Aug. 10, 1971. The appeal right is meaningless, because the CSC takes the position that it has no right to overrule Blue Cross/Blue Shield in an individual case. If benefits are denied in violation of the contract, the CSC will "straighten things out" at future contract negotiations. The CSC sees its only powers as ones of persuasion. 1972 FEBP Hearings, Pt. II, supra n. 321, at pp. 152–53.

365. The only time in FEBP history when the CSC had independent actuarial information was when it hired the Wyatt Co. in 1971. The CSC does not audit Blue Cross/Blue Shield on a regular basis. 1972 FEBP Hearings, Pt. II, supra n. 321, at pp. 45–46.

366. 5 U.S.C. §8909(b)(1).

367. 1972 FEBP Hearings, Pt. II, supra n. 321, at p. 44. After the debacle of 1972, the CSC requested $2,422,000 for administration of the program in 1973. This was an increase of about 40%. Id. at p. 171.

368. 5 U.S.C. §8911 (1967). Members of the Advisory Committee must be enrolled subscribers or elected officials of employees' organizations. The members are appointed by the CSC, and its only powers are advisory.

369. The Advisory Committee meets only two or three times a year and does not perform a program review function. *Administration of Federal Health Benefit Programs,* Hearings before a Subcommittee of the House Committee on Government Operations, 91st Cong., 2nd Sess., Pt. II, Blue Cross-Blue Shield, p. 310 (May 21, June 30, July 1, 1970).

370. *Council for the Advancement of the Psychological Professions and Sciences Inc. v. Blue Cross Ass'n Inc.,* District Court for the District of Columbia, filed Aug. 16, 1973.

371. In general, see I. Wolkstein, "The Legislative History of Hospital Cost Reimbursement," in HEW, SSA, Office of Research and Statistics, *Reimbursement Incentives for Hospital and Medical Care, Objectives and Alternatives,* Report No. 26 (1968); N. J. Skidmore, *Medicare and the American Rhetoric of Reconciliation* (University, Ala.: University of Alabama Press, 1970).

372. Commission on Hospital Care, *Hospital Care in the United States* (N.Y.: The Commonwealth Fund, 1947), p. 174. See also Michael M. Davis and C. Rufus Rorem, *The Crisis in Hospital Finance* (Chicago: University of Chicago Press, 1932), pp. 109–15.

373. N. Sinai and O. Anderson, *EMIC: A Study of Administrative Experience* (Ann Arbor, Mich.: Bureau of Health Economics, University of Michigan, 1948), p. 57, cited in J. Thompson, "On Reasonable Costs of Hospital Services," 46 *The Milbank Memorial Fund Quarterly,* No. 1, Pt. 2, p. 38 (January 1968).

374. Id. at p. 39. In a 1947 editorial, *Hospital Management* said, "This rule is so reasonable, and yet so entirely unusual, that it struck hospital people everywhere as one of those wonderful things which somebody should have thought of much earlier." Cited in J. Thompson, supra n. 373, at pp. 39–40.

375. From 1950 to 1959 the number of Blue Cross plans paying retail hospital charges declined from 29 to 22. During the same period the number of plans paying a negotiated per diem rate, unrelated to costs, decreased from 25 to 8. By 1959 49 Blue Cross plans were making payments on the basis of "reasonable costs." Eilers, supra n. 15, at pp. 179–96.

376. Id. at p. 184.

377. AHA/BCA, Principles of Payment for Hospital Care, 1963, §§1.100, 1.200, 1.400, 1.500.

378. The section entitled "Determination of Reimbursable Cost" states that "the determination of reimbursable cost requires acceptance and use of uniform definitions, accounting, statistics, and reporting," and AHA publications "should be used as guides." Costs should be reimbursed according to some formula. Research expenses, not related to patient care, are not to be included. A "reasonable" amount for medical, nursing, and other education may be included in determining costs. "Bad debts, the unpaid costs of care of the indigent and the medically indigent, and courtesy allowances should not be included in reimbursable cost." Ordinary remodeling expenses should be included as an expense, but remodeling that enhances capital should be capitalized. "Depreciation on buildings and equipment . . . should be included in reimbursable cost, identifiable on the books of the hospital and acceptable for certification, and reimbursement for depreciation should be used for capital purposes." "Net interest at a reasonable rate incurred on capital or other indebtedness should be included in determining reimbursable cost."

The final section on "Obligations in Applying Principles of Reimbursable Cost Payment" requires that the hospitals and third-party payors cooperate in doing studies, share information, and cooperate with each other and other agencies. The principles conclude with the requirement that the method and amount of reimbursement "should be established by mutual agreement of the parties concerned and should be based on the Principles of Payment for Hospital Care." However, the comment to this section notes that "if

a hospital's costs or utilization depart substantially from other hospitals of similar size, scope of services and utilization, maximum reimbursement may be established through agreement reached between third-party purchasers and hospitals."
    379. Vocational Rehabilitation Act as amended. 1943, 29 U.S.C. §31 et seq. Reasonable costs. 29 U.S.C. §34(c), Act of July 6, 1943, ch. 190 §2(q), 57 stat. 374.
    380. Social Security Act, Title V, §§505(a)(6), 42 U.S.C. §705(a)(6).
    381. Dependents' Medical Care Act of June 7, 1956, ch. 374, 70 stat. 250 et seq.
    382. For example, $31 million in federal funds were paid under the Vocational Rehabilitation Program in 1956. Fifteen million dollars were paid under the Title V Crippled Children Program in 1957. A. Brewster, *Health Insurance and Related Proposals for Financing Personal Health Services: A Digest of Major Legislation and Proposals for Federal Action, 1935-57* (Washington, D.C.: HEW, SSA, 1958), pp. 40-43.
    383. In response to a question by Chairman Mills on how the government would determine reasonable costs, Robert Ball introduced the AHA principles, which he stated would generally be followed. Executive Hearings before the House Committee on Ways and Means on H.R.1, 89th Cong., 1st Sess., p. 142 (1965). See also pp. 145-51, 247-52, 293-96, 302-06. The AHA witness suggested that the reasonable cost provision be amended "to *require* the Secretary to consult *only* with the AHA" on determination of reasonable costs. Id. at p. 229.
    Before the Senate Finance Committee, HEW Secretary Celebrezze stated, "The reimbursement of hospitals by third parties on a reasonable cost basis has been the subject of extended and painstaking consideration for more than a decade, and principles governing such reimbursement have been developed which have been widely used and which have met with a large measure of acceptance." Hearings on H.R. 6675, 89th Cong., 1st Sess., Pt. 1, p. 95.
    384. See Somers and Somers, *Medicare and the Hospitals,* supra n. 187 at pp. 154-58. See also Wolkstein, supra n. 371, at pp. 6-10. The earlier King-Anderson bill had also called for hospital payments on the basis of reasonable costs. H.R. 4222 and S. 902, 87th Cong., 1st Sess. (1961).
    385. 1965 Executive Hearings before the House Committee on Ways and Means, supra n. 383, at pp. 138-51.
    386. Id. at pp. 139-40.
    387. Id. at p. 145.
    388. Ibid. See also AHA/BCA, Principles of Payment for Hospital Care, 1963, §3.4000.
    389. Ibid.
    390. Social Security Act, §1814(b), 42 U.S.C. 1395f(b) (1973).
    391. Social Security Act, §1861(v)(1)(A), 42 U.S.C. §1395x(v)(1)(A) (1973).
    392. Social Security Act, §1861(v)(1), 42 U.S.C. §1395(v)(1). The word "consider" was chosen deliberately. Wilbur Cohen stated, "it is true that the bill requires us to consult on the principles, but it doesn't say if it is necessary to follow them in every detail." Hearings before the House Committee on Ways and Means on H.R. 1, 89th Cong., 1st Sess., Pt. 1, p. 784 (1965).
    393. Social Security Act, §1861(v)(1)(A), 42 U.S.C. §1395f(v)(1)(A) (1973).
    394. Social Security Act, §1861(v)(1)(A)(ii), 42 U.S.C. §1395x(v)(1)(A)(ii).
    395. Social Security Act, §1861(v)(2)(A), 42 U.S.C. §1395x(v)(2)(A).
    396. Executive Hearings before the Senate Finance Committee on Reimbursement Guidelines for Medicare, 89th Cong., 2nd Sess., pp. 118, 120-22 (1966). Hereinafter cited as 1966 Senate Medicare Hearings.
    397. This report is printed in id. at pp. 2-40 (May 25, 1966).
    398. Ibid.

399. Id. at p. 43.

400. Herman Somers, "Medicare and the Cost of Health Services," in William G. Bowen, ed., *Princeton Symposium on the American System of Social Insurance* (N.Y.: McGraw-Hill, 1967), p. 124.

401. 1966 Senate Medicare Hearings, supra n. 396, at p. 69.

402. Id. at pp. 32, 45, 50.

403. Somers states, "Another review, in August 1965, just after passage of Medicare, resulted in a new affirmation." *Medicare and the Hospitals,* supra n. 384, at p. 156. It would seem more accurate to characterize the 1965 revision as a tailoring to the massive public funds available.

404. 1966 Senate Medicare Hearings, supra n. 396, at p. 46. See infra p. 66 et seq.

405. Id. at p. 60.

406. Sen. Douglas said, "I don't see how we can compel the Social Security Administration to revise its formula at this late date. I think we have to let them go ahead with what they have done. But I think there should be a public discussion of half a dozen points involved, and that sometime during the year the committee should . . . express its point of view, so as to be a guideline for revision." Id. at p. 122.

407. Dorothy Rice and Barbara Cooper, "National Health Expenditures, 1929–71," 35 *Social Security Bulletin,* No. 1, p. 11 (January 1972).

408. The Hospital Statement of Reimbursable Costs, Joint Form #1. Herman Somers, supra n. 400, at p. 128.

409. 20 C.F.R. §405.415(a)(2).

410. See testimony of Robert Meyers, 1966 Senate Medicare Hearings, supra n. 396, at p. 58.

411. 20 C.F.R. §405.415(d)(2).

412. 20 C.F.R. §405.417.

413. 20 C.F.R. §405.418.

414. Somers, supra n. 400, at p. 129.

415. Comptroller General, *Report to the Senate Committee on Finance on Payments to Hospitals and Extended Care Facilities for Depreciation Expense Under the Medicare Program,* B-142983, pp. 18–19 (Aug. 21, 1970).

416. Title VI of the Public Health Act, 42 U.S.C. §291 et seq. (1964). A 1964 amendment emphasized the need for metropolitan and area planning as well as planning on the state level and authorized $22.5 million over a five-year period for the cost of developing comprehensive area and regional plans. 42 U.S.C. §§291d(a)(3), and (4) (1964). P. L. 88-443, 78 Stat. 447, amending 42 U.S.C. §§247c, 291d (1964).

417. 42 U.S.C. §246.

418. See W. Dickey, J. Kestell, and C. Ross, "Comprehensive Health Planning—Federal, State, Local: Concepts and Realities." 1970 *Wisc. L. Rev.* 839; *Heal Yourself,* Report of the Citizens Board of Inquiry into Health Services, pp. 37–44 (1970).

419. Somers and Somers, supra n. 384, at p. 171.

420. Figures were arrived at by the following calculation:

   $4,442 million—total Part A Medicare payments
   $128 million—total Part B Medicare (outpatient reimbursement)
   $5,605 million—Medicaid

From 35 *Social Security Bulletin* 49, 50, 57 (March 1972). The total of $10,175 million × .06 = $610.50 million. The figures for Hill-Burton and Comprehensive Health Planning are from *Federal Role in Health,* Report of the Senate Committee on Government Operations, p. 206 (April 30, 1970).

421. 1966 Senate Medicare Hearings, supra n. 396, at p. 10.

422. Id. at p. 92.

423. Social Security Act, §1861(e)(9), 42 U.S.C. §1395x(e)(9) (1973). Where the Joint Committee on the Accreditation of Hospitals (JCAH) has standards on a particular subject, the authority of the secretary was limited. However, the JCAH standards do not go to the question of hospital coordination with area planning. See Joint Commission on Accreditation of Hospitals, *Accreditation Manual for Hospitals* (Hospital Accreditation Program, 1971). Also, the act has now been amended to allow the secretary to promulgate standards higher than those set by the JCAH. Social Security Act, §§1864 and 1865(b), 42 U.S.C. §§1395aa and 1395bb(b).

424. Report of the Senate Finance Committee to Accompany H.R. 6675, Sen. Rpt. No. 404 (June 30, 1965), reported in 1965 U.S. Code, *Congressional and Administrative News,* vol. 1, p. 1977. Senator Anderson said, "We ought to be able to say we are going to give you money for depreciation which you have to set up in a fund and plan for it properly and have your plans approved . . . If someone doesn't want to take the money on that basis, they can turn it back to the Federal Treasury. I would say when there is no prohibition on putting controls on these things, you ought to try to put it on, and let somebody take it into court and see if they can take it off. I think they would have a hard time doing it. But at least you would have tried to do something that is in accordance with ordinary, reasonable precautions." 1966 Senate Medicare Hearings, supra n. 396, at p. 113.

425. 1970 Senate Finance Committee Report, supra n. 236, at p. 53.

426. Id. at p. 53.

427. 20 C.F.R. §405.415(a)(3) (1971).

428. IV. Provisions Relating to Medicare-Medicaid and Maternal and Child Health, Excerpt from S. Rept. 92-1230, Report of the Committee on Finance to Accompany H.R.1, The Social Security Amendments of 1972, 92nd Cong., 2nd Sess., p. 185. Hereinafter cited as 1972 Senate Finance Committee Report.

429. The amendment authorizes the secretary to withhold or reduce reimbursement amounts to providers of services under Title XVIII for depreciation, interest, and, in the case of proprietary providers, a return on equity capital related to capital expenditures that are determined to be inconsistent with state or local health facility plans. (Similar authority is provided with respect to the federal share of payment for inpatient hospital care under Titles V and XIX.) Capital expenditures include expenditures (1) for plant and equipment in excess of $100,000; (2) which change the bed capacity of the institution; or (3) which substantially change the services provided by the institution. The secretary would act on the basis of findings and recommendations submitted to him by various qualified planning agencies. If he determines, however, after consultation with an appropriate national advisory council, that a disallowance of capital expenses would be inconsistent with effective organization and delivery of health services or effective administration of Titles V, XVIII, or XIX, he would be authorized to allow such expenses. H.R.1, §221, amending Social Security Act, §1122 (1973).

430. The Health Law Project questionnaire to Blue Cross plans, supra n. 146, asked, "As a matter of policy would you refuse to provide services to your subscribers at a hospital which had been constructed or expanded without the approval of the local planning agency? Have you in fact ever done this? Please describe the circumstances."

The BCA responded: "At the present time, 20 Plans have conformance clauses in their provider contracts that make the approval of a planning agency (for new building or expansion of facilities or services) as a condition of participation and reimbursement. If this condition is not met by a new facility, no contactual agreement is possible. If it is not met by an existing contracting hospital, its reimbursement level would be adversely effected [sic] for that portion of the facility. However, in the case of a new facility with which no contract is possible, 'non-member hospital' benefits (much lower) are paid on the subscribers' behalf. Very few Plans have been tested on their refusal to contract with a certain hospital. The most notable case involved the Michigan Plan, which successfully defended in court its Standards of Participation document and its right to contract with whom it sees fit. There are other examples of Plan refusals in California and around the country, but they seldom reach the courts."

431. For example, the Pennsylvania Insurance Commissioner required the insertion of a provision in the 1972 Blue Cross agreement with Philadelphia hospitals obligating the hospitals to seek approval of the local Hill-Burton agency for major construction or expansion. The planning agency is supported by contributions from hospitals that are reimbursed by Blue Cross.

432. Adjudication of Thomas Thacher, Superintendent of Insurance, State of New York, *In the Matter of Two Amended 1960 Applications of Associated Hospital Service of New York,* Sept. 12, 1960, p. 9. Cited in Eilers, supra n. 15, at p. 186.

433. BCA, Summary of Provider Payment Methods of Blue Cross Plans, April 1970. The BCA response to the Health Law Project questionnaire, supra n. 146, states that with respect to costs for private subscribers 41 plans require that depreciation be funded, and 28 plans pay accelerated depreciation.

434. 20 C.F.R. §405.428 (1971).

435. 1966 Senate Medicare Hearings, supra n. 396, at p. 56.

436. On April 20, 1968, the *Chicago American* reported that, "Bill S. Byrd, Chief of HEW's health insurance professional relations, speaking to the [nursing home administrator's] groups, had suggested that while neither profits nor interest would be allowed in payments for Medicare patients, sums formerly designated as profits might possibly be included in such items as administrator's salaries." Reported and discussed, 1966 Senate Finance Hearings, supra n. 396, at pp. 72–77.

437. 1966 Senate Medicare Hearings, supra n. 396, at p. 30.

438. Social Security Act, §1861(v)(1)(B), 42 U.S.C. §1395x(1)(B) (1973) added by P.L. 89-713, Sec. 7, effective Nov. 2, 1966.

439. The plus factor was condemned by the National Governors' Conference and the Advisory Commission on Intergovernmental Relations. See 1970 Senate Finance Report, supra n. 236, at p. 48. It was deleted in 20 C.F.R. §405.428, 34 *Fed. Reg.* §9927 (June 27, 1969).

440. The 8.5% nursing cost differential is allowed by 20 C.F.R. §405.430 as amended by 37 *Fed. Reg.* §10353 (May 20, 1972) for periods after July 1, 1969 (the date on which the plus factor was suspended).

441. 20 C.F.R. §405.451(c)(3) (1971).

442. HEW, SSA, *Health Insurance for the Aged,* Provider Reimbursement Manual, Part A HIM-15, §2138.1 and 2138.2.

443. Part A Intermediary Manual §1100. For example, membership in trade, business, technical, and professional organizations is an allowable cost, as are the costs of attending or conducting meetings for "the dissemination of technical information or stimulation of production." Id. at §§1152.1 and 1152.2. Legal, accounting, and other costs of professional services are allowed under general rules, e.g. "the past pattern of such costs." Id. at §1142. Labor relations costs, including "costs of shop stewards, labor-management committees, employee publications, and other related activities," are allowed. Id. at §1134.

444. *Health Insurance for the Aged,* supra n. 442, at §§2138.1 and 2136.

445. J. Seldin, "Blue Cross Pays the Bills," *The Nation,* July 14, 1969, p. 48.

446. Id. at p. 50.

447. *New York Times,* Nov. 3, 1971, p. 23, col. 1.

448. *Physician's Training Facilities and Health Maintenance Organizations,* Hearings before the Subcommittee on Health of the Senate Committee on Labor and Public Welfare, Pt. 3, p. 1039 (Nov. 2, 1971).

449. For example, a report of the HEW Audit Agency for the 12-month period ending April 30, 1969, revealed that 72 Part A intermediaries and Part B carriers had claimed administrative costs totaling about $38 million under Medicare. At 56 plans, the Audit Agency questioned expenses totaling $1,134,400. The report found that "Medicare was charged for employees who were not hired to work in Medicare activities, did not receive training for Medicare work, and did not perform work related to Medicare activities. In still other cases Medicare was charged for overtime work in amounts greater than the intermediaries had actually incurred. . . . Some intermediaries charged Medicare for the cost of first-class air travel even though less expensive air accommodations were available. One intermediary claimed a portion of the printing and mailing costs of more than three million contracts for its regular subscribers. Other intermediaries charged Medicare for entertainment, donations, and various other personal expenses." At 10 intermediaries, depreciation costs were questioned. HEW, SSA, Audit Agency, *Summary Report on Audits of Administrative Costs Incurred and Benefit Payments Made by Fiscal Intermediaries Under the Health Insurance for the Aged Act* (Feb. 5, 1970).

450. Extrapolated from figures in *Length of Stay in PAS Hospitals* (Ann Arbor, Mich.: Commission on Professional and Hospital Activities, 1970), pp. 4–5.

451. See Hearings before Senate Finance Committee on H.R. 6675, 89th Cong., 1st Sess., p. 351 (1965); Executive Hearings before the House Committee on Ways and Means on H.R.1, 89th Cong., 1st Sess., pp. 252, 295 (1965); Dr. Edwin Crosby, Executive Vice President, AHA: "The average daily cost for the aged is probably lower than the average daily cost for the acutely ill, the non-aged" and "If you get into the over 65, their average daily cost will apparently be lower in most instances than the others, because they will be getting room and board and nursing care, basically, rather than expensive diagnostic and the usual procedures. It will certainly not be open heart surgery."

452. Social Security Act, §1861(v)(1)(A), 42 U.S.C. §1395x(v)(1)(A) (1973). See also 20 C.F.R. §405.403(e).

453. 20 C.F.R. §405.403(e).

454. Hearings before the House Committee on Ways and Means on H.R.1, 89th Cong., 1st Sess., pp. 192–93 and 890 (January 1965).

455. Somers, *Medicare and the Cost of Health Services,* supra n. 400, at p. 125.

456. 20 C.F.R. §405.452(a)(1) and (2). For cost reporting periods before January 1, 1969, providers were allowed a third method of apportioning costs "based on the ratio of beneficiary inpatient charges to total inpatient charges applied to the total costs of all services." 20 C.F.R. §405.453(d)(4). This option was provided for hospitals that lacked the accounting capacity to utilize the other methods of apportionment.

457. For example:

Departmental charges to Medicare beneficiaries = $50,000
Departmental charges to all patients = $100,000
Departmental total costs (direct and indirect) = $80,000

$$\frac{\$50,000}{\$100,000} \times \$80,000 = \$40,000$$

Medicare dollar reimbursement for department = $40,000

458. For example:

Step 1
a. Total costs for inpatient routine services = $500
b. Total inpatient days = 10
c. Average per diem rate for routine services = $50

d. Total Medicare inpatient days = 5
e. Total reimbursement for routine services = $250

$$\frac{a}{b} = c \qquad \frac{\$500}{10} = \$50 \qquad \begin{array}{l} c \times d = e \\ \$50 \times 5 = \$250 \end{array}$$

Step 2

f. Total ancillary charges for all Medicare patients = $900
g. Total ancillary charges for all patients including Medicare patients = $1200
h. Total costs for all ancillary services = $1000
i. Total Medicare reimbursement for ancillary services = $750

$$\frac{f}{g} \times h = i$$

$$\frac{\$900}{\$1200} \times \$1000 = \$750$$

Step 3

Add Medicare reimbursement for routine services to Medicare reimbursement for all ancillary services (e + i) to arrive at the total amount reimbursable to the hospital for the "reasonable cost" of providing services to beneficiaries.

In this instance: $250   routine
                     750   ancillary
                   ─────
                   $1000   Total Medicare reimbursement

459. Executive Hearings before the House Committee on Ways and Means on H.R.1, 89th Cong., 1st Sess., Pt. 1, pp. 150–51 (1965).

460. Id. at pp. 144 and 148. The Senate Finance Committee Report notes that at some hospitals "charges are set according to prevailing rates in the area, or are based on other considerations and not solely on the actual costs of the particular items and services rendered. Except where a close correlation of cost and charges would be shown, other methods would have to be applied to achieve equitable reimbursement." Report No. 404, 89th Cong., 1st Sess. (1965).

461. "The need for other (non-medical) necessities is more or less regular and predictable: The consumer knows that he must eat a certain number of times a day and that he needs certain kinds of clothing. The need for medical care is, in contrast, irregular and unpredictable. Second, the consumer can exercise a good deal of control over the price he pays for other necessities . . . The costs of medical care are usually not within his control. The third, and perhaps most important, distinction between medical care and other goods or services is . . . the difference between a desired good and an undesired necessity." Feingold, "Medical Care for the General Population," in *Issues in Social Policy* (Englewood Cliffs, N.J.: Prentice-Hall, 1968), p. 172. Each of these points has especial force with respect to hospital services.

462. In addition to traditionally lower charges for obstetrics and pediatrics, hospitals have also undercharged for room, board, and nursing services and made up the difference by overcharging on ancillaries. Somers, *Medicare and the Cost of Health Services,* supra n. 400, at p. 127.

463. Somers and Somers, *Medicare and the Hospitals.* They add, "The word was out early that some hospitals were already redoing their charge structures to take advantage of the RCC formula." Supra n. 384, at pp. 168–69.

464. A frank article by a New York Blue Cross official in the official AHA magazine explains in simple terms that "the more charges piled on to Medicare patients or the fewer the charges to all patients in the hospital, the more money the hospital will receive. . . . . Who sets the charges in a hospital? The answer, of course, is administration. . . . One hospital in New York has been contemplating establishing a charge for the use of *bedrails* at *$10* a day. The charge would apply to all patients regardless of age. Of course, it is something more than a coincidence that patients 65 years old and over use bedrails more frequently than any other group of patients. . . . Most hospitals in New York charge $4 or $5 for a sedimentation rate test. One hospital making a study of its rate structure found that two-thirds of its sedimentation rate tests were given to patients 65 years old and over, whereas only one third of the patient days were for such patients. That charge for a sedimentation rate was raised to $12. One might ask why the hospital stopped at $12. Only its own sense of self-discipline intervened." J. C. Ingram, "The Case Against RCC," 41 *Hospitals* 38, 39–40 (April 16, 1967).

465. Chart, Ancillary Costs Computed by Combination and Departmental RCC Methods for the Same Hospital, in General Accounting Office, *Lengthy Delays in Settling the Costs of Health Services Furnished Under Medicare,* B-164031, p. 22 (June 23, 1971).

466. Wilbur Cohen of HEW assured the Ways and Means Committee, "We don't have anything to do nor is any authority given to the Secretary vis-a-vis charges." 1966 Hearings before the House Committee on Ways and Means, supra n. 383, at p. 139. And Mr. Robert Ball, "As far as charges are concerned—that is, what the hospital charges a patient who comes in and is not under the social security program—what they charge per day for a room, say is of absolutely no concern to us under this bill. . . . We will not reimburse on the basis of charges at all, but rather through the development of cost information from that particular hospital about the cost of services, not charges." Id. at p. 140.

467. The regulations state simply that "Implicit in the use of charges as the basis for apportionment is the objective that charges for services be related to the cost of the services." 20 C.F.R. §405.452(a)(4).

468. J. C. Ingram, "The Case Against RCC," 41 *Hospitals* 38, 39 (April 16, 1967). Misallocation can also result from incorrect attribution of costs. A recent GAO study of 14 hospitals showed that generally from 20% to 35% of the hospitals' inpatient costs and from 1% to 10% of the outpatient costs were charged to Medicare. Five hospitals used inaccurate square footage figures to allocate maintenance, depreciation, plant operation. Six hospitals allocated entirely to inpatient services personnel costs that should have been prorated between inpatient and outpatient. These misallocations had escaped Blue Cross audits. Comptroller General, Report to the Congress, *Problems Associated with Reimbursements to Hospitals for Services Furnished Under Medicare,* No. B-164031(4) (Aug. 3, 1972). 2 CCH Medicare and Medicaid Guide, ¶26,495.

469. Testimony of Thomas M. Tierney, *Administration of Federal Health Benefit Programs,* Hearings before a Subcommittee of the House Committee on Government Operations, 91st Cong., 2nd Sess., Pt. 1, p. 39 (1970).

470. HEW, SSA, Audit Agency, *Summary Report on Audits of Administrative Costs Incurred and Benefit Payments Made by Fiscal Intermediaries Under the Health Insurance for the Aged Act,* p. 14 (September 1969).

471. General Accounting Office, *Lengthy Delays in Settling the Costs of Health Services Furnished Under Medicare,* B164031, p. 28 (June 23, 1971). Hereinafter cited as GAO Report to the Congress.

472. Unreleased document dated Feb. 5, 1970, as quoted by James R. Naughton, Counsel to the Intergovernmental Relations Subcommittee of the House Committee on

Governmental Operations, *Administration of Federal Health Benefit Programs,* supra n. 469, p. 44 (Feb. 17, 1970). See also *Washington Post,* May 20, 1971, §G, p. 1.
    473. SSA comments on HEW Audit Report, supra n. 470 at pp. 6–7.
    474. Ibid.
    475. In 1967 the General Counsel's Office had questioned the legality of inclusion of costs of private rooms and delivery costs through the use of the combination method. When questioned about the SSA decision to retain the combination method, BHI Director Thomas Tierney said, "I made the decision. It had the approval of my superiors." He was asked, "Is it true that the Blue Cross Association in Chicago, after the 1967 letter by your General Counsel questioning the legality of this, recommended that its plans continue to use this method, which includes the costs of delivery rooms?" Tierney replied, "Not only the Blue Cross Association of Chicago, but the hospital systems of the Nation and all other intermediaries involved, as well as members of my staff were very much concerned that the elimination of this method would result in a substantial underpayment of hospital costs in the country." *Administration of Federal Health Benefit Programs,* supra n. 469, at p. 43.
    476. GAO Report to the Congress, supra n. 471, pp. 26–27 (June 23, 1971).
    477. Id. at p. 27.
    478. HEW Audit Report, supra n. 470, at p. 14. Thomas Tierney, Director of SSA's Bureau of Health Insurance, estimated in 1970 that only 8.2% of participating hospitals were using the departmental allocation method. *Administration of Federal Health Benefit Programs,* supra n. 469, at p. 47.
    479. In 1967 one intermediary wrote to BCA showing that a hospital would receive additional reimbursement of about $528,000 annually through the use of the combination method. The intermediary concluded that, "Because there is an apparent loophole in the Medicare method of reimbursement, this matter is being called to your attention for whatever action you might wish to take." GAO Report to the Congress, supra n. 471, at p. 23.
    480. Ibid.
    481. 20 C.F.R. §§405.452(c), 405.452(e)(2)(ii), and 405.452(e)(3)(iii).
    482. See *Administration of Federal Health Benefit Programs,* supra n. 469, pp. 33–35.
    483. 1 CCH Medicare and Medicaid Guide, ¶6049.
    484. GAO, *Evaluation of HEW Proposed Regulation Changes Affecting Medicare Reimbursements to Institutions,* Report to the Senate Finance Committee (March 24, 1972). The report notes that HEW has recognized that the actual cost differential between private and semi-private rooms is far smaller than the charge differential typically imposed. However, allocation between private and semi-private rooms based on actual cost finding in each hospital would add an administrative burden inconsistent with the Senate Finance Committee's expressed desire to simplify Medicare cost-finding requirements. The alternative proposed by the GAO is "to establish a standard private-room cost differential—based on a study of a random sample of hospitals—which could be applied uniformly by all hospitals on the basis of the number of their private rooms." If adopted, this proposal would eliminate the need for reliance on hospitals' arbitrarily determined room charge structure.
    485. 20 C.F.R. §405.430, adopted 36 *Fed. Reg.* 12606 (July 2, 1971), corrected 36 *Fed. Reg.* 13206 (July 26, 1971).
    486. Letter to author from an official, Bureau of Health Insurance, March 20, 1972; Letter to author from an official, AHA. The AHA study is reported in J. Thompson, S. Jacobs, S. R. Ratchin, G. Anderson, "Age a Factor in Amount of Nursing Care Given, AHA Study Shows," 42 *Hospitals* 33 (March 1, 1968); S. Jacobs, "Older Patients Get More Care," 43 *Hospitals* 68 (Dec. 16, 1969).

487. R. Rosenthal, *Experimenter Effects in Behavioral Research* (N.Y.: Appleton-Century Crofts, 1966).

488. A more recent study considers the relationship between nursing workload and length of hospital stay, indicates that there are reasons to expect nursing requirements to increase as the length of hospital stay decreases, and cites some studies to support the expectation. The study warns against placing too much reliance on the quantitative aspects of the studies, given their lack of objective means of measuring nursing needs. B. Moores, "The Effect of Length of Stay on Nursing Workload," *International Journal of Nursing Studies*, 81–89 (1970). Such a relationship between nursing workload and length of hospital stay may shed light on the relationship between nursing workload and age of patients. However, more study is needed in this area.

489. The Senate Finance Committee Staff Report in 1970 noted, "blanket recognition of increased nursing and clerical time should be avoided. It appears illogical, for example, to pay a plus factor for increased nursing time to institutions which do not fully meet the conditions for Medicare participation, particularly those with staffing deficiencies." Supra n. 236, at p. 46.

490. Phase II Guidelines limit hospital price increases to 6% of the previous year's aggregate revenues. 6 C.F.R. §300.18(c). Regulations and reporting forms contain provisions that allow adjustments to take into consideration fluctuations in the volume of services provided. The volume index formula allows a hospital to aggregate changes in prices and volume of inpatient and outpatient services. Outpatient services are both more numerous and inexpensive, and this aggregation of apples and oranges permits hospitals to greatly increase prices for inpatient care, while staying within the Phase II and III Guidelines through adjustment in outpatient volume and prices.

For example, one of the cases cited in a complaint filed before the Cost of Living Council showed that a New Jersey hospital increased its Blue Cross Medicaid per diem rate by 14.0% ($103.37 to $117.88), while its inpatient admissions declined by 14.0%. (Complaint filed by Gary G. Grindler, A. Ernest Fitzgerald, and Health Research Group, before the Cost of Living Council on Feb. 22, 1973, p. 8). The outpatient procedures rate increased 14.2% but comprised only 10 to 14% of the hospital's total costs. (Ibid.) When these figures were aggregated on the Phase II Reporting Form S-52 and adjusted by the volume index formula, the resulting price increase was only 5.39% (Ibid.) As of this writing no action has been taken on the complaint.

491. According to the American Hospital Association the surplus of net total revenues over total expenses in voluntary hospitals was as follows:

	(in millions)
1960	$116
1961	91
1962	−3
1963	131
1964	115
1965	227
1966	239
1967	340
1968	314
1969	400

Note the marked change beginning in 1965. Reported in H. Paxton, "Can We Stop Our Hospitals from Pricing Themselves Out?" 48 *Med. Economics* 79, 143 (Aug. 16, 1971).

492. N. Doherty, "Excess Profits in the Drug Industry and Their Effect on Consumer Expenditures," 10 *Inquiry* 19 (1973); *The Medical Care Industry* (N.Y.: Goodbody and

Co., 1969); *The American Health Empire,* prepared by the Health Policy Advisory Center (N.Y.: Random House, 1970), pp. 95–108.

493. See DuPont Walston, Institutional Research Report, Health Care, July 27, 1973, S and P 425: 123.23. This report summarizes, "The drug/health industry has distinguished and desirable characteristics for investment purposes: 1) Immunity to economic recessions from diversified consumer products marketed worldwide; 2) A high degree of earnings predictability; 3) Superior individual company and industry growth rates for sales and profits stemming from sophisticated technology and marketing; 4) Conservative, cash-rich balance sheets that provide financial strength for the future. The outlook for 1973 is one of earnings gains of 15% or better—the 25% increase in first quarter '73 profits clearly is not sustainable."

The following table demonstrates the relative performance in the stock market of drugs and industrials, 1965–73 (source: Standard and Poor's):

Year	S and P Indexes		Price:Earnings Ratios	
	Drugs	425 Industrials	Drugs	425 Industrials
1973	282.8	120.6	35	17
1972	213.9	122.6	34	19
1971	172.0	107.6	30	18
1970	144.7	89.3	27	17
1969	146.5	107.0	28	18
1968	125.7	106.6	27	17
1967	119.8	95.8	27	17
1966	98.9	89.3	23	15
1965	94.9	92.5	25	17

The DuPont Walston report also notes, p. 11, that "the pharmaceutical industry has clearly outperformed all manufacturing companies as to growth rates for sales and earnings as well as in profitability ratios."

The following table compares the net return on equity capital (source: Federal Trade Commission, *Quarterly Financial Report for Manufacturing Corporations):*

Year	All Manufacturing	Pharmaceutical Industry
1973 E*	12.4%	20.4%
1972 E*	11.5	20.0
1971	9.8	19.1
1970	8.7	17.5
1969	11.3	17.8
1968	12.8	18.9
1967	12.5	18.9
1966	13.4	19.8
1965	13.7	21.5
1964	12.4	18.5
1963	11.4	16.8
1962	10.5	16.4
1961	10.5	16.6

* 1973 figures are estimates. 1972 figures for the pharmaceutical industry are also estimates because of a change in FTC statistical sampling procedure and reclassification of companies due to their product diversification.

With respect to long-term prospects, the DuPont Walston report states, "Although projected revenue growth of the drug industry in the 1970s in the United States has been indicated within a 7% to 9% annual rate of gain by ICN Pharmaceutical Corp. and by the U.S. Department of Commerce, growth after 1976–77 could accelerate if public funding for a national health care maintenance system is established. Implicit is greater government pressures on pricing policy of drug manufacturers—*but volume gains could more than compensate for price concessions!*" Id. at p. 14.

494. Commonwealth of Pennsylvania, Department of Insurance, *Supplemental Guidelines for Inclusion in Blue Cross Contract with Delaware Valley Hospital Association* (1971).

495. Hospital Agreement between Participating Philadelphia Hospitals and Blue Cross of Greater Philadelphia, July 1, 1971.

496. HEW, SSA, Bureau of Health Insurance, Intermediary Letter No. 393. Subject: Identifying unreasonable costs—application of the "Prudent Buyer Concept."

497. The average yearly earnings in community hospitals in the United States increased from less than $1,500 a year in 1946 to over $5,000 a year in 1969. See *Basic Facts on the Health Industry,* Report by the Staff of the House Committee on Ways and Means, 92nd Cong., 1st Sess., pp. 54–55 (1971).

498. From 1955 to 1968 average labor costs per patient day increased 156.7% while nonlabor costs per patient day went up 179.6%. M. Feldstein, *The Rising Cost of Hospital Care* (Washington, D.C.: Information Resource Press, 1971), p. 17.

499. U.S. Department of Labor statistics show that professional nurses' wages have increased at a more rapid rate than lower-paid workers'. For example, from 1963 to 1966 national average wage increases were:

professional nursing	19.0%
clerical	12.5%
nonprofessional nursing	14.5%
housekeeping	16.1%

The Department of Labor does not have data on increases to administrators or professionals not on salary. See Department of Labor Bulletin #1688, March 1969, pp. 6–8; Department of Labor Bulletin #1409, September 1963, pp. 4–6.

500. Hart Committee Hearings, Pt. I, supra n. 121, at pp. 233–35.

501. Id. at pp. 237–41. R. Kessler, "The Hospital Business, Part 5: Pathologist Paid a Percentage of the Profit in Department," *Washington Post,* Nov. 1, 1972, p. 1, offers the following comparative statistics:

Test	Washington Hospital Center	Independent Lab A	Independent Lab B	Average Difference
Routine urinalysis	$ 5	$ 2.50	$ 1.00	186%
Complete blood count	7	3.75	2.00	143%
Pregnancy test	11	3.75	3.50	204%
Mono test	6	3.50	5.50	33%
Routine tissue	18	10.00	15.00	44%
12 channel (SMA 12)	25	5.00	5.00	400%

502. See Pathology Services, Standards I and II, pp. 1, 2, *Accreditation Manual for Hospitals,* prepared by the Joint Commission on Accreditation of Hospitals (1971).

503. *United States v. College of American Pathologists,* Civ. No. 66 C 1253, filed July 7, 1966, U.S. Dist. Ct. Northern District, Ill.

504. R. Kessler, "The Hospital Business, Part 5: Pathologists Paid a Percentage of the Profit in Department," *Washington Post,* Nov. 1, 1972, p. 1.

505. C. Hardwick and H. Wolfe, "A Multifaceted Approach to Incentive Reimbursement," 8 *Medical Care* 173, 186 (1970).

506. The 1972 amendments to the Social Security Act make some minor changes in the standard for determining reasonable hospital costs under Medicare. The amendment adds the underscored words to Sec. 1861(v)(1) of the Social Security Act, 42 U.S.C. §1395x(v)(1), supra n. 391. "The reasonable cost of any services shall be *the cost actually incurred, excluding therefrom any part of incurred costs found to be unnecessary in the efficient delivery of needed health services.*" Sec. 1866(a)(2)(B) of the Act, 42 U.S.C. §1395cc(a)(2)(B), is amended to allow hospitals to charge individuals for services furnished, after notice to the public and to the individual, where the hospital furnishes "items or services which are more expensive than the items or services determined to be necessary in the efficient delivery of needed health services."

The Senate Finance Committee Report indicates that under these sections HEW is authorized to "set limits on costs recognized as reasonable for certain classes of providers in various services areas." 1972 Senate Finance Committee Report, supra n. 428, at p. 188. This authority would be exercised on a prospective, class, and presumptive basis. The Finance Committee suggests, "Hotel services may be easiest to establish limits for and be among the first for which work can be completed." Id. at p. 189.

This vague amendment contributes little to the control of rising hospital costs. Examination of the pre-1965 legislative history shows that HEW has always had authority to exclude costs that were substantially out of line. Supra n. 387–389. Further, in an industry in which exorbitancy is the rule rather than the exception, disallowance of costs that are substantially out of line does not go to the main problem.

507. See Medical Committee for Human Rights, *Outlines of a National Health Plan* (February 1971). Available from the Health Law Project, 133 So. 36th Street, Philadelphia, Penn.19174.

508. "If hospital costs are not to go totally out of control, third parties must stipulate ahead of time the outer limits of reimbursement . . . The incestuous marriage between Blue Cross and the hospitals must be broken up. If third parties begin to protect their interests, I believe that the rise in hospital costs can be moderated." Dr. Eli Ginzberg, "Hospital Costs: Sense and Nonsense," 54 *Rhode Island Medical J.* 409, 411–12 (1971).

509. "It is evident, however, that beyond some point, reimbursement at cost offers no incentives to a hospital for achieving reductions in operating expenditures and no penalties for higher ones." Herbert K. Klarman, "Reimbursing the Hospital—The Differences the Third Party Makes," 36 *Journal of Risk and Ins.*, no. 5, p. 563 (December 1969).

510. Id. at p. 557.

511. A well-known proposition about hospital use, known as Roemer's Law, states that when hospital care is financed through prepayment an increasing number of hospital beds tends to be used whether the prevailing level of use is high, intermediate, or low. Max Shaine and Milton I. Roemer, "Hospital Costs Relate to the Supply of Beds," 92 *Modern Hospital* 71 (April 1959); Milton I. Roemer, "Bed Supply and Hospital Utilization: A Natural Experiment," 35 *Hospitals* 36 (Nov. 1, 1961).

512. HEW, SSA, Provider Reimbursement Manual, HIM-15, §§2400, 2409.

513. BCA 1970 Contract, supra n. 237, art. V, §3(A).

514. BCA 1970 Contract, supra n. 237, art. IX.

515. As of January 31, 1970, 16,240 Medicare audits had been completed. Of these 12,108 were done under contract with auditing firms, and 4,132 were done by the intermediaries. Thomas Tierney, testifying at 1970 Hearings, *Administration of Federal Health Benefit Programs*, supra n. 469, at p. 135.

516. HEW, SSA, Audit Agency, *Summary Report on Audits of Administrative Costs Incurred and Benefit Payments Made by Fiscal Intermediaries Under the Health Insurance for the Aged Act*, February 1970, p. 11.

517. Statement of Thomas Tierney, id. at p. 136.

518. Auditors employed by the HEW Audit Agency earn between $13,300 and $24,000 a year. Auditors employed under Medicare subcontracts earn an average of $15 an hour, with some earning over $50 an hour. Assuming a 40-hour work week, the *average* private auditor's salary would be $31,000 a year. Id. at p. 167. Despite the apparent high cost of private auditors, some intermediaries explain that the long delays in auditing result because "less-than-standard rates were negotiated with the public accounting firms with the understanding that the intermediaries would not require that Medicare audits be given top priority during the accounting firms' busy season." GAO Report to the Congress, supra n. 471, at p. 67.

519. *Administration of Federal Health Benefit Programs,* supra n. 469, at p. 141.

520. Social Security Administration, Bureau of Health Insurance, Contract Performance Review, St. Louis Blue Cross, August 31–September 4, 1970, at p. 3.

521. *Administration of Federal Health Benefit Programs,* supra n. 469, at p. 22. See also GAO Report to the Congress, supra n. 471. On Sept. 20, 1970, over 3 years after the end of the reporting periods for the first year under Medicare, final settlements for the cost of care had been made for only 68% of the hospitals included in the GAO study.

522. HEW, SSA, Audit Agency, Report on Massachusetts Blue Cross, Inc. No. 10092-01, May 1971.

523. HEW, SSA, Audit Agency, Report on Hospital Service of Southern California, No. 0005-09, April 30, 1970.

524. GAO Report to the Congress, supra n. 471, at pp. 15–18. SSA must approve subcontracts with auditing firms, and this has also caused delays. Id. at pp. 62–63.

525. Id. at pp. 38–46.

526. Contract Performance Review of St. Louis Blue Cross, supra n. 520, at p. 3.

527. GAO Report to the Congress, supra n. 471, at pp. 75–76.

528. 1970 BCA Contract, supra n. 237, art. II, ¶J. The Provider Appeals Committee is composed of five members, three of whom are representatives of BCA appointed by the president of BCA and two of whom are designated by the president of BCA from persons nominated by national associations selected by the president. A hearing may be conducted by, and the decision thereon rendered by, three members, but at least one of those present shall be a vice president of BCA. Temple University Hospital has challenged the composition and conduct of this committee as violative of constitutional requirements of due process. The suit alleges that the committee is not impartial, that committee members are briefed by BCA staff prior to the hearing itself, that the secretary of HEW abused his discretion in delegating final reviewing authority to BCA. *Temple University v. Associated Hospital Service of Philadelphia,* Civ. No. 7-3119, U.S. Dist. Court, E.D. Pa. 1971.

529. Social Security Act, §1878. This provision requires the secretary of HEW to establish a Provider Reimbursement Review Board to review disputes between an intermediary and a provider when the amount in controversy is at least $10,000 and other requirements are met. The board may also review disputes between an intermediary and a group of providers when the amounts in controversy aggregate $50,000 or more (even though each provider may be involved in a dispute of less than $10,000), common issues are involved, and the other requirements are met.

530. Mr. O'Leary, Chairman of the Massachusetts Rate Commission, explains, "Without in any sense suggesting wrongdoing on the part of these 11 men [representing providers]—many of whom are known to me personally as fine, honorable men who act only according to deeply held convictions—I believe their mere duality of roles weakens the resolve of Blue Cross in its dealings with hospitals. . . . I propose that hospital-connected persons be excluded from the governing body of Blue Cross, and . . . that instead, the Blue Cross legislation be modified to provide for a hospital advisory committee to Blue Cross." Hart Committee Hearings, supra n. 121, at p. 131.

531. BCA states that most plans negotiate with individual providers rather than with a hospital association but would not provide concrete information on this. BCA response to Health Law Project questionnaire, supra n. 94. Many of the major plans negotiate with hospital associations, including Philadelphia Blue Cross, Massachusetts Blue Cross, New Jersey Blue Cross. In Michigan, Illinois, and Washington, D.C., Blue Cross negotiates several standard contracts with the hospital association and then deals with individual hospitals to determine which contract each will use.

532. Statement of John O'Leary, Hart Committee Hearings, supra n. 121, at p. 133.

In the 1971 negotiations between Philadelphia Blue Cross and the Delaware Valley Hospital Council (DVHC), the state insurance commissioner insisted on a contract provision allowing reimbursement for depreciation only to hospitals providing a community service, such as emergency rooms and outpatient departments. Ten hospitals agreed to the provision and left the DVHC negotiations. A few days later the remaining hospitals got Blue Cross and the commissioner to agree to straight-line depreciation on all assets. The new provision was extended to all hospitals including the ten that had agreed to the original provision. "Hospitals Agree to Cost-Cutting Measures in Blue Cross Pact," *Modern Hospital,* October 1971, p. 40.

533. Associated Hospital Service of New York City negotiates with individual hospitals. One plan official indicated that while AHS has substantial leverage with respect to cost control in any individual hospital, it has not utilized this leverage in the past because if Blue Cross were to push too hard for reform the hospitals could mount organized resistance. In 1968, eight proprietary hospitals on Long Island banded together and threatened to dissociate from Blue Cross unless substantial changes were made in reimbursement. Blue Cross negotiated changes to the satisfaction of the hospitals. Interview with Paul Tully, Health Law Project, July 16, 1971. The New York Cost Control Law, infra p. 104, now provides some leverage and duty for AHS control of hospital costs.

534. *Mass. Gen. Laws* ch. 176A, §5, as amended by St. 1969, §1, approved, Aug. 29, 1969.

535. Statement of the Massachusetts Hospital Association, reported in Hart Committee Hearings, supra n. 121, at p. 128.

536. Statement of John O'Leary, Chairman, Mass. Rate Setting Commission, id. at p. 129.

537. Id. at p. 130.

538. *Philadelphia Inquirer,* March 18, 1971, p. 1, col. 8. The guidelines of the Pennsylvania insurance commissioner are available from his office in Harrisburg, Pa. or from the Health Law Project, 133 So. 36th St., Phila., Pa. 19174.

In requiring renegotiation of the contract, Commissioner Dennenberg said, "When an insurance commissioner agreed to give away the subscribers' money, Blue Cross would spend it, and the hospitals would gobble it up as fast as it became available." *Modern Hospital* June 1971, p. 33. "We are literally committing murder when we waste money which might otherwise buy life-saving medical and hospital care. We are not only throwing away money on our wasteful medical system—we are throwing away our most valuable and irreplaceable possession—the life and health of our people." Statement at Hearings on the Application for a Rate Increase by Blue Cross of Lehigh Valley, April 19, 1971, p. 1.

539. "Blue Cross May Up Rate Despite Pact," *Philadelphia Inquirer,* March 15, 1972, p. 57, col. 6.

540. Agreement between Philadelphia Blue Cross and Participating Hospitals, July 1, 1971, Sec. 2.3. See p. 129 infra.

541. Id. at Sec. 11.1.

542. Id. at Sec. 18.1.

543. The agreement provides, Sec. 28, that "Provider and Blue Cross mutually agree

that the public at large has a significant and continuing interest in the development of an effective, cost-efficient medical service program which is responsive to consumer needs. To ensure that the public is advised of the plans, programs and undertakings of both the Provider and Blue Cross, each party agrees that during the term of this Agreement they shall individually make available information relating to costs, facilities, services available and other pertinent financial and statistical data with respect to their own operations, and continue appropriate measures to assure adequate consumer participation in their respective activities.''

544. It is estimated that the new provisions of the contract cut the rate of increase of hospital costs for Philadelphia Blue Cross subscribers by 50% and saved the plan over 55 million dollars a year. "Blue Cross May Up Rate Despite Pact," *Philadelphia Inquirer,* March 15, 1972. p. 57, col. 6. Furthermore, the year 1972 evidenced "a new element of judiciousness on the part of both physicians and patients in the use of hospitalization." *Annual Report '72,* Blue Cross of Greater Philadelphia, p. 1. In 1972, Philadelphia Blue Cross hospital claims increased by only 2.5%, compared to an increase of almost 16% for 1971 and 25% for 1970. Ibid. This slow-down was accomplished in part by an increase in the ratio of outpatient to inpatient cases. Ibid., p. 2. Blue Cross believes that the "beneficial reductions, which have eliminated some of the unnecessary and costly care, were directly influenced by the new hospital contract." Ibid., p. 1.

545. Supra n. 94.

546. 1970 Senate Finance Committee Report, supra n. 236, at p. 116.

547. See "Dual Track: Social Inequality in the Urban Teaching Hospital," Paper on file at the Health Law Project, 133 S. 36th Street, Philadelphia, Penn. 19174.

548. In 1961 31.4% of the accommodations in community hospitals were in rooms of 3 or more beds. In 1972, only 20.1% of the accommodations were in such rooms. Letter to author from an official, AHA, Sept. 6, 1972.

549. "Dual Track: Social Inequality in the Urban Teaching Hospital," supra n. 547.

550. Delays in Medicaid payments are common. Medicaid often does not provide advance payments on the basis of estimated costs, as does Medicare. See "Medicaid: The Patchwork Crazy Quilt," 5 *Col. J. of L. and Social Probs.* 62, 82 (1969). See also *Meyers v. Massachusetts Eye & Ear Infirmary,* 300 F. Supp. 1328 (D. Mass. 1971).

551. Blue Cross also gives lower priority to the auditing of nursing home cost reports. The justification offered for this is that hospitals do a larger dollar volume of business. GAO Report to the Congress, supra n. 471, at pp. 77–80.

552. Social Security Act, §1902(a)(13)(B), 42 U.S.C. §1396(a)(13)(B).

553. Social Security Act, §1902(a)(13)(D), 42 U.S.C. §1396(a)(13)(D) said that the state plan must provide: "for payment of the reasonable cost (as determined in accordance with standards approved by the Secretary and included in the plan) of inpatient hospital services provided under the plan."

554. 45 C.F.R. §250.30(b)(1)(i).

555. Ibid.

556. HEW, Report of the Task Force on Medicaid and Related Programs, p. 8 (1970). See also *Heal Yourself,* Report of the Citizens Board of Inquiry into Health Services for Americans, p. 35 (1970).

557. *Catholic Medical Center v. Rockefeller,* 305 F. Supp. 1256 (E.D.N.Y. 1969), vacated and remanded, 397 U.S. 820 (1970), order reentered, 305 F. Supp. 1268 (E.D.N.Y. 1970), affirmed per curiam 430 F.2d 1297 (2nd Cir. 1970), appeal dismissed, 400 U.S. 931 (1970).

558. For example, in response to efforts by poor people to enforce the requirement of the Hill-Burton Act that hospitals receiving construction funds under that act provide a reasonable volume of free or below cost care to persons unable to pay, hospital adminis-

trators frequently cite inadequate Medicaid payments as a form of below cost hospital care to the poor. See Defendant Answers, in *Cook v. Ochsner Hosp.* 319 F. Supp. 603 (E.D.La. 1970). Testimony of the Colorado Hospital Assn. before the Colorado Board of Health Hearings on the Hospital Survey and Construction Act, Sept. 15, 1971.

559. In response to a Senate staff questionnaire, 11 state governors said that tying Medicaid reimbursement to Medicare standards imposed no unreasonable burdens, while 26 governors said that it did. Massachusetts objected that "the payment of full costs is in effect a blank check to hospitals to meet any cost they may undertake." Rhode Island said, "because of the two percent incentive and depreciation allowance the State in most cases pays over one hundred percent of changes." Hawaii said, "States are subjected to payments exceeding 100 percent of the cost at times and this method of reimbursement neither encourages provider institutions to practice economy of operations nor insures high quality care." 1970 Senate Finance Committee Report, supra n. 236, at p. 51.

560. *Intergovernmental Problems in Medicaid,* Report of the Advisory Commission on Intergovernmental Relations, pp. 73–75 (September 1968).

561. 1970 Senate Finance Committee Report, supra n. 236, at p. 50.

562. See R. Duff and A. Hollingshead, *Sickness and Society* (N.Y.: Harper & Row, 1968), p. 152.

563. 45 C.F.R. §250.30(b), 35 *Fed. Reg.* 21591 (Nov. 11, 1971).

564. Social Security Act, §1902(a)(13)(D), 42 U.S.C. §1396(a)(13)(D).

565. 38 *Fed. Reg.* 25450, Sept. 13, 1973. The author does not understand the purpose of the proposed regulations. Why would a hospital choose to set its customary charges at a level below reasonable costs and thereby suffer a loss in Medicaid payments? Under the proposed regulations hospitals retain autonomy in setting their charges, and the regulations make provision for retroactive adjustment where hospital charges in past years were less than reasonable costs.

566. The 1967 National Conference on Medical Costs concluded that "Cost-based reimbursement to hospitals is an open-ended invitation to increase expenditures. The development of satisfactory alternate methods of reimbursement is enormously complicated by the fact that the end products of improved health and quality care have thus far defied logical measurement. However, there was no dissent from the view that measures of quality must be found that will permit the development of cost-saving incentives and stop paying for whatever inefficiencies may exist." *Intergovernmental Problems in Medicaid,* Report of the Advisory Commission on Intergovernmental Relations, p. 74. (September 1968).

HEW's 1966 report to the President on Medical Care Prices stated, "The present Medicare reimbursement scheme, based on 'reasonable cost,' does not provide hospitals and other health facilities with adequate incentive to be efficient. The Medicare and Title XIXI reimbursement formulas, as well as the reimbursement formulas of some private insurance plans, tend to maintain institutions that are inefficient in size, plant layout, and equipment."

See A. R. Somers, *Hospital Regulation: The Dilemma of Public Policy* (Princeton, N.J.: Princeton University, Industrial Relations Section, 1969): "Reimbursement Incentives for Hospital and Medical Care," Research Report No. 26, Office of Research and Statistics, 35 *Social Security Bulletin,* No. 1, p. 9 (January 1972). See also *Hospitals, Journal of the American Hospital Association,* Guide Issue, p. 460 (1971).

567. P.L. 90-249, §402(a)(3), Social Security Amendments of 1968.

568. Only five programs were established under this section. The general approach is to guarantee reimbursement under existing payment formulas and pay institutions that effectuate economies a bonus over and above their costs. One demonstration was conducted by the Connecticut Hospital Association in conjunction with the local Blue Cross, with 17

hospitals participating. Each hospital department submits its budget for approval by a Budget Approval Board. If the cost for any department falls more than 10% below the cost of the same department in other hospitals, then the hospital receives the budgeted amount plus 2% of year-end costs as a reward or incentive. If a department's costs are above average, it still receives its costs. However, the experiment has not worked as planned, because the accounting procedures required were so complex that accounting costs exceeded the 2% bonus incentive, and in 1972 audits had been completed for only the first of three years' data.

A second experiment conducted by California Blue Cross/Blue Shield, Medi-Cal, and 25 participating hospitals uses industrial engineering techniques to cut costs by increasing labor productivity. A third project involves New York's Health Insurance Program (HIP) and includes 9 HIP groups and 6 hospitals providing Medicare services through prepaid group practice. Medicare provides an initial capitation payment, and if HIP utilization and cost experience is less than the general Medicare community HIP is paid the difference or a supplemental capitation. HIP is an innovative means of organizing health services, but it was so wholly apart from the influence of Medicare. Interview, Carl Slutter, SSA, BHI, Program Experiments Section.

In a fourth experimental project about one-third of the hospitals in Maryland participate in a program under which consulting services are offered to individual hospital departments that have high costs. The experimental program of the Birmingham Regional Hospital Association pools groups of hospitals by size and encourages them to share "innovative" programs. Eventually it is hoped to lead to joint purchasing arrangements and a pooling of resources. Interview, Howard Jackson, SSA, BHI, Projects Experiment Section.

See also *Reimbursing Hospitals on Inclusive Rates,* The Boston Consulting Group, Boston, Mass., Contract HSM 110-70-53, National Center for Health Services Research and Development.

569. Social Security Act, §222(a)(1). See 1972 Senate Finance Committee Report, supra n. 478, at pp. 224–26.

570. New York, New Jersey, Massachusetts, Maryland, Rhode Island, Arizona, and California have cost control legislation. See "Survey of State Laws Regulating Hospital Costs," *Hospital Week,* Nov. 5, 1971.

571. See C. Hardwick and H. Wolfe, "A Multifaceted Approach to Incentive Reimbursement," 7 *Medical Care* 173 (1970).

572. The act was passed in 1969 with the cooperation and support of the New York Hospital Association. The N.Y. State Department of Health actively sought the cooperation of the Hospital Association and obtained it, in part, because of a promise of liberal administration of the current payments provisions of the Medicaid freeze legislation that was subsequently struck down by the U.S. Supreme Court. See supra n. 557. Interview by P. Tully with an official, Associated Hospital Service of New York, July 16, 1971.

573. *N.Y. Pub. Health Law* §2807(2) (Supp. 1973).

574. Id. at §2807(3).

575. Ibid.

576. Title 10, New York Code Rules and Regulations (NYCRR), Parts 86.15 and 86.16.

577. 10 NYCRR 86.13.

578. 10 NYCRR 86.11 and 86.(14).

579. 10 NYCRR 86.15(b). Some price guidelines used for various items are the New York State Department of Civil Service Annual Salary Survey of Hospitals, the U.S. Department of Labor, Bureau of Labor Statistics, the Wholesale Price Index, the Consumer Price Index, and Geographical Price Differentials.

580. 10 NYCRR 86.14(b).

581. Greater New York's Blue Cross, Associated Hospital Service of New York, *Plan for Changes in Rates and Benefits,* sec. A, table 1 (unpublished report, Dec. 21, 1970).

582. Letter to author from an official, Associated Hospital Service of New York. The low rate for payments to teaching hospitals was $88.84.

583. "Corpus Delecti—Hospitals' Corporation," *Health/Pac Bulletin,* December 1971, pp. 1, 8, 9; M. Tolchin, "The Changing City: A Medical Challenge," *New York Times,* June 2, 1969.

584. *New York Times,* Sept. 24, 1972, p. 62, col. 1.

585. "The problem is not that anybody is selfish or antisocial but that under the changed circumstances of prepayment financing the individual hospital's interests and the social interest no longer jibe." H. E. Klarman, "Reimbursing the Hospital—the Differences the Third Party Makes," 36 *J. of Risk and Ins.* 553, 557 (1969).

586. Incentives "might save money; but at best it would have no effect on the patterns of care in the institutions, on the relations of the institution to the community, on the quality of care, etc. In fact unless very stringent community controls were introduced, the likely result would be that the hospital would cut down on service in order to save money and pick up its incentive reward." J. Ehrenreich and O. Fein, "National Health Insurance: The Great Leap Sideways," *Social Policy,* January 1971, pp. 5, 9.

587. H.R.1, Sec. 223(a), amends the previous language of §1861(v)(1) of the act, "the reasonable cost of any service shall be determined in accordance with regulations" to read "The reasonable cost of any services shall be the cost actually incurred excluding therefrom any part of incurred costs found to be unnecessary in the efficient delivery of needed health services, and shall be determined in accordance with regulations."

This language does not require incentive reimbursement, but legislative history explains that the amendment gives the secretary authority to approve costs on a "prospective rather than retroactive basis." Report of the House Committee on Ways and Means, House Rpt. No. 92-231, 92nd Cong., 1st Sess., pp. 83–84 (1971). 1972 Senate Finance Committee Report, supra n. 428, at p. 187.

588. "While it is clear, for example, that prospective rate setting will provide incentives for health care institutions to keep costs at a level no higher than the rates set, it is not clear that the rates set would result in Government reimbursement at levels lower than, or even as low as, that which would result under the present retroactive cost finding approach. Providers could be expected to press for a rate that would cover all the costs, including research costs and bad debts, as well as margins of safety in the prospective rates that might result in reimbursement—if their requests were met—in excess of the costs that would have been reimbursed under the present approach. Moreover, any excess of reimbursement over costs to voluntary providers would probably be used to expand services, and the new level of expenditures might be reflected in setting higher prospective rates for future years." 1972 Senate Finance Committee Report, supra n. 428, at p. 224.

589. "Also to be considered is the fact that under prospective reimbursement it will be necessary to take steps to assure that providers do not cut back on services necessary to quality care in order to keep actual costs down and thus increase the difference between costs and the prospective rate established. The development of adequate and widely-agreed-upon measures of quality of care will clearly be needed to provide that assurance and should be immediately developed by the Department." Id. at p. 525.

590. Note, "The Role of Prepaid Group Practice in Relieving the Medical Care Crisis," 84 *Harv. L. Rev.* 887 (1971); R. Holley and R. Carlson, "The Legal Context for the Development of Health Maintenance Organizations," 24 *Stanford L. Rev.* 644 (1972); *State Laws Affecting the Establishment of Health Maintenance Organizations* (Minneapolis, Minn.: Institute for Interdisciplinary Studies, American Rehabilitation Founda-

tion, 1971). *Health Maintenance Organizations,* Senate Finance Committee Staff Questions with Responses of the Department of Health, Education and Welfare, CCH Medicare and Medicaid Guide, Supp. No. 51, Oct. 8, 1971; A. Somers, *The Kaiser Permanente Medical Care Program: A Symposium* (N.Y.: The Commonwealth Fund, 1971).

591. GAO Report to the Congress, *Study of Health Facilities Construction Costs,* pp. 25–27, 75–83 (1972). Hereinafter cited as 1972 GAO Report.

592. For example, the Health Insurance Plan of Greater New York provides comprehensive outpatient benefits, and persons enrolled have a hospital utilization rate well below that of comparable groups without outpatient coverage. However, since HIP does not own its own hospitals, HIP subscribers purchase Blue Cross for hospital coverage. As a result of this bifurcation of benefit coverage, HIP has found it difficult to operate an economically sound program. Interview, Dr. Harry Becker, Health Economist, Albert Einstein College of Medicine, March 15, 1971. 1972 GAO Report, supra n. 591, at pp. 81–82. "HIP's Troubles: Is the Cure Worse Than . . . ?" *New York Times,* April 30, 1972, Sec. 4, p. 9, col. 1.

593. C. Havighurst, "Health Maintenance Organizations and the Market for Health Services," 35 *Law and Cont. Prob.* 716 (1970). Hereinafter cited as Havighurst.

594. 1972 GAO Report, supra n. 591, at pp. 5, 10–11.

595. L. Bellin, "Realpolitik in the Health Care Area, Standard Setting of Professional Services," 59 *Am. Jour. of Pub. Health,* No. 5, p. 820 (May 1969).

596. Member groups of Kaiser-Permanente, particularly labor union groups, have pressed for Kaiser to allow them representation on the board of directors. So far they have had no success. Members are not provided with information about impending rate increases. Frank Jones, Kaiser executive, says, "I can see how members would want to be better informed, but the budgeting process we go through isn't completed until late in the year. Once our projected operating costs are figured, we stack them up against the anticipated dues structure. If the expenditures are greater than the dues, then it means we must have a dues increase." G. Williams, "Kaiser, What Is It? How Does It Work? Why Does It Work?" *Modern Hospital,* February 1971, p. 87. Of course, the budgeting process is not as mechanistic as the description indicates but rather involves choices affecting the scope and quality of care to be provided.

597. §1876 of the Social Security Act, 42 U.S.C. §1395mm and Social Security Act, §1903(k), 42 U.S.C.§1396b(k), which authorize qualified HMOs to provide services to Medicare and Medicaid beneficiaries respectively, give no decision-making power to enrollees. Although recipients are entitled to a hearing on grievances (Social Security Act, §1876(f), 42 U.S.C. §1395mm(f) for Medicare, and Social Security Act, §1902(a)(3), 42 U.S.C. §1396a(3) and 45 C.F.R. §205.10 for Medicaid), these provisions are far from being consumer-control measures.

598. Social Security Act, §1876, 42 U.S.C. §1395mm.

In order to qualify for Medicare participation an HMO must provide all the Medicare-covered services that are generally available in the area served. The HMO must hold an annual enrollment period and accept applicants on a nondiscriminatory basis, unless acceptance of all applicants would result in an HMO enrollment of more than 50% of individuals over age 65.

There are two methods of reimbursement. Substantial, established HMOs can be paid a capitation rate based on the same reimbursement principles as present Medicare providers, including reimbursement for administrative costs that would otherwise go to the fiscal intermediary and carrier. If the HMO realizes a savings, it is shared between the HMO and the federal government. If the HMO experiences a loss, it is carried over to subsequent years and can be set off against subsequent savings. The second method, which must be used by newly established HMOs and may be used by any HMO, provides for interim monthly capitation payments subject to adjustment at the end of the year reflecting the HMOs actual costs of providing Medicare-covered services under ordinary reimbursement principles.

599. 1972 Senate Finance Committee Report, supra n. 428, at p. 229.

600. The act requires that at least half of the individuals enrolled be under age 65. Social Security Act, §1876(b)(7), 42 U.S.C. §1395mm(b)(7). HMOs may avoid this requirement for up to three years by showing that they are "making continuous efforts and progress toward achieving compliance." Social Security Act, 1876(h), 42 U.S.C. §1395mm(h). The act does not explicitly prohibit HMOs from enrolling Medicaid and FEBP beneficiaries to make up the other 50%, but since the enrollment of only the federally fianced poor and aged would seem to defeat the congressional purpose, it is hoped that HEW will prohibit such a result through regulation.

The act also requires that constituent parts of the HMO, e.g. hospitals and nursing homes, meet the normal Medicare conditions of participation (§1876(b)(2), 42 U.S.C. §1395mm(b)(2)) and that services be provided "promptly and appropriately" and "measure up to quality standards" to be established by regulation (§1876(b)(8), 42 U.S.C. §1395mm(b)(8)). Medicare conditions of participation have not been adequate to assure that beneficiaries receive services of minimally decent quality even where the financial incentives are geared to encourage spending and utilization. See W. Worthington and L. Silver, "Regulation of Quality of Care in Hospitals: The Need for Change," 35 *Law and Cont. Problems* 305 (1970).

601. Havighurst, supra n. 593.

602. Id. at pp. 729–32.

603. For comment on the monopolistic nature of the health industry, see Sen. Edward Kennedy, *In Critical Condition* (N.Y.: Simon and Schuster, 1972), pp. 183–86.

604. It is not clear whether the federal antitrust laws apply to Blue Cross. Under the federal McCarran-Ferguson Act, the business of insurance is subject to the antitrust laws only "to the extent that such business is not regulated by State law," except that the Sherman Act applies to "boycott, coercion or intimidation." 15 U.S.C. §§1012(b), 1013(b) (1964). Federal law governs the definition of the "business of insurance." *SEC. v. National Securities, Inc.*, 393 U.S. 453, 458–61 (1969). There are federal cases holding that Blue Cross is in the insurance business, supra n. 39 et seq.

One federal circuit court of appeals has held that Blue Cross is not subject to the Sherman Act. Travelers Insurance Company complained that Blue Cross in the Pittsburgh area had enrolled over half of the population of the relevant market area and purchased 62% of the days of hospital service. Hospitals charged non-Blue Cross patients 14% more than Blue Cross subscribers. Blue Cross paid lower per diem rates to nonparticipating hospitals than to Blue Cross participating hospitals. The district court held that Blue Cross was in the business of insurance and was regulated by state law. It also found that the Blue Cross contract with hospitals was negotiated and not obtained through "boycott, coercion or intimidation." Most interestingly, the district court observed that "The enjoining of Blue Cross activities, would necessarily produce a result inconsistent with the basic and ultimate goal of the federal anti-trust laws—consumer protection. The seller's protection is apposite only to the extent that it is not inconsistent with the public's attainment of the highest quality products and services at the lowest possible price." In effect the court found that, in the hospital market, competition is not as helpful as Blue Cross pressure backed by state regulation. *Travelers v. Blue Cross of Western Pennsylvania*, 481 F.2d. 80 (3rd Cir. 1973).

605. Havighurst, supra n. 593, at p. 789.

606. Connecticut General Insurance Co. is opening an HMO in Columbia, Maryland; Equitable Life Insurance Company and at least ten other major insurance firms are studying HMO development. 6 *Medicare Report,* No. 17, p. 4 (Dec. 18, 1972).

607. "Professional Briefs: There's a School for H.E.W.-Promoted Group Practice," 47 *Med. Economics,* Pt. 2, p. 42 (July 20, 1970).

608. BCA, *Alternative Delivery Systems Status Report,* March 31, 1972; "Blues to Assume Responsibility for Detroit CHA Program," *Michigan Hospitals,* December 1971, p. 15 (describing the dissolution of a group prepaid practice with members moving to Blue Cross); "The Blues Are Rolling out Their Own Bandwagon," *Med. Economics,* Nov. 8, 1971, p. 267. Rochester, N.Y., has three HMOs, all of which are being marketed by Blue Cross, *New York Times,* Aug. 19, 1973, p. 35.

609. Walter McNerney, A Statement on Health Maintenance Organizations presented to the Subcommittee on Public Health and Environment of the House Committee on Interstate and Foreign Commerce, 92nd Cong., 2nd Sess., pp. 1–2 (May 10, 1972).

610. *Health Maintenance Organizations: An Introduction and Survey of Recent Developments* (Washington, D.C.: Lawyers' Committee for Civil Rights Under Law, October 1972), p. 93.

611. Id. at p. 100.

612. Id. at p. 98.

613. Interview with Dr. Newton Spencer, Nov. 6, 1972.

614. *Health Maintenance Organizations,* supra n. 610, at p. 95. Interview with Larry O'Brian, Executive Director, South Philadelphia Health Action, Nov. 28, 1972.

Public perception of the importance of having a card with the Blue Cross insignia is probably correct. Members of the Temple University HMO are issued cards that do not indicate that they are insured by Blue Cross. People holding Temple HMO cards have presented themselves for emergency treatment at Temple University Hospital and have been turned away because of doubt as to whether the treatment would be reimbursed. Interview, Staff member Temple University Health Services Research Institute, Jan. 7, 1972.

615. "The HMO organizations, as now conceived, cannot act on behalf of the community in planning the total complex of services from preventive services for children to home care for the homebound chronically ill. It cannot reach out into the community to make its services known and available to those who might not otherwise hear of them, [and] it cannot cope with any of the major community problems such as drug abuse, alcoholism or mental disorders." Dr. Harry Becker, quoted in "Nixon Health Plan Is Called Unrealistic," *New York Times,* Oct. 12, 1971, p. 31, col. 1.

616. W. Killin, "Herbert S. Denenberg—A New Kind of Impact on Insurance," 72 *Bests Rev. of Life and Health Ins.* 30 (July 1971); C. Rosenberg, "The Government Official Who's Socking It to Doctors," *Medical Economics,* Oct. 11, 1971, p. 83.

617. LL.B., Creighton University Law School, B.S., Johns Hopkins, LL.M., Harvard Law School, Ph.D. in insurance, University of Pennsylvania.

618. Pennsylvania Department of Insurance, News Release, Feb. 26, 1971.

619. *New York Times,* March 28, 1971, p. 50, col. 3.

The 32 guidelines issued in 1972 contained suggestions on the elimination of duplicative and underutilized facilities and services, elimination of unsafe and substandard beds, financing of resident and intern salaries, limitations on depreciation, limitation on the number of employees, prospective rate setting, budgetary review, adoption of cost-saving devices such as preadmission testing, changes in compensation arrangements for ancillary services, elimination of payments for membership in some organizations, consumer control of hospitals, elimination of arbitrary limits on physician admitting privileges, use of generic drugs, reimbursement for general management surveys, better accounting for noncovered research costs, public disclosure of information, better utilization review, patient protection from charges for unnecessary services, more uniform accounting, use of prudent buying practices, and several other matters. Twenty-five additional guidelines were proposed for Blue Cross-hospital negotiations in March 1973. They called for a hospital ombudsman, a patients' bill of rights, personnel to facilitate discharge planning, itemized hospital bills, conflict-of-interest statements by hospital boards and administrative personnel, elimination of interest-free advance payments from Blue Cross to hospitals, and other reforms. H. Denenberg, *Guidelines for Inclusion in Blue Cross Contract with Delaware Valley Hospital Association,* March 2, 1973.

620. See, e.g., Statement by Dr. Herbert Denenberg on Consumer Control of Hospitals at the Sixth Negotiating Session, June 4, 1971. Pennsylvania Department of Insurance, News Release, June 8, 1971, on Hospital Council refusal to allow insurance commissioner to present a statement on progress of negotiations to member hospitals.

621. *Philadelphia Bulletin,* Oct. 12, 1971, p. 1, col. 6.

622. Pennsylvania Department of Insurance, News Release, March 15, 1972.

623. Philadelphia Blue Cross subscriber rates increased 21% in 1970, 18.4% in 1971, 12.3% in 1972, and 7.8% in 1973. The head of Philadelphia Blue Cross said, "A dramatic change has been made. Our rate of increase must be among the lowest in the country." Savings to Blue Cross subscribers were apparently not effected by shifting costs to private paying patients. A *Philadelphia Inquirer* survey of semi-private room charges for uninsured patients showed a 4.13% increase in 1972, a reduction in inflation credited mostly to the federal price freeze. *Philadelphia Inquirer,* Aug. 27, 1972, p. 12, col. A.

624. Relying on the public information provision of the Blue Cross hospital contract, the *Philadelphia Inquirer* requested simple information on hospital costs of 44 hospitals. Four provided no information; others gave only partial answers. Of those answering all of the questions, most gave inaccurate information, in all cases understating their costs. *Philadelphia Inquirer,* Aug. 27, 1972, p. 12, col. A.

Blue Cross's refusal to make public information requested by Commissioner Denenberg is discussed in Sen. Abraham Ribicoff, *The American Medical Machine* (N.Y.: Saturday Review Press, 1972).

625. *Guidelines for Review and Approval of Rates for Health Care Institutions and Services by a State Commission,* Accepted by AHA Board of Trustees, Feb. 9, 1972.

626. "Pa. Doctors Demand Ouster of Official, Talk of Boycott," *Washington Post,* Oct. 31, 1972, p. A2, col. 4; "Doctors Protest in Pennsylvania," *New York Times,* Oct. 29, 1972, p. 80, col. 1; "Shapp Backs Denenberg; Hits Doctors," *Philadelphia Inquirer,* Oct. 31, 1972, p. 13, col. 8. See also *Modern Hospital,* November 1972 p. 42; *Pennsylvania Medicine,* November 1972, p. 11.

627. Pennsylvania Governor Milton Shapp frequently introduces himself at political gatherings saying, "You may not know who I am but I'm the guy that brought Herb Denenberg into state government."

628. Philip Elman, who served as a commissioner with the Federal Trade Commission, said, "During my years at the Federal Trade Commission it became increasingly evident that the Commission was failing to fulfill its role as protector of the public interest in the market place." Philip Elman, "Administrative Reform of the Federal Trade Commission," 59 *Georgetown Law Journal* 777, 777 (March 1971).

See also Nicholas Johnson, "Consumer Rights Are the Regulatory Crisis," 20 *Catholic University Law Review* 424, 426 (Fall 1970); Louis M. Kohlmeier, Jr., *The Regulators: Watchdog Agencies and the Public Interest,* (N.Y.: Harper and Row, 1969), pp. 6, 265; Statement of Marver H. Bernstein, Dean of the Woodrow Wilson School of Public and International Affairs, Princeton University, before the Subcommittee on Antitrust and Monopoly of the House Committee on the Judiciary, Hearings on Monopoly Problems in Regulated Industries, 84th Cong., 2d. Sess., Pt. 1, Vol. 1, pp. 60–64 (1956); Marver H.

Bernstein, *Regulating Business by Independent Commission* (Princeton, N.J.: Princeton University Press, (1966), pp. 157–62.

629. Cases of denial of hospital benefits to Blue Cross subscribers are collected in the files of the Health Law Project, 133 So. 36th St., Philadelphia, Penn. 19174. Each of these cases came to the HLP in the form of hospital collection actions for payment for services that Blue Cross refused to cover. See Anne Taylor, "Report on the Works of the Health Consumers' Committee, June and July 1971," in Health Law Project, "Preliminary Materials on Health Law," Sec. 7, p. 279 (1971).

630. Blue Cross of Philadelphia most commonly denies coverage on the ground that the care provided was diagnostic. In these cases the subscriber receives a form letter that says, "Subscription Agreements provide that inpatient hospital care primarily for diagnostic studies is not covered when the studies can properly be provided on an outpatient basis, considering the individual circumstances of the ‚ase. This provision is followed to protect all subscribers against any unnecessary increase in Blue Cross rates." When such cases are appealed to the Blue Cross Review Board and the denial is sustained, the review record (which is not provided to the subscriber) is equally abrupt, e.g., "The medical record indicates that the patient was admitted primarily for studies, all of which could have been done on an outpatient basis. Benefits are not being granted." From the files of the Health Law Project, supra n. 629.

631. In 1970 the mean income of white men in America was $10,634; for black men it was $6,773; for white women $5,965; and for black women $4,943. U.S. Department of Commerce, Bureau of the Census, *Consumer Income,* Current Populatio⁊ Reports, Series P-6, No. 80 (Oct. 4, 1971). The Bureau of Labor Statistics estimated that in 1970 an urban family of four needed $10,664 to live at a moderate level. Of this $564 was allocated for medical care. U.S. Department of Labor, *Handbook of Labor Statistics,* p. 291 (1971).

By contrast, the average length of hospitalization for all cases is 8.2 days. In 1970 the average cost per day was $81.01, or $664.28 per hospitalization. 45 *Hospitals,* Guide Issue, pp. 454–62 (1971). This does not include physicians' fees or pre-and post-hospital expenses. A single hospitalization would require the family's entire medical budget and would leave the rest of the family without medical resources for the year.

632. See Taylor, supra n. 629, at pp. 279–82.

633. Richard D. Lyons, "Medicare Costs Below Estimate," *New York Times,* Nov. 26, 1970, p. 26.

634. A similar de facto reduction in benefits to federal employees is discussed supra nn. 353–59.

635. In 1970, while 80.3% of the population had private insurance coverage for hospital care, and over 70% had coverage for inhospital service such as surgical costs, physicians' visits, and X-ray and laboratory examinations, only 49.7% had insurance for prescribed drugs, 52.4% had it for visiting nurse services, 49.4% had private-duty nursing coverage, and 16% had nursing home care coverage. Although these latter figures represent outpatient coverage for a sizable proportion of the population, it must be noted that the actual protection against costs represented by this insurance varies from substantial to very little. In fact, during 1970 private health insurance met only 5.5% of consumer costs for outpatient services, as compared to 71% of hospital costs and 48% of physicians' services expenditures that were met in the same year. Marjorie Smith Mueller, "Private Health Insurance in 1970," 35 *Social Security Bulletin,* No. 4, p. 19 (February 1972). See also A. Somers, *Health Care in Transition: Directions for the Future* (Chicago: Hospital Research and Education Trust, 1971), pp. 44–48.

636. H. Paxton, "Whatever Happened to the Hospital Bed Shortage?" 13 *Medical Economics* 34 (Feb. 28, 1972).

637. Average lengths of stay have gone up marginally from 7.6 days in 1960 to 8.2 days in 1970. Despite the advent of Medicare and Medicaid, hospital admission per thousand population increased only from 139 to 156 in the same ten-year period. 45 *Hospitals,* Guide Issue, p. 447 (1971).
For the 65 and over age group average length of stay increased from 13.4 days in 1966 to 14.2 days in 1968; discharges per thousand increased from 277.1 in 1966 to 300.8 in 1968. "Inpatient Utilization of Short-Stay Hospitals in Each Geographic Division," HEW, National Center for Health Statistics, *Vital and Health Statistics,* Ser. 13, No. 10, pp. 7 and 12 (1972).
638. 45 *Hospitals,* Guide Issue, p. 454 (1971). The General Accounting Office reports that "Medicare payments for care provided by hospitals and extended-care facilities increased from $2.5 billion in fiscal year 1967 to $4.7 billion in fiscal year 1970. The potential significance of control over the utilization of medical services is illustrated by [an unofficial HEW estimate] that Medicare costs could be reduced by as much as $400 million annually if each Medicare patient's hospital stay could be reduced by a single day." GAO Report to the Congress, *Improved Controls Needed over Extent of Care Provided by Hospitals and Other Facilities to Medicare Patients,* p. 1 (July 30, 1971).
639. Social Security Act, 42 U.S.C. §1395, §1801.
640. For example, the federal statute requires that extended care facilities and hospitals meet certain conditions of participation, including the establishment of utilization review committees, which did not exist previously. The statute requires payment of "reasonable costs" under principles established by the secretary. In these and other areas, the specific statutory mandates plainly apply even though they necessarily involve federal "interference." There has been no formal administrative or judicial interpretation of the meaning of the preamble.
641. Social Security Act, §§1861(a), (i), and (n), 42 U.S.C. §§1395x(a), (i), and (n).
642. No payment shall be made for services for which the individual has no obligation to pay, services paid for by the government, services not provided within the United States, services required as a result of war, services rendered by relatives or members of the beneficiary's household. Social Security Act, §§1862(a),(2),(3),(4),(5), and (11), 42 U.S.C. §§1395y(a),(2),(3),(4),(5), and (11).
643. No payments shall be made for routine physical checkups, routine foot care or dental care, cosmetic surgery, orthopedic shoes, or personal comfort items. Social Security Act, §§1862(a)(6),(7),(8),(10),(12), and (13), 42 U.S.C. §§1395y(a)(6), (7),(8),(10),(12), and (13).
644. Social Security Act, §1862y(a)(1), 42 U.S.C. §1395y(a)(1).
645. Social Security Act, §1862y(a)(9), 42 U.S.C. §1395y(a)(9).
646. Social Security Act, §1814(a)(3), 42 U.S.C. §1395f(a)(3).
647. Social Security Act, §1814(a), 42 U.S.C. §1395f(a).
648. The Senate Finance Committee Report states, "The committee's bill provides that the physician is to be the key figure in determining utilization of health services—and provides that it is a physician who is to decide upon admission to a hospital, order tests, drugs, and treatments, and determine the length of stay. For this reason the bill would require that payment could be made only if the physician certifies to the medical necessity of the services furnished. If services are furnished over a period of time to be specified in regulations, recertification by the physician would be necessary." Report of the Senate Committee on Finance to accompany H.R. 6675, Social Security Amendments of 1965, Senate Report No. 404, 89th Cong., 1st Sess., Pt. I, p. 46 (June 30, 1965).
649. Utilization review committees as defined in Social Security Act, §1861(k), 42 U.S.C. §1395x(k), are required for participating hospitals, §1861(e)(6), 42 U.S.C.

§1395x(e)(6), and for extended care facilities, Social Security Act, §1861(j)(8), 42 U.S.C. §§1395x(j)(8).

650. Social Security Act, §§1861(k)(1) and (3), 42 U.S.C. §§1395x(k)(1) and (3). See also C.F.R. §405.1035.

651. Section 1861(k)(4) of the Social Security Act states that the utilization review plan of hospital of nursing home must provide for "prompt notification to the institution, *the individual,* and his attending physician of any finding (made after opportunity for consultation to such attending physician) by the physician members of such committee or group that further stay in the institution is not medically necessary." (Emphasis added.) 42 U.S.C. §1395x(k)(4). 20 C.F.R. §405.1035(g) requires that notice must be given within 48 hours.

652. The Social Security Act, §1814(a)(7), 42 U.S.C. §1395f(a)(7), provides that payments may not be made for services rendered after a finding has been made by the utilization review committee that "further inpatient hospital services or further post-hospital extended care services, as the case may be, are not medically necessary; except that, if such a finding has been made, payment may be made for such services furnished before the 4th day after the day on which the hospital or extended care facility, as the case may be, received notice of such finding."

653. Section 1866(b)(2) on Agreements with Providers of Services states, "An agreement with the Secretary under this section may be terminated . . . by the Secretary at such time and upon such reasonable notice to the provider of services *and the public* as may be specified in regulations but only after the Secretary has determined . . . that [the] provider is not complying [with the conditions of participation]." (Emphasis added.) 42 U.S.C. §1395cc(b)(2).

654. Section 1866(b)(3), Social Security Act, provides: "Any termination [of the agreement] shall be applicable—in the case of inpatient hospital services . . . or post-hospital extended care services, with respect to services furnished after the effective date of such termination, except that payment may be made for up to thirty days with respect to inpatient institutional services furnished to any eligible individual who was admitted to such institution *prior to the effective date of such termination.*" (Emphasis added.) 42 U.S.C. §1395cc(b)(3).

655. Social Security Act, §1866(d), 42 U.S.C. §1395cc(d) provides: "If the Secretary finds that there is a substantial failure to make timely review in accordance with Section 1861(k) of long-stay cases in a hospital or skilled nursing facility, he may, in lieu of terminating his agreement with such hospital or facility, decide that, with respect to any individual admitted to such hospital or facility *after a subsequent date* specified by him, no payment shall be made under this title for inpatient hospital services . . . after the 20th day of a continuous period of such services or for post-hospital extended care services after such day of a continuous period of such care as is prescribed in or pursuant to regulations, as the case may be." (Emphasis added.)

656. A decision to bar payments after the 20th day "may be made effective only after such notice to the hospital, or (in the case of a skilled nursing facility) to the facility and the hospital or hospitals with which it has a transfer agreement, *and to the public,* as may be prescribed by regulations." (Emphasis added.) Ibid.

657. The Social Security Act, §1814(a)(6), provides that payments may not be made for services rendered after the 20th continuous day if, *"at the time of admission of such individual . . .* [there was in effect] a decision under Section 1866(d)." (Emphasis added.) 42 U.S.C. §1395f(a)(6).

658. Rep. Ullman noted, "Professional people seem to be very reluctant to move in and contradict any judgment that has been made by a fellow professional. The way this thing is set up you have doctors reviewing doctors, and I just can't conceive of it working

the way it is supposed to work." Robert Ball, Under Secretary of HEW, replied, "I think
. . . that you are right, that this is a delicate area, the review of a professional judgment,
but it seems to me that it would be making the problem even more difficult if the review of
the professional judgment were to be made by anyone other than the members of the profession." Executive Hearings on H.R.1 before the House Committee on Ways and
Means, 89th Cong., 1st Sess., Pt. 1, p. 107 (1965).

659. Id. at p. 68.

660. Social Security Act, §1816(b)(1)(B), 42 U.S.C. §1395h(b)(1)(B).

661. Report on H.R. 6675, House Committee on Ways and Means, Rep. No. 213,
89th Cong., 1st Sess., p. 45; Senate Finance Committee Report No. 404, p. 52 (1965).
Walter J. McNerney described the function of Blue Cross with respect to utilization
review as working "together with hospitals and physicians [to] fashion a grid for that
type of review . . . [developing] runs on age, sex, and diagnosis, to see how stay differs, and how use of services differs, and how admission rates differ, and where we find
extreme variation ask a question, 'What is this about?' . . . [and to] have built within
each hospital a utilization committee." Executive Hearings on H.R.1, House Committee
on Ways and Means, 89th Cong., 1st Sess., Pt. 1, p. 176 (1965).

The contract between BCA and SSA provides that the intermediary shall: "Assist providers of services in the development of procedures relating to utilization practices and
make studies of the effectiveness of such procedures, including the appraisal and evaluation of the results of provider utilization review activity and recommendations for necessary changes in provider utilization practices and procedures; and assist in the application
of safeguards against unnecessary utilization of services." Agreement No. SSA-70-110-
1 (BCA-7/70), art. II, sec. 3(d).

662. The following exchange between Kenneth Williamson of the AHA and Committee Chairman Wilbur Mills spells out the role of utilization review:

The Chairman: What do you understand is involved in this matter, anyway, utilization review? . . .

Mr. Williamson: It is involved in insuring that patients receive care for the period
that they need it; and that they do not remain in hospitals longer than their care
demands . . .

Chairman: . . . Whether you have Blue Cross in it or not, what the legislation requires
in the definition of a hospital, among other things, is that it have the utilization review
committee . . . [and] that utilization review committee . . . would be made up of this
group of doctors. . . . It is the very group that today in a big hospital makes decisions
with the physician of the patient as to the length of stay of that patient. That would be the
same operation under this program, would it not?

Dr. Crosby: My judgment would be yes.

Chairman: Blue Cross would exercise the judgment of the committee, is that the point?

Dr. Crosby: Whether the committee was being effective in this operation or not."
Executive Hearings on H.R.1 before the House Ways and Means Comm., 89th Cong.,
1st Sess., pp. 287–88 (1965).

663. Shortly after the passage of Medicare, Arthur Hess, then Director of BHI, spoke
of the role of the fiscal intermediary: "When the fiscal intermediary comes on center stage
in the near future, we will rely heavily on the intermediary to participate with the medical
profession in the long-run measures that will result in assurance that utilization review
does in fact function in the ways that it was indicated it would function at the time of certification of the institution. . . . *This assurance, we believe, may be fully supported by
statistical analyses and consultations based on questions arising out of day-to-day claims
administration, rather than requiring audits of the individual case judgments of review
committees.*" (Emphasis added.) Address by Arthur Hess, Seventh Annual Medical Ser-

vices Conference, American Medical Association, Philadelphia, Pa., Nov. 27, 1965, as quoted in Associated Hospital Service of New York, *Medicare Advance Information Letter,* No. 12 (March 24, 1966).

664. In 1965, the SSA actuarial estimate of the projected annual costs of Medicare by 1970 was $3.1 billion. In 1967 this figure was revised upward to $4.4 billion, in 1969 to $5 billion, and finally in 1970 to $5.8 billion. In 1965, the SSA believed that adequate financing of Medicare could come from a levy of 1.23% of taxable payroll subject to social security taxes, with a maximum of $6600 of taxable payroll subject to the Medicare tax. After three years of experience, this figure had to be raised to 2.27% of taxable income with a $7800 maximum for the hospital tax. 1970 Senate Finance Committee Report, supra n. 236, at pp. 3–4, 35–36. In 1973 HEW estimates that Medicare will cost $9.8 billion for the current year, $12.4 billion in 1974, $15 billion in 1975, $19.4 billion in 1977, and $24.5 billion in 1979. HEW, "Health Program Memorandum—Fiscal Year 1975 Budget," *Cong. Rec.* (daily ed), July 24, 1973.

665. See Report of the Senate Special Committee on Aging, S. Rep. No. 91-875, 91st Cong., 2d Sess., p. 87 (May 15, 1970).

666. The Senate Finance Committee staff found that "utilization review requirements have, generally speaking, been of a token nature and ineffective as a curb to unnecessary use of institutional care and services. Utilization review in Medicare can be characterized as more form than substance." 1970 Senate Finance Committee Report, supra n. 236, at p. 105; 1972 Senate Finance Committee Report, supra n. 428, at p. 255.

667. "Intermediaries have not been performing these functions satisfactorily despite the fact that the Secretary may not, under the law, make agreements with an intermediary who is unwilling or unable to assist providers of services with utilization review functions." 1972 Senate Finance Committee Report, supra n. 428, at p. 256.

668. Comptroller General, *Report to the Congress,* No. B-164031(4), pp. 14–15, 22–24 (July 30, 1971). 2 CCH Medicare and Medicaid Guide, ¶26,339.

A sample of hospitals studied by SSA in 1968 showed that: 10% of the hospitals were not conducting a review of extended care cases; 47% of the hospitals were not reviewing any admissions; 42% did not even maintain an abstract of the medical record or other summary form that could provide a basis for evaluation utilization by diagnosis or other common factor. Id. at p. 107.

An SSA study of one intermediary found that while the intermediary made pro forma semiannual reviews of each provider's utilization review program, "the results are not too meaningful in terms of an effective utilization review program. The approach results in reports showing proper compliance with the regulations but does not indicate to Plan management a true picture of what the UR committees are in fact doing. In addition, irregularities noted are seldom reported to the State Agency or the BHI Regional Office." SSA, BHI, *Contract Performance Review, St. Louis Blue Cross,* p. 4, Aug. 31–Sept. 4, 1970.

Federal District Judge Irving BenCooper made similar observations in enjoining New York from reducing Medicaid services on the ground that compliance with utilization review requirements is a prerequisite to reduction in benefits. *Bass v. Richardson,* 338 F. Supp. 478 (S.D.N.Y. 1971). The court's opinion relied upon a report on the New York utilization review system made by federal investigators in May 1971, which noted: "[I]t was found in districts reviewed that there is essentially no formal utilization review activity performed prior to the payment of bills. In many districts the claims clerks use their judgment and experience to assess utilization priorities in the absence of any guidelines or defined procedures which would assure a degree of uniformity. . . . [Utilization review is done on a] sporadic basis. The local medical directors are not following any Statewide guidelines for conducting or reporting utilization review activities. There appear to be no periodic reports of local U.R. activities required either by the Regional or Central Office of the State Health or Social Services Department." Id. at 488. The court summarized, "New York's utilization review program, even to a charitable eye, is woefully inadequate under federal Law." Id. at 487.

669. Interview with officials in Division of State Operations, Bureau of Health Insurance, Social Security Administration, July 14 and 17, 1972. One official stressed that few if any hospitals or extended care facilities will be dropped from the Medicare program solely for having a nonfunctioning or nonexistent utilization review mechanism, because such institutions usually have additional serious defects—e.g. inadequate nursing or dietary facilities—which, taken together, necessitate termination of the Medicare connection. This preference for complete termination of noncomplying facilities was also given as a reason for the lack of reliance by the SSA on 20-day orders. He noted further that 20-day orders were not favored by the SSA because of the requirement that a hearing must precede their issuance.

670. GAO Report, supra n. 668, at pp. 33–34.

671. BHI Intermediary Letter No. 257 (Aug. 14, 1967) is set forth in full in Hearings before the Senate Finance Committee on H.R. 12080, 90th Cong., 1st Sess., Pt. 2, p. 1042 (1967).

672. 20 C.F.R. §§405.126–129, 36 Fed. Reg. 10848 (June 4, 1971). These regulations abandon the justification of claims review in terms of "custodial care" and instead address the broader question of what are covered and noncovered care. Like Intermediary Letter 257 these regulations ask whether: (1) the patient's condition medically requires the skilled services and care available in a hospital setting, and (2) his admission has as its primary purpose the securing of such services.

673. The letter recognizes that "In light of the limited amount of information available at the time of the bill review, considerable skill and sound judgment must be exercised if the intermediary is to successfully identify cases involving custodial care." "Consideration" should be given to "length of stay in the institution," "diagnosis," "history of in-patient usage," "adverse utilization review decision," death or discharge, and the characteristics of the institution. Of course, when the utilization review committee has made an adverse determination, care provided after that point is not covered, but, in addition, an adverse determination "would raise a presumption that care in the *prior* period may not have been covered."

The opinion of the attending physician is not given much weight in claims review. "In border line cases the intermediary should *consider* consulting the doctor." Contrast §1861(k) of the Social Security Act, 42 U.S.C. §1395y(k), which *requires* the utilization review committee to consult with the attending physician.

674. Blue Cross "recommended that Section 1814 of the Act be amended to provide that physicians' certification serve as presumptive evidence of covered care subject to review by the Secretary through the intermediary." Blue Cross officials said statutory change was needed because "there appears to be a fundamental conflict between our ability to administer exclusions under the law and the mandate given to utilization review committees under Section 1861(k) and others." Hearings before the Subcommittee on Medicare/Medicaid of the Senate Finance Committee, 91st Cong., 2nd Sess., Pt. 2, pp. 294 and 303 (1970).

675. The issue of Blue Cross authority to perform claims review has not received full judicial consideration. A hospital or extended care facility suffering economic loss as a result of the ex post facto denial of claims would be a likely plaintiff. However, the author has been told by hospital administrators and attorneys that, despite the financial penalty that falls on the hospital as a result of claims review, "the hospital cannot afford to bite the hand that feeds it," i.e. Blue Cross.

Alternatively, the issue can be raised defensively by a beneficiary denied payment by the intermediary. However, any court is likely to try to decide an individual claim on the basis of the facts presented, rather than adjudicate the validity of an entire administrative structure. For example, one district court, while deciding that on the facts of the case the care provided was covered by Medicare, noted in dicta: "Although the Secretary does not directly question the physician's certification, nor do I think he intends to, his decision seems to have that effect. This is a medical judgment which Congress placed in the hands of medical men, not the Secretary or his subordinates. Congress has provided that even the review of the necessary duration of post-hospital stay is not by the Secretary but by the physician members of the 'committee or group' administering a 'utilization review plan.' " *Lascaris v. Richardson*, 2 CCH Medicare and Medicaid Guide, ¶¶10,352 and 10,355 (N.D.N.Y. 1972).

Another district court stated, without explication, that: "The purpose of the utilization review plan is to promote the efficient use of services and facilities of a hospital rendering care for a person under Medicare health benefits. It does not supplant the Secretary's statutory authority to determine whether certain costs are reimbursable under the Act, but assists the Secretary in making that decision." *Baker v. Richardson*, 2 CCH Medicare and Medicaid Guide, ¶¶10,361 and 10,364 (W.D.Mo. 1972).

An affirmative class action challenging the authority of Blue Cross to overrule provider utilization review examinations has been filed on behalf of a group of Medicare beneficiaries whose claims for payment were denied by Michigan Blue Cross. *Himmler v. Richardson*, Civ. No. 39294, D.C. Mich. filed Nov. 6, 1972.

676. HEW, SSA, *Selected ECF Data*, p. 1 (June 15, 1971); HEW, SSA, *Report of Intermediary Level of Care Determinations for ECFs* (Aug. 16, 1971).

677. *Selected ECF Data*, Id. at p. 2.

678. Archer, "Medicare and Extended Care Facilities," 44 *Hospitals* 48, 51 (1970).

679. Seventy-one extended care facilities dropped out of the Medicare program in the third quarter of 1970. Ninety more facilities dropped out in the last quarter of that year, and 114 dropped out in the first quarter of 1971. *Report of Intermediary Level of Care Determinations for ECFs*, supra n. 676.

680. Preadmission deposits are prohibited under Medicare, 20 C.F.R. 405.610(b), because they discriminate against needy beneficiaries. Nonetheless, the author knows that half a dozen facilities in the Philadelphia area in fact charge deposits and believes that the practice is widespread.

681. Affidavit of David Heath, M.D., June 10, 1971, on file at the Health Law Project, 133 So. 36th St., Philadelphia, Penn. 19174.

682. The Medicaid act sets no floor on the minimum amount that states can pay for skilled nursing home services. Social Security Act, §§1905(a)(4)(A) and (b), 42 U.S.C. §§1396d(a)(4)(A) and (b). The Commonwealth of Pennsylvania pays $15 per day for skilled nursing home services. *Pennsylvania Bulletin* 205 (Oct. 30, 1971). Clerks Medical Assist. Manual, §9424, App. I, Annex A (in *Bulletin*—1292).

The 1972 amendments to the Social Security Act eliminate this difference. States must pay for skilled nursing home services under Medicaid on a "reasonable cost related basis." §1902(a)(13)(E), 42 U.S.C. §1396a(a)(13)(E). The secretary may utilize the state-determined reimbursement rate in paying for nursing home services under Medicare, §1861(v)(1)(E), 42 U.S.C. §1395x(v)(1)(E), except that nursing homes affiliated with hospitals must be paid their full reasonable costs. See 1972 Senate Finance Committee Report, supra n. 428, at p. 287.

683. In his affidavit of June 10, supra n. 681, the attending physician stated, "In my professional judgment as Mr. W.'s attending physician, the services of skilled medical

personnel in an extended care facility were and are medically necessary for the patient. At the time of discharge from the hospital, Mr. W. was still suffering from cardiac failure, a condition complicated by his liver problem. Although auto-amputation of the gangrenous toes was anticipated, these also required nursing care. With cardiac patients of this kind, there is a strong possibility of recurrent heart failure. The continuing observation by medically trained personnel is essential to the early detection of changes in the patient's condition which indicate further deterioration. Observation of signs such as swelling in legs, chest pains, shortness of breath, and lethargy, enables immediate emergency preventative measures to stabilize the condition. . . . In addition to the presence of trained medical personnel, the presence of at least some rudimentary laboratory facilities in a skilled nursing home make it easier to monitor the patient's problems.''

684. On June 10 the attending physician averred, "Without the availability of such skilled nursing services, the chances of recurrent heart failure requiring another period of hospitalization are significantly increased. . . . The inability of the hospital to secure transfers at the appropriate time results in unnecessary utilization of hospital facilities which is far more costly than care in extended facilities.'' On June 13, Mr. W. was readmitted to the hospital.

685. Social Security Act, §1869(b)(1)(C), 42 U.S.C. §1395ff(b)(1)(C), provides, "Any individual dissatisfied with any determination . . . as to the amount of benefits under Part A (including a determination where such amount is determined to be zero) shall be entitled to a hearing thereon by the Secretary to the same extent as is provided in Section 205(b) [of the Social Security Act].'' However, the next paragraph, Social Security Act, §1869(b)(2), 42 U.S.C. §1395ff(b)(2), provides, "Notwithstanding the provisions of subparagraph (C) of paragraph (1) of this subsection, a hearing shall not be available to an individual by reason of such subparagraph (C) if the amount in controversy is less than $100.'' Social Security Act, §205(b), 42 U.S.C. §405(b) requires the secretary to "make findings of fact, and decisions as to the rights of any individual applying for a payment under this title,'' and provides that "Upon request by any such individual . . . who makes a showing in writing that his or her rights may be prejudiced by any decision the Secretary has rendered, he shall give such applicant . . . reasonable notice and opportunity for a hearing.''

686. 20 C.F.R. Subpart J, §405.702, Part A Intermediary Manual, Health Insurance Manual—13 Sects. 3780–89.

687. The beneficiary whose claim has been denied by the intermediary receives a notice advising him of his right to a reconsideration of the initial determination by filing a written request with the SSA. 20 C.F.R. §§405.702, 405.711. The reconsideration process entails a review of the request for payment, the evidence and findings upon which the intermediary based its determination, and any additional evidence submitted to the administration or otherwise obtained by the intermediary or the administration. 20 C.F.R. §405.715. The review is conducted by the intermediary, and a summary of the review action is sent to the Reconsideration Section of the Bureau of Health Insurance. The beneficiary receives written notice of the reconsidered determination, setting forth the basis for the action and the beneficiary's hearing right. 20 C.F.R. §405.716. If the amount in controversy is more than $100 the beneficiary may then request a hearing from the SSA within six months. 20 C.F.R. §405.722. The administration is not a party and is normally not represented. The hearing officer normally develops the facts for both sides and makes a written decision, containing findings of fact and a statement of reasons, or recommends the case to the Appeals Council for final decision. 20 C.F.R. §405.939.

688. Interview by H. Makadon, Health Law Project, with an official, Associated Hospital Service of New York, June 11, 1971.

689. Ibid.

690. HEW, SSA, *Status of Implementation of Contract Performance Review, AHS of New York City,* p. 6 (May 20, 1971).

691. *Report of Intermediary Level of Care Determinations for ECFs,* supra n. 676. In the second quarter of 1970, AHS rejected 15.3% of the ECF claims; in the third quarter the rate was 8.6%; in the fourth quarter it was 14.0%; in the first quarter of 1971 it was 6.4%.

692. *Status of Implementation of Contract Performance Review,* supra n. 690, at p. 7.

693. Ibid.

694. Interview with AHS official, supra n. 688.

695. *Status of Implementation of Contract Performance Review,* supra n. 690, at p. 6.

696. Id. at p. 8.

697. M. S. Mueller, "Enrollment, Coverage and Financial Experience of Blue Cross and Blue Shield Plans, 1969," *Research and Statistics Note,* No. 4 (Washington, D.C.: HEW, SSA, April 21, 1971), Table 6.

698. Cronyism and the natural reluctance of professionals to review each other were cited as reasons that utilization review does not work. Interview by M. Gilbride, Health Law Project, with an official, Philadelphia Blue Cross, July 12, 1971. The official also noted that commercial data services are willing to provide hospitals with length of stay and other utilization information, but that Blue Cross does not consider the provision of such data as part of its function.

699. *Wall Street Journal,* Oct. 12, 1960, p. 14, Col. 2 (continued from p. 1, col. 6).

700. Longer stays are allowed in teaching hospitals, although plan officials could not explain the justification for this policy. Interview with Philadelphia Blue Cross official, supra n. 698.

701. In an average month in 1973, Philadelphia Blue Cross reviewed 3,000 claims under Medicare, Medical Assistance, and their private business. Of these, 50 were rejected. Of the 3,000 claims, 2,500 were reviewed inhospital and 500 were reviewed by the plan's medical director and two part-time physicians. Data provided by an official, Blue Cross Association of Philadelphia. Even making the overgenerous assumption that the three doctors each worked a 40-hour week on claims review, this means that they had an average of 14 minutes to review each claim.

702. *Report of Intermediary Level of Care Determinations for ECFs,* supra n. 676.

703. Interview by H. Makadon, Health Law Project, with an official, Medicare Division, Hospital of the University of Pennsylvania, April 14, 1971.

704. Interview by H. Makadon, Health Law Project, with an official, Medical Records Department, Philadelphia General Hospital, April 14, 1971.

705. There is little hard or comprehensive data on Blue Cross delays in claims processing. But, for example, in December 1970, in all but 10 of the 83 fiscal intermediaries more than 5% of the bills pending at the end of the month had been pending for more than 30 days. In 42 of the intermediaries, over 10% of the bills pending at the end of the month had been pending for more than 30 days. In 6 intermediaries more than 30% of the bills pending had been pending for more than 30 days. HEW, SSA, *Evaluation of Part A, Intermediary Performance,* table 1b-4 (March 19, 1971).

706. For example, in discussions with extended care facility administrators and hospital social workers Health Law Project personnel have found a widespread belief that care for chronic illness is not covered by Medicare. Intermediary letters have consistently stated that chronic conditions are covered, provided there is a need for skilled services. Even though the belief that chronic cases are not covered is mistaken, services are often denied on this basis.

707. For example, New York Blue Cross did no screening of hospital bills with regard

to length of stay in relation to diagnosis, high ancillary charges, or questionable diagnoses leading to unnecessary admissions, while nursing home bills received 100% review. Supra n. 690, at p. 31.

708. The American Nursing Home Association withdrew its early support of the Medicare extended care facility program, denouncing it as a "hoax perpetrated on the elderly" and claiming that the restrictive Blue Cross interpretation of what was covered extended care facility care resulted in a 70% drop in the use of extended care facility benefits between January 1968 and January 1970 with fewer than 5% of the 340,000 Medicare extended care facility beds in use. 45 *Hospitals* 130 (Feb. 16, 1971).

SSA data indicate that days of care declined from 1 million in 1969 to 700,000 in 1970, and program spending on extended care facilities fell from $318 million to $188 million. *Social Security Bulletin,* May 1971, as quoted in the *U.S. Statistical Abstract, 1971,* p. 281, table 445. Of the Part A dollar in 1969–70, 94 cents went to hospitals, while 4 cents went to extended care facilities. *Social Security Bulletin,* October 1970.

A St. Louis nursing home administrator testifying before a Senate subcommittee stated that that area "has slightly over 9,000 acute general hospital beds, with a daily census of approximately 7,800 patients of whom more than 2,600 are Medicare patients. This compares with approximately 100 Medicare patients in St. Louis area non-hospital ECF's, or a ratio of 25 in hospitals to 1 in ECF's." Hart Committee Hearings, supra n. 121, at p. 3.

709. HEW, SSA, *Selected ECF Data,* June 15, 1971, shows that extended care facility admissions as a percentage of hospital admissions for 1968, 1969, and 1970 were 7.6%, 8.5% and 7.7%, respectively. During the period from October 1968 to December 1969 the length of covered stay in short-stay hospitals dropped slightly from 13.1 days to 12.8 days.

HEW Division of Intermediary Operations states, "from the data, no conclusions could be made regarding the often repeated allegations that patients are being kept in hospitals rather than being transferred to ECFs to avoid the possibility of a denial of the ECF bills."

710. Only 28% of Blue Cross subscribers have any nursing home coverage. A 1971 BCA survey of 71 local plans shows that 52 plans offer optional nursing home benefits. Forty-seven plans offer extended care facility coverage in copayment policies supplementary to Medicare. Of those persons 65 or over who are Blue Cross subscribers, 66 per cent have extended care facility coverage of some sort. Data furnished on request by the Blue Cross Association, 840 N. Lake Shore Drive, Chicago, Ill. 60611.

711. "The retroactive denial of claims is a basic underlying reason for the decline in ECF use. Moreover, the decline in use has resulted in the decline in the number of participating ECFs by about 700 and by 64,000 beds between December 1969 and December, 1971. This decline is unfortunate for, as noted previously, there is considerable need for long-term-care facilities." 1972 GAO Report, supra n. 591, at pp. 799–800.

712. A GAO review of seven fiscal intermediaries found that only two Medicare agents had procedures for denying doctor bills in cases in which hospital claims were rejected as unnecessary. Comptroller General, Report to the Congress, *More Needs to Be Done to Assure that Physician's Services—Paid for by Medicare and Medicaid—Are Necessary,* No. B-164031(4), ch. 5 (Aug. 2, 1972).

The level of review coordination between Blue Cross and Blue Shield is so small that BCA itself has no significant data on the subject. All that BCA could tell the author was that some plans cooperated on Medicare claims review, some on all claims, and some not at all. Most plans—particularly the 42 plan areas in which Blue Cross and Blue Shield have separate corporate identities—have no effective means of coordination. BCA also noted, however, that a joint proposal sponsored by the Blue Cross and Blue Shield associations is before a joint cost containment committee at this time. It is expected that this proposal will be implemented shortly on a trial basis. Blue Cross of Philadelphia already has such a plan in operation, but one observer has noted that its effect is lessened considerably by Blue Shield's practice of paying physician claims even when the hospital is *not* paid by Blue Cross. See memo by Anne Taylor in Health Law Project, "Preliminary Materials on Health Law," vol. 7, pp. 284–85 (1971).

713. Blue Cross of Greater Philadelphia, *Hospital Agreement,* Sec. 2.3 (July 1, 1971).

714. See *Albert Einstein Medical Center v. Lipoff and Blue Cross of Great Philadelphia,* Common Pleas Court of Phila., Trial Div., Jan. Term 1972, No. 3872 X, filed March 13, 1972. The court held the doctor liable, stating: "the Court's decision was made primarily on the theory that Dr. Brecher had placed his patient in a position where the patient was liable for medical expenses, when in the opinion of his peers, that is, three physicians from Blue Cross and six physicians from the Philadelphia County Medical Society, all found that the admission was not necessary. This matter is simply a case of a physician failing to use reasonable care under the circumstances, as result of which his patient has been financially injured."

In a second case, in which there was no written opinion, the Court held the hospital liable. See *Medical Economics,* May 22, 1972, pp. 101–16; *Medical World News,* May 5, 1972, p. 13; *American Medical Association News,* March 20, 1972, p. 1; *Philadelphia Bulletin,* Jan. 18, 1972, p. 1, and March 8, 1972, p. 13; *Philadelphia Inquirer,* Jan. 19, 1972, p. 1. Both cases are now on appeal.

715. Philadelphia hospitals objected to the imposition of liability for the cost of services judged to be medically unnecessary on the ground that the hospital had no power to control the physician. The objection is not convincing. Hospitals *can* control the conduct of physicians. See *Darling v. Charleston Community Hospital,* 211 N.E.2d 253, 33 Ill.2d 326 (1965). Alternatively the hospital could shift the risk of nonpayment to the patient or the physician by giving clear advance notice in cases in which the physician and patient seek an admission which the hospital believes is unwarranted.

716. Social Security Act, §1155 (a) (1), 42 U.S.C. §1320c-4(a) (1).

717. "The committee would stress that the approach recommended does not envisage Blue Cross or Blue Shield or other insurance organizations or hospital or medical association review committees, assuming the review responsibilities for the professional standards review organizations. Where Blue Cross or Blue Shield or other insurers, or agencies have existing computer capacity capable of producing the necessary patient, practitioner, and provider profiles in accordance with the parameters and other requirements of the PSRO, on an on-going expeditious and economic basis, it would certainly be appropriate to employ that capacity as a basic tool for the professional standards review organizations." 1972 Senate Finance Committee Report, supra n. 428, at p. 265.

718. Social Security Act, §1152(b) (2), 42 U.S.C. §1320c-1(6) (2).

719. Social Security Act, §1152(a), 42 U.S.C. 1320c-1(a). If physician organizations are not interested in forming PSROs, HEW can seek alternate applicants from "state and local health departments, medical schools, and failing all else, carriers and intermediaries or other health insurers." 1972 Senate Finance Committee Report, supra n. 428, at p. 260.

720. Social Security Act, §§1162 and 1163, 42 U.S.C. §§1320c-11 and c-12.

721. Social Security Act, §1155(a) (2), 42 U.S.C. §1320c-4(a) (2).

722. Social Security Act, §1156(a), 42 U.S.C. §1320c-5(a). The norms may reflect regional differences.

723. Social Security Act, §1156(d) (1) (A), 42 U.S.C. §1320c-5(d) (1) (A).

724. Social Security Act, §§1152(e) and 1155(e) (1), 42 U.S.C. §§1320c-1(e), and c-4(e) (2).

725. Evaluation of that impact is beyond the scope of this book. See Health Law Project, "Utilization Review and Quality of Care" (1973).

726. Social Security Act, §1879, 42 U.S.C. §1395pp.

727. "Where both the provider and beneficiary exercised due care (i.e., they did not know, and had no reason to know, that noncovered services were involved), the liability would shift to the Government and payment would be made as though covered services had been furnished. However, in making such a payment it would be necessary to make certain that the provider and patient are put on notice that the service was noncovered with the result that in subsequent cases involving similar situations and further stays or treatments in the given case (or similar types of cases in the instance of the provider) they could not show they had exercised due care. Thus, the Government's liability would be progressively limited." 1972 Senate Finance Committee Report, supra n. 428, at p. 294.

728. Social Security Act, §1879(b), 42 U.S.C. §1395pp(b).

729. Part A Intermediary Letter No. 73-30. BHI Telegraphic Message to Part A Intermediaries, Aug. 15, 1973. Reported in 2 CCH Medicare and Medicaid Guide ¶24,353.

In December 1972, HEW instructed intermediaries that "pending receipt of specific instructions, claims involving the above disallowances [of claims for services that were determined to be not reasonable or necessary or did not meet level-of-care requirements] *should be processed in the present manner,* but identified for *possible* future action." Part A Intermediary Letter No. 72-27; Part B Intermediary Letter No. 72-31. It is not clear what was done with these claims.

730. Part A Intermediary Letter No. 73-30, BHI Telegraphic Message to Part A Intermediaries, Aug. 15, 1973. 2 CCH Medicare and Medicaid Guide ¶24,353.

731. The requirement that information be submitted within from 5 to 7 days of admission or request for further information will be applied on an institutional basis. Thus even though all information in a particular case is submitted on time, the provider will nonetheless not be entitled to the statutory limitation unless it has established "a pattern of timely submittal of materials" in all cases. I.L. No. 73-30, Section III(D), para. 5. However, intermediaries are urged to be "tolerant in situations where a provider occasionally submits an item after the established time frame." Ibid.

732. Very few providers now participating in the Medicare program will be able to meet this requirement if it is enforced. Supra nn. 666–69 and accompanying text.

733. I.L. No. 73-30, Sec. III (A–C).

734. Supra n. 676 and accompanying text.

735. The HEW letter says, "Until final instructions are issued, the presumption applies to all categories of claims submitted by a provider. . . . In the future, it may be possible to apply the presumption selectively so that, for example, Part A claims submitted by a hospital involving surgery are entitled to the presumption while those involving general medical care are not." I.L. No. 73-30, Sec. II.

736. Supra n. 406.

737. Social Security Act, §§1160(a) (2) (B) (ii). This provision does not change the definition of what constitutes covered hospital service but rather exempts the physician and hospital from penalty when an individual is kept in the hospital because there is no nursing home available for transfer.

738. 1972 Senate Finance Committee Report, supra n. 428, at p. 295.

Because the attending physician has a much greater familiarity with the patient's needs, considerable weight should be given to his professional judgment concerning the moment when an individual no longer requires care at the hospital level.

739. 1972 Senate Finance Committee Report, supra n. 428, at p. 295.

740. Actuarial estimates were adjusted to reflect a substantial anticipated increase in the use of nursing home services. 1972 Senate Finance Committee Report, supra n. 428, at p. 285.

741. Social Security Act, §1814(a) (2) (C), 42 U.S.C. §1395f(a) (2) (C).

742. 1972 Senate Finance Committee Report, supra n. 428, at p. 284.

743. Social Security Act, §1814(h) (1), 42 U.S.C. §1395f(h) (1). It is arguable that such a presumption has always existed in the statute but has simply not been honored by Blue Cross and HEW.

744. Supra n. 694 and accompanying text.

745. 1972 Senate Finance Committee Report, supra n. 428, at pp. 283–84.

746. Miller, "Phasing out Medicare: Changing Definitions of Skilled Nursing Care and Custodial Care," 18 *J. Amer. Geriat. Soc.* 937, 945 (1970); Health Law Project, "Medicare Level of Care Determinations," 6 *Clearinghouse Rev.* 234 (1972); Lorenz, "Background, Experience, and Models for the Concept of Extended Care in Medicare Legislation," 19 *J. Amer. Geriat. Soc.* 417 (1971); Brahna, "Home Health Services and Health Insurance," 9 *Med. Care* 89 (1971).

747. Social Security Act, §1160(a) (1), 42 U.S.C. §1320c-9(a) (1).

748. Social Security Act, §1160(b), 42 U.S.C. §1320c-9(b).

749. Social Security Act, §1160(b) (2), 42 U.S.C. §1320c-9(b) (2).

750. Social Security Act, §1814(h) (2), 42 U.S.C. §1395f(h) (2).

751. Social Security Act, §1871, 42 U.S.C. §1395hh, gives the secretary general authority to promulgate regulations to implement the purposes of the Medicare program.

752. Social Security Act, §1877, 42 U.S.C. §1395nn.

753. Social Security Act, §1155(a), 42 U.S.C. §1320c-4(a).

754. Social Security Act, §1814(h) (1), 42 U.S.C. §1395f(h) (1).

755. Social Security Act, §1159(a), 42 U.S.C. §1320c-8(a).

756. Social Security Act, §1159(b), 42 U.S.C. §1320c-8(c).

757. The discussion here is confined to review of a determination by an attending physician that institutional services are medically required and covered by the act. In a perfect system, patients might also be afforded some form of review of the judgments of their individual physicians. See Freidson, *Professional Dominance* (N.Y.: Atherton Press, 1970).

758. *Goldberg v. Kelly,* 397 U.S. 254, 269–71.

759. The development of effective sanctions against an administrator who fails to act in a timely fashion is a difficult problem. One solution is to create a presumption that if there is no determination within a fixed period of time the services proscribed are approved. Another solution is to impose fines upon the administrative agencies, payable to the claimant. See *Rodriguez v. Swank,* 318 F. Supp. 289 (N.D.Ill., 1970), aff'd 403 U.S. 901 (1971), 2 CCH Pov. L. Rpt. ¶26,280 (N.D.Ill., 1973) (contempt).

760. H. Somers, "Hospital Utilization Controls: What Is the Way?" *New England Journal of Medicine,* June 22, 1972, p. 1362.

761. HEW, SRS, Medical Services Administration, *Medicaid: Medical Assistance Manual,* provides that the review of requests for prior authorization involves evaluation of whether the services "to be provided are actually needed, that all adequate less expensive alternatives have been given consideration, and that the proposed service and materials conform to commonly accepted community standards of the profession involved." Pt. 5, p. 2, §5-30-20 A.

762. 45 C.F.R. §205.10(a) (3) (1972).

763. E. Brian, "Government Control of Hospital Utilization: A California Experience," *New England Journal of Medicine,* June 22, 1972, p. 1342; "Screening Programs Effects Disputed," *American Medical News,* Oct. 16, 1972, p. 8.

764. "Doctors' Views of Medi-Cal," *New England Journal of Medicine,* Sept. 21, 1972, p. 618.

765. "Screening Program's Effects Disputed," supra n. 763, at p. 8.

766. "Doctors' Views of Medi-Cal," supra n. 764, at p. 618.

767. 1972 Senate Finance Committee Report supra n. 428, at p. 200.

768. 20 C.F.R. §405.129. The procedure was originally set forth in Intermediary Letter No. 328 (June 1968). The intermediary must give the extended care facility notice "as promptly as possible."

769. 20 C.F.R. §405.129(b). In addition, the extended care facility's past performance must indicate that it does not seek payment of clearly noncovered care. As of March 1971, 2,134 extended care facilities, or 48% of all participating ones, were utilizing the assurance of payment procedure. In 33% of the cases in which this extended care facility filed information under the assurance of payment procedure, the intermediary held that the care needed was not covered. HEW, SSA, *Report of Intermediary Level of Care Determinations for ECFs* (Aug. 16, 1971).

770. 20 C.F.R. §405.129(d). The regulation provides for termination of the period for which coverage is assured by whichever of the following occurs first: (1) intermediary notice of noncoverage; (2) intermediary request for additional supporting evidence; or (3) a change in the patient's condition such that he clearly does not need covered care. Id.

771. *Flemming v. Nestor*, 363 U.S. 603 (1960).

772. Social Security Act, §1812(a), 42 U.S.C. §1395d(a).

773. *Goldberg v. Kelly*, 397 U.S. 254, 264.

774. The Senate Special Committee on Aging reported that, as of 1970, 4.7 million aged persons had incomes that fell below the poverty level, representing nearly one-fourth of the elderly population of the U.S., as compared to one out of nine persons under 65 whose incomes fell below the poverty line. Thirty-eight per cent of the elderly had incomes of less than $4,000 per year and another 12% had incomes between $4,000 and $5,000 per year. The Bureau of Labor Statistics has fixed the moderate level of income for elderly couples at $4,489 per year. Even if an aged person were to receive the maximum benefits allowed under social security, benefits would still fall $650 short of the BLS moderate income level if they were the only source of income.

The number of elderly poor are increasing. Between 1969 and 1970 the number of aged poor rose by 100,000. The lion's share of this increase represented increased numbers of poor people aged 60 to 64, who had left or been forced out of jobs earlier but were still ineligible for many benefits accruing to persons 65 or older. *Report of the Senate Special Committee on Aging,* S. Rept. 92–505, 92d Cong., 1st Sess., pp. 7–8 (1971).

775. See *Boddie v. Connecticut*, 401 U.S. 371 (1971) in which the Supreme Court held that court costs that effectively excluded the poor from access to the courts in matrimonial actions denied the poor equal protection and substantive due process of law.

776. For analogous situations where coverage, participation, or benefits cannot be terminated without a hearing, see *Escalera v. New York City Housing Authority*, 425 F. 2d 853 (2 Cir. 1970) (tenancy in public housing); *Crow v. Calif. Dept. of Human Resources*, 325 F. Supp. 1314 (N.D.Calif., 1972) (enemployment compensation); *Tindall v. Hardin*, 337 F. Supp. 563 (W.D.Pa., 1972) (food stamps).

777. A factor that influenced the court in *Goldberg*, that of "brutal need," is equally applicable to Medicare benefits in arguing for the necessity of a pretermination hearing. As the court noted in *Goldberg:* "While post-termination review is relevant, there is one overpowering fact which controls here. By hypothesis, a welfare recipient is destitute, without funds or assets . . . suffice it to say that to cut off a welfare recipient in the face of 'brutal need' without a prior hearing of some sort is unconscionable, unless overwhelming considerations justify it." 397 U.S. at 261, quoted from *Kelly v. Wyman*, 294 F. Supp. 893, 899–900 (S.D.N.Y., 1968).

778. See, e.g., *Williams v. Robinson*, 432 F.2d 637 (D.C.Cir., 1970) (mental patient's right to a hearing to contest transfer to maximum security ward); *In Re Banard*, 455 F.2d 1370 (D.C.D.C., 1971) (patient committed to hospital by court order for seven-day

emergency observation and diagnosis entitled to hearing within first two days of this period); *Wyatt v. Stickney,* 325 F. Supp. 781 (D.C.Ala., 1971) (involuntarily committed mental patient has right to hearing on failure to provide adequate treatment).

779. Prior notice and hearing are needed to protect the *eligible* beneficiary's right to uninterrupted receipt of health care services. Of course, if the initial determination that the beneficiary is no longer entitled to prescribed services is correct, individuals will receive payment for services to which they would not otherwise be entitled during the time it takes to provide notice and opportunity for a hearing. If the individual has money, the government may recoup these payments. However, it is likely that, as in the case of public assistance recipients, many aged Medicare beneficiaries will be judgment proof and recoupment will be impossible.

As the court found in *Goldberg v. Kelly,* 397 U.S. 254, at 266, "the interest of the eligible recipient in uninterrupted receipt of public assistance, coupled with the State's interest that his payments not be erroneously terminated, clearly outweighs the State's competing concern to prevent any increase in its fiscal and administrative burdens. Much of the drain on fiscal and administrative resources can be reduced by developing procedures for prompt pre-termination hearing and by skillful use of personnel and facilities."

780. *Armstrong v. Manzo,* 380 U.S. 545, 552 (1962).

781. The principle that a hearing must be timely is ancient. "The laws of God and man both give the party an opportunity to make his defence, if he has any. I remember to have heard it observed by a very learned man upon such an occasion, that even God himself did not pass sentence upon Adam, before he was called upon to make his defence." *The King v. The Chancellor, Masters and Scholars of the University of Cambridge,* 1 Str. (K.B.) 557, 567, 93 Eng. Rpts. 698, 704 (1723) (Fortescue, J.).

The principle is oft stated. "The demands of due process do not require a hearing at the initial stage or at any particular point or at more than one point in an administrative proceeding *so long as the requisite hearing is held before the final order becomes effective.*" (Emphasis added.) *Opp. Cotton Mills v. Administrator,* 312 U.S. 126, 152–53 (1941). "Those who are brought into contest with the government . . . are entitled to be fairly advised of what the Government proposes and to be heard upon its proposals *before it issues its final command.*" (Emphasis added.) *Morgan v. United States,* 304 U.S. 1, 25 (1938). "It needs no extended argument to conclude that absent notice and prior hearing . . . pre-judgment garnishment violates the fundamental principles of due process." *Snaidach v. Family Finance Corp.,* 395 U.S. 337, 342 (1969). "It is enough that opportunity was given for a full and fair hearing before the order became operative." *Wilson v. Standefer,* 184 U.S. 399 (1902). See also *Londoner v. Denver,* 210 U.S. 373 (1910); *Nickey v. Mississippi,* 292 U.S. 393 (1934); *U.S. v. Illinois Central Railroad Co.,* 291 U.S. 457, 463 (1934).

782. 397 U.S. at 267–68.

783. 397 U.S. at 271.

784. 397 U.S. at 267.

785. *Cafeteria & Restaurant Workers Union v. McElroy,* 367 U.S. 886, 895 (1961), quoted in *Goldberg v. Kelly,* 397 U.S. 254, 263. The norms of due process are flexible, *Hannah v. Larche,* 363 U.S. 420, 442 (1960), and "cannot . . . be tested by mere generalities or sentiments abstractly appealing." *Joint Anti-Fascist Refugee Comm. v. McGrath,* 341 U.S. 123, 163 (1951).

786. The testimony of a physician member of a utilization review committee in a case in which the determination of the committee was retroactively reversed by Blue Cross is illuminating: "'Our rule of thumb . . . was this: If the patient would have been in the hospital because of the medical condition prior to Medicare, then the patient should be here after Medicare; if he would not have stayed in the hospital this length of time before

Medicare, then he shouldn't stay that way now." (T. 77) Asked whether the patient required the constant availability of physician services, the doctor replied: "I don't think the question is fair, because this is not why people are in the hospital. It is one small part of it. We've got people there who are monitored in the intensive care unit, and they are in need of having a doctor pretty quickly available. This is maybe 12 patients. But you've got a whole hospital full of people that don't need doctors that quickly available. We've got them there because out of 600 there are going to be a few. But the majority of them do not need that. That is not why they are in the hospital as a rule." (T. 80).

There was a good deal of confusion on the part of both physician and hearing examiner as to the meaning of the standard. The hearing examiner asked, "In the medical profession . . . does the phrase 'skilled nursing services on a continuing basis' have an accepted meaning?" The physician answered, "I don't think it does. . . . I interpret it to mean that skilled nursing services were needed 24 hours a day, but maybe that is not what it means. What does it mean to you?" (T. 85) *In Re Clara S.,* Social Security Administration Hearing, Dayton, Ohio, March 30, 1972. In the files of the Health Law Project, 133 So. 36th St., Philadelphia, Penn. 19174.

787. See *Martinez v. Richardson,* (D.N.Mex.Civ. No. 8990, Aug. 5, 1971) (TRO reinstating services to plaintiffs terminated from home health services until after a hearing could be had). Aff'd 2 CCH Medicare and Medicaid Guide ¶26,603 (10th Cir. 1973).

788. The agency role of the intermediary as administrator of Medicare is recognized in the federal regulations, which provide, "In the performance of their contractual undertakings, the fiscal intermediaries act on behalf of the Secretary, carrying on for him the administrative responsibilities imposed by law. The Secretary, however, is the real party in interest in the administration of the program and will endeavor to safeguard the interests of his contractual representatives with respect to their actions in the fulfillment of commitments under the agreements entered into by them with the Secretary." 20 C.F.R. §405.651. The contractual arrangement with the intermediary does not per se make them an agent of the government. Rather the key factors are the close degree of control which the secretary is to exercise over the intermediary under the terms of the statute. Social Security Act, §§1816, 1874(a), 42 U.S.C. §§1395h, 1395kk(a). See *Kuenstler v. Occidental Life Ins. Co.,* 292 F. Supp. 532 (C.D.Calif., 1968), *Allen v. Allen,* 291 F. Supp. 312 (S.D.Iowa, 1968).

789. Blue Cross might also be viewed as a public utility in light of the public function it performs and its special status under state law. Several courts have held that public utilities—electric, gas, and telephone companies—are agents of the state for constitutional purposes and as such must provide their customers with due process prior to the termination of services. In general see Note, "Constitutional Safeguards for Public Utility Customers: Power to the People," 48 *N.Y.U.L. Rev.* 493 (1973).

790. 42 U.S.C §1302 specifically authorizes the secretary of HEW to "make and publish such rules and regulations not inconsistent with this chapter as may be necessary to the efficient administration of the functions with which [he] is charged." The scope of this rule-making power was considered in *Opelika Nursing Home v. Richardson,* 448 F.2d 658 (5th Cir., 1971), remanded, 323 F. Supp. 1206 (1971) (dismissed for lack of jurisdiction and failure to state a claim).

791. The PSRO amendments prohibit release of information gathered in the review process unless such release would "carry out the purposes" of the PSRO legislation or unless authorized by the secretary of HEW but only if "the rights and interests of patients, health care practitioners, or providers of health care" are protected. Social Security Act, §1166, 42 U.S.C. §1320c-15. Violations of this provision are punishable by fine or imprisonment. Social Security Act, §1166(b), 42 U.S.C. §1320c-15. These provisions should not inhibit the secretary from requiring that beneficiaries have access to the information in

their own cases and the decisions, without identification of beneficiary or doctor, in prior cases.

792. According to an HEW study, of the 280 health care institutions which reported that they maintain a patient advocate, ombudsman, or "formal complaint function," 36.1% have done so for 6 years or more (i.e. since 1966); 19.3% have maintained a patient advocate for 11 years or more (i.e. since 1961). Fargo Thompson, Andrew Lupton, Richard Renck, James Felderman, "Patient Grievance Mechanisms in Health Care Institutions," *Medical Malpractice,* Report of the Commission on Medical Malpractice, DHEW Publication No. (OS73-89) (Washington, D.C.: HEW, Jan. 16, 1973), Appendix, pp. 761, 779.

793. Neighborhood health centers, established with federal funds in areas where there is an acute unmet need for health services, have done innovative work in developing patient advocate services. See *Healthright Programs: The Neighborhood Health Center,* OEO Pamphlet 6128-9 (Washington, D.C.: Office of Health Affairs, Office of Economic Opportunity, March 1970), p. 7; "Comprehensive Health Services: Career Development," 1 *Technical Assistance Bulletin,* No. 6, pp. 1–2 (April 1970).

The secretary's Commission on Medical Malpractice recommends that each state establish an "Office of Consumer Health Affairs" and that "Federal financial assistance be made available to the states to encourage the establishment of such offices at the earliest possible date." *Medical Malpractice,* Report of the Commission on Medical Malpractice, DHEW Publication No. (OS 73–88) (Washington, D.C.: HEW, Jan. 16, 1973), p. 86.

794. 1972 GAO Report, supra n. 591, at p. 802.

795. In 1974 the enactment of national health insurance seemed more imminent than in either 1972 (when the text was written) or in 1973. The cooling of interest that occurred in 1972 and 1973 probably resulted from the following factors: health did not become an important issue in the 1972 election; there was growing recognition of the massive problems that accompany the enactment of health benefits programs with little or no rationalization of provider resources and no desire to increase those problems exponentially; the enormous costs of a comprehensive national health insurance program caused concern at a time of continuing inflation. The year 1974 looked promising for national health insurance, since the administration made health a high priority in its domestic agenda and the House and Senate committees with jurisdiction promised early hearings. Of course the continuing impact of Watergate and the widely shared opinion that the 1974 congressional elections would lead to a more Democratic 94th Congress would affect the legislative timetable.

796. President Nixon says, "Good health care should be readily available to all of our citizens." *Health Message from the President of the United States,* H.R. Doc. No. 94-49, 92nd Cong., 1st Sess., p. 2 (1971). Sen. Edward Kennedy says, "I believe that in America today, health care is a right for all, not just a privilege for the few." *Health Security for America,* speech, U.S. Senate, Jan. 25, 1971, *Cong. Rec.,* Vol. 117, Pt. 1, p. 284, 92nd Cong., 1st Sess. The A.M.A. is on record saying, "It is a basic right of every citizen to have available to him adequate care." Resolution, A.M.A. House of Delegates, December 1969, reprinted in pamphlet, *Medical and Health Care for All.* See also Milton I. Roemer, "Nationalized Medicine for America," *Trans-Action,* September 1971, pp. 31–36.

797. S. Kelman, "Toward the Political Economy of Medical Care," 8 *Inquiry* 30 (September 1971).

798. Id. at p. 33.

799. Id. at p. 34.

800. Ibid. G. Kolko, *The Triumph of Conservatism* (N.Y.: Free Press of Glencoe, 1963). E.g. "Pennsy Estimates Needs for Aid by Government," *New York Times,* Feb. 2, 1973, p. 39, col. 7.

801. R. R. Alford, "The Political Economy of Health Care: Dynamics Without Change," 2 *Politics and Society* 127 (1972).

802. See, e.g., D. W. Pettengill, "Writing the Prescription for Health Care," *Harv. Business Rev.*, November–December 1971, p. 37; H. Schwartz, "Health Care in America: A Heretical Diagnosis," *Saturday Review*, Aug. 14, 1971, p. 14.

803. A. Somers, "Call It Anything, but the Hospital Is the System," *Modern Hospital*, June 1971, p. 110. M. I. Roemer, "Nationalized Medicine for America," *Trans-Action*, September 1971, p. 31.

804. Alford, supra n. 801, at pp. 136–37.

805. R. G. Noll, *Reforming Regulation: An Evaluation of the Ash Council Proposals* (Washington, D.C.: The Brookings Institution, 1971), p. 41.

806. Id. at pp. 39–46. See also N. Johnson, "A New Fidelity to the Regulatory Ideal," 59 *Georgetown L.J.* 869, 875–90 (1971); P. Elman, "Administrative Reform of the Federal Trade Commission," 59 *Georgetown L.J.* 777, 788–94, 853–58.

807. Alford, supra n. 801, at p. 133.

808. See, for example, Medical Committee for Human Rights, *Outline of a National Health Plan*, available from the Health Law Project, 133 S. 36th St., Philadelphia, Penn. 19174.

809. Noll, supra n. 805, at p. 92. He suggests that in the case of industries in which widespread deregulation or the status quo of more or less weak regulation "yield seriously deficient performance, nationalization is surely worthy of dispassionate study."

810. One useful definition of the term *public interest* is "the policies government would pursue if it gave equal weight to the welfare of every member of society." Noll, supra n. 805, at p. 15. This definition does not explain who is to define the welfare of each individual or weigh the importance of allowing each individual opportunity to define his or her own welfare. Furthermore, individual perceptions of self-interest change as people acquire knowledge.

811. Noll, supra n. 805, at p. 34.

812. Ibid.

813. Johnson, supra n. 806, at p. 875.

814. Elman, supra n. 806, at p. 788.

815. *The Regulatory Process: A Personal View*, address by Commissioner Philip Elman, FTC, before the American Bar Association, St. Louis, Mo., Aug. 11, 1970, *Wall Street Journal*, Aug. 12, 1970, p. 12, col. 6. See also R. Leone, "Public Interest Advocacy and the Regulatory Process," 400 *Annals of the Am. Academy of Pol. and Soc. Sci.* 46 (1972); H. Green, "Nuclear Power Licensing and Regulation," 400 *Annals of the Am. Academy of Pol. and Soc. Sci.* 116 (1972); Comment, "Public Participation in Federal Administrative Proceedings," 120 *U. of Pa. L.R.* 702 (1972); E. Gelhorn, "Public Participation in Administrative Proceedings," 81 *Yale L.J.* 359 (1972).

816. The OEO health backup center, the National Health Law Program at UCLA, employs five lawyers and is in danger of extinction. The OEO Health Law Project at the University of Pennsylvania employed six lawyers and a sociologist and is also in danger of extinction. Ralph Nader's Health Research Group employs three lawyers, a doctor, and a health specialist.

A survey of legal services attorneys conducted by the National Legal Services Training Program in 1971 showed that "health law" was near the bottom on a list of subjects on which these lawyers wanted training. The survey also showed that fewer than 30 legal services attorneys in the United States considered themselves actively involved in health law work.

817. The most comprehensive statement of the Nixon administration's position on this issue is contained in a confidential memo by Marshall Boarman entitled "Issues concerning Legal Services," September 1972. It defines the proper function of legal services as

seeking justice in individual cases within the confines of existing law and would prohibit legal action or advocacy to bring about "fundamental social change." See "Memos Show New Plans to Narrow U.S. Legal Aid," *New York Times*, Feb. 19, 1973, p. 16, col. 3.

818. W. Johnson, supra n. 806, at p. 897.

819. "Because the community is not self-conscious and knowledgeable about health facilities, and because the members of the community are likely to give food, jobs, housing, and schools priority over doctors and hospitals—since only a small proportion of the community needs health care at any given time—the equal-health advocates are likely to have a great deal of autonomy in representing community needs to official agencies. Advocates are not under much surveillance, there is little reaction to their decisions, and their victories have little collective impact. Thus, the isolation of equal-health advocates from the community increases the chances of their being co-opted into advisory boards, planning agencies, and other devices for advertising the representative character of 'community participation' without much chance, let alone guarantee, that the community will be able to evaluate and control the actions of their advocates, let alone the health providers." Alford, supra n. 801, at p. 146.

820. For example, Alford concludes his analysis of the political economy of health care saying, "Change is not likely without the presence of a social and political movement which rejects the legitimacy of the economic and social base of pluralist politics," supra n. 801, at p. 164. J. Ehrenreich and O. Fein deem all current proposals for national health insurance irrelevant, concluding, "No matter how hard the public insurers tried to persuade the controllers of the private delivery system to change that system, no attempt would be made to take control away from them . . . National health insurance would not be a move in the direction of a national health system; it would be more of a shuffle sideways." "National Health Insurance: The Great Leap Sideways," *Social Policy*, January 1971, p. 9.

821. " 'The House of Representatives,' said one of its members, 'does not have the computer capacity of the State Bank of Kenosha, Wisconsin.' The Senate has one computer that, in accordance with its priorities, it uses for sending news letters." E. Drew, "Why Congress Won't Fight," *New York Times Magazine*, Sept. 23, 1973, p. 90.

822. "There has been," says Representative Tom Foley (D.-Wash.), a "subtle and imperceptible change in the *Zeitgeist*. But frankly, I don't see the Congress yet really wanting to change its role from the passive one to the active one of being makers of policy. It has become accustomed to passivity. It still waits for the department to come up with proposals. The basic reasons for this are tradition and convenience. It's what most of the members have always known." Id. at p. 86. See, e.g., E. Sparer, "On the Matter of Community Relations: The Consumer Movement in Health Care," Albert Einstein Medical Center, Long Range Planning Seminar, June 12, 1971 (unpublished draft available from the Health Law Project).

823. The A.M.A.'s Medicredit plan would offer a tax credit against the individual's federal income tax to encourage purchase of private health insurance. The poor would receive federal vouchers to cover insurance premiums. S. 1623, 92nd Cong., 2nd Sess. The Health Insurance Association of America would provide incentive tax deductions, with the states purchasing policies for the poor. S. 1490. State commissions would review rates charged by health care providers. Senator Javits has introduced a proposal to strengthen Medicare and extend it to the entire population. The role of the intermediaries and carriers would remain essentially the same, although it allows contracting out in the case of employer-employee plans and alternative health insurance policies developed by private insurance companies. Public insurance corporations could be set up to administer the program if the private companies did not function properly. S. 836. The Nixon ad-

ministration proposal is a collection of programs, including preservation of Medicare for the aged, preservation of portions of Medicaid for the indigent aged, blind, and disabled. The National Health Insurance Standards Act would require employers to purchase private health insurance for their workers and would allow self-employed persons to purchase an equivalent plan to be developed by the private insurers. Under the Family Health Insurance Plan the government would purchase private insurance coverage for needy families. S. 1623. Companion bills provide loans and grants to encourage the use of HMOs, S. 1182, and to increase health manpower and facilities, S. 1183.

824. J. Simons, "National Health Insurance Legislation and the 92nd Cong.," 7 *N. Eng. L. Rev.* 25, 31 (1971).

825. *Report on Commercial Banks and Their Trust Activities* (Patman Report), House Committee on Banking and Currency, 89th Cong., 2nd Sess. (1966). Wright Patman, "Bank Trust Activities Threaten America," 215 *Commercial and Financial Chronicle,* No. 7214, p. 1 (June 22, 1972).

826. H. Somers, "National Health: A Critical Era of Debate," *Trial Magazine,* January–February 1972, n. 34 at pp. 39–40.

827. For example, the secretary of HEW can waive statutory requirements of Title XIX for the purpose of trying experimental and demonstration programs, and funds are appropriated for such programs. 42 U.S.C. 1115.

828. Although state and local taxes have increased markedly, the gap between the city governments' revenue needs and revenue expectations (including revenues obtained through intergovernmental aid, as well as those raised through local taxes) has also increased. This gap has been estimated as follows (in billions of dollars):

Fiscal year	1966	1967	1968	1969	1970	1971	1972	1973	1974	1975
Revenue gap	$4.5	$7.9	$12.0	$16.7	$22.2	$28.5	$34.5	$40.1	$45.4	$50.3

The regressivity of state and local taxes is shown by the following:

State and Local Taxes as a Percentage of Total Income for
All Families by Income Class, 1965

Income Class	Under $2000	$2000-2999	$3000-3999	$4000-4999	$5000-5999	$6000-7499	$7500-9999	$10,000-14,999	$15,000- & over
State and local taxes as a percentage of income	15.1%	12.7%	12.6%	11.8%	11.5%	10.8%	10.1%	9.6%	9.1%

Tax Burdens and Benefits of Government Expenditures by Income Class, 1961 and 1965 (N.Y.: Tax Foundation, Inc., 1967), p. 20.

829. The National Health Security Bill uses a trust fund device and is financed in part from general revenues, in part from payroll taxes, and in part from a tax on nonwage income. See National Health Security Bill, S. 3, §61, 92nd Cong. 1st Sess., printed in *Cong. Rec.,* Jan. 25, 1971. Hereinafter cited as Health Security Bill.

830. Health Security Bill, supra, n. 829, §§21–28.

831. Id. §11.

832. Id. §§201–204.

833. Remarks, Sen. Edward Kennedy, U.S. Senate, 92nd Cong., 1st Sess., Jan. 25, 1971. 117 *Cong. Rec.,* Pt. 1, p. 286.

834. Health Security Bill, supra, n. 829, §121.

835. It provides that "members who are representatives of consumers of such care shall be persons not engaged in and having no financial interest in the furnishing of health services, who are familiar with the needs of various segments of the population for personal health services and are experienced in dealing with problems associated with the furnishing of such services." Id. §125(a)(2).

836. Id. §125(c).

837. Id. §126.

838. Id. §101.

839. Id. §101, 102. If the state comprehensive health planning agency does not operate effectively, the secretary may assume responsibility for planning within the state.

840. Id. §83(b).

841. Id. §134.

842. Id. §87.

843. Inpatient hospital care is provided for an indefinite duration, if certified as necessary by a physician. Domiciliary or custodial care is explicitly excluded. Id. §24(b) and 24(e). Skilled nursing home care, certified as necessary by a physician, is covered for 120 days in each benefit period, except that the period may be extended for homes affiliated with hospitals or comprehensive health organizations. Id. §24(b) and 24(e). Utilization review requirements are similar to those under the current Medicare program. Id. §§43(g) and 51. Since within the negotiated budget hospitals would continue to be paid on the basis of the amount of service rendered, the providers would continue to have economic incentives to retain patients beyond the point when services are medically required, and the health security administrators would be inclined to deny payments for these services. It is not clear where the risk of loss would fall in this situation. Although the bill provides the right to notice and a hearing prior to the termination of eligibility for benefits, it is not clear whether beneficiaries could obtain review of determination of entitlement to specific benefits. Id. §132(e).

844. Id. §83(a). The Social Security Amendments of 1972 require for the first time that hospitals prepare annual budgets. Social Security Act, §1861(z), 42 U.S.C. §1395x(z).

845. Some of the present specific problems of reasonable cost reimbursement should probably be solved by congressional action. For example, it seems unreasonable to expect that a new administrative agency would have the political strength to take on entrenched nationwide patterns of excessive hospital expenses. With respect to drugs, the bill requires that the Health Security Board establish an approved list of drugs, §25, and set maximum prices for the drugs listed, §86. The bill says that maximum prices are to be fixed so as to encourage bulk purchasing by providers. There are no other standards, and unless the Health Security Board exercised initiative, patient fees would continue to provide open-ended support to drug company profits, research, advertising, and name brand differentiation. The bill specifically authorizes presently existing patterns of compensation for pathologists, radiologists, and other physicians. Id. §83(c).

846. Id. §63.

847. Id. §64.

848. Id. §65(a).

849. Id. §124(b).

850. Id. §125(b) (national advisory board), §126 (regional advisory boards).

851. Id. §83(d).

852. Comprehensive Health Service Organizations, HMOs under the Health Security

NOTES TO PAGES 158–159

Bill, must make "periodic consultation with representatives of its enrollees regarding the policies and operation of the organization." Id. §47(a)(6).

853. Sen. Abraham Ribicoff says, "Yet heightened interest for the consumer is nowhere near enough. The consumer doesn't need 'interest.' He needs a place to go, a complaint bureau, an ombudsman who works for him instead of for the providers, an office and a staff that takes him seriously and investigates his complaints." *The American Medical Machine* (N.Y.: Saturday Review Press, 1972) p. 153.

854. See M. Kotler, "The Politics of Community Development," 36 *Law and Cont. Prob.* 3 (1971); S. M. Miller, M. Rein, "Participation, Poverty, and Administration—Decentralism: A Model for Rapproachment in Los Angeles," 58 *Geo. L.J.* 901 (1970).

855. The selection of delegates to the National Democratic Convention of 1972 demonstrates that there is a variety of techniques for allowing popular selection of representatives while at the same time assuring that all segments of the relevant population are represented. Tom Wicker, "Guidelines, Quotas, and the Future," *New York Times,* July 23, 1972, §IV, p. 11, col. 1.

The Commonwealth of Pennsylvania has proposed regulations requiring that the members of a hospital governing board "shall be broadly representative of the total community population it serves . . . [and] shall be selected on the basis of their demonstrated awareness of community needs and shall be committed to serving all segments of that community." 2 *Pa. Bull.* 1134, §2.1.3.2. (June 24, 1972).

856. Havighurst notes that it is practically impossible to construct a regulatory structure capable of preventing a single enterprise from subsidizing unregulated activities from regulated, monopoly business. With respect to hospitals and HMOs he concludes that, "In no event could cost accounting be depended upon to protect the public from possible abuse since it could not supply the precision necessary to police transactions and joint-cost allocations between a hospital and its captive HMO." Havighurst, supra n. 593, at p. 765.

857. Growing discontent is difficult to document when it has no forum for expression, but, for example, Congresswoman Griffiths says, "I was asked one morning to speak in a very conservative church and one of the questions asked me concerning my bill, was what was the provision in it for insurance companies. I said, 'Well, sir my bill doesn't have insurance companies in it. When my bill is passed then Blue Cross and Blue Shield are gone,' and to my amazement and the questioner's, there was instant and complete applause from everybody. You might try this on one of these people. It is one way to get an ovation." Hearing on National Health Insurance Proposals before the House Committee on Ways and Means, 92nd Cong., 1st Sess., Pt. 2. p. 367 (1971).

858. See Report on Washington Representation Task Force, Sept. 10, 1971, and Remarks by George J. Kelly at Blue Cross Program Session, AHA Convention, Chicago, Ill., Aug. 24, 1971, Confidential BCA documents printed in Hearings on Physician Training Facilities and Health Maintenance Organizations before the Subcommittee on Health of the Senate Committee on Labor and Public Welfare, 92nd Cong., 1st Sess., Pt. 3, pp. 1030–33 (1971).

INDEX

Aged: hospital utilization patterns, 75–77, 82–84, 87–88; nursing costs, 86–88. *See also* Medicare

Alabama, 47

Allowable costs: depreciation, 66–70; plus factor, 70–72; public relations costs, 72–74

American Association for Labor Legislation, 179 *n*.173

American Hospital Association: and fiscal intermediary concept, 36–46; and hospital charges, 81; and hospital service plans, 7–8; and local Blue Cross plans, 18–24; and national health insurance, 32–41; and plus factor allowance, 71; promotes growth of Blue Cross, 10–11; and public regulatory agencies, 113; and reimbursement principles, 60–61, 62, 63–65; relationship to Blue Cross, 19–20; standards for group hospitalization plans, 7–8

American Hospital Association Nursing Activity Study Project, 86–87

American Medical Association: Eldercare, 39; position on national health insurance, 31–32

American Nursing Home Association, 227 *n*.708

Anderson, Senator, 64, 198 *n*.424

Annual Contract Evaluation Reports, 45–46

Associated Hospital Services (Blue Cross of New York City), claims review, 125–26

Assurance of Payment procedure, 138, 142

Auditing of hospital cost reports, 94–97

Ball, Robert, 61–62, 64, 77

Baylor (University) Plan, 7, 168 *n*.60

Blue Cross: and allowable costs, 65–74; and antitrust laws, 215 *n*.604; and auditing of hospital cost reports, 94–97; claims review under Medicare, 122–30; consumer influence on, 4, 27–28; and cost allocations among patients, 74–89; denial of coverage, 115–17, 130–31; distinguished from commercial insurance companies, 11–12; enrollment in, 11; failure as regulator of hospitals, 148; and health maintenance organizations, 107–11; history and growth, 6–13; and hospital charges, 81; and hospital cost control, 24, 104–14; and hospital purchasing practices, 89–93; name and insignia, 19–21; operating expenses, 1; premium costs, 90 *n*.303; Professional Standards Review Organization created, 130; public regulation of, 4, 13–18, 63–64; and reimbursement methods, 76–85; reimbursement negotiations with hospitals, 97–100; reimbursement for private care and for Medicare and Medicaid compared, 100–02; and reimbursement principles, 63–65; relationship to Blue Shield, 5; role in national health insurance, 145–46, 153–56, 158–60; secrecy, 25, 30; tax exemption, 9–13. *See also* Blue Cross Association; Blue Cross boards of directors; Local Blue Cross plans; State supervision of Blue Cross

Blue Cross Association (BCA): budget, 20; External Relations Division, 20; and Federal Employee Benefit Program,